Hegemony Now

Hegemony Now

How Big Tech and Wall Street Won the World
(and How We Win It Back)

Jeremy Gilbert and Alex Williams

VERSO

London • New York

First published by Verso 2022
© Jeremy Gilbert and Alex Williams 2022

1 3 5 7 9 10 8 6 4 2

Verso
UK: 6 Meard Street, London W1F 0EG
US: 388 Atlantic Avenue, Brooklyn, NY 11217
versobooks.com

Verso is the imprint of New Left Books

ISBN-13: 978-1-78663-314-9
ISBN-13: 978-1-78663-316-3 (UK EBK)
ISBN-13: 978-1-78663-317-0 (US EBK)

British Library Cataloguing in Publication Data
A catalogue record for this book is available from the British Library

Library of Congress Cataloging-in-Publication Data
A catalog record for this book is available from the Library of Congress

Typeset in Sabon by Biblichor Ltd, Edinburgh
Printed and bound by CPI Group (UK) Ltd, Croydon CR0 4YY

CONTENTS

INTRODUCTION

The old is dying and the new cannot be born; in this inter-
regnum a great variety of morbid symptoms appear.

—Antonio Gramsci[1]

In the years since 2016, it has seemed at times as if the world
was coming apart. From the election of Donald Trump to the
presidency of the United States, to the UK's vote to leave
the European Union, and from the global COVID-19 pandemic to the early signs of catastrophic climate collapse, the
world seemed to be running the script of a particularly unsub-
tle dystopian fiction. Where previously order, of a sort, had
reigned, now everywhere disorder was spreading. The 'rules'
that were deemed to govern politics and economics were rapidly discarded. What once seemed impossible rapidly became
inevitable. All the signs have become present that we are
living through an epochal crisis. This is the global crisis of
neoliberalism.

Neoliberalism, which is the political system that has ruled
almost the entirety of the planet since the 1990s, is everywhere in decline, if not ruination. Meanwhile, its successors
scrabble in the debris left behind for new forms of power. As
this global political crisis collides with a planetary health
crisis, against the backdrop of an intensifying environmental
crisis, the systems of order that regulate our political world
have been plunged into disarray. We are in a moment of grand
realignment, where different cycles of world history have
clicked together to produce a rare instant where more or less
anything could be possible.

We are writing this book as something of a guide as to what we, the political left, should do in these uncertain times. To understand this era requires thinking much more broadly than we are accustomed to, to go beyond our commonplace obsessions and reflexes. We have to think about how power actually works, not just in specific circumstances, such as during an election or the emergence of a social movement, but in general.[2] To do so we need to be thinking about politics through the idea of *hegemony*.

Power and Hegemony

Today, the term 'hegemony' is used fairly commonly, but in quite different ways.[3] Perhaps most often it is used to describe the domination or influence of one nation-state over another (e.g., 'American geopolitical hegemony'). This is indeed the root meaning of the term, as it emerges from ancient Greek. Sometimes too we might hear it being used to describe an influential social norm (e.g., 'hegemonic masculinity'). But perhaps the most significant development of the idea of hegemony, and the one we will be using for the most part in this book, was developed by the Italian communist writer, politician, and journalist Antonio Gramsci.

Gramsci was one of the founders of the Italian Communist Party and spent much of the end of his life as a political prisoner under the despotic rule of Benito Mussolini's fascists. His writings roamed over many topics, such as political history, philosophy, and culture. Underpinning them all was an emerging idea about how power worked, which he termed 'hegemony'. In a sense this was all about political leadership, of a collective and emergent kind. How was it, Gramsci asked, that relatively small groups come to rule large, complex societies as a whole? How was it, for example, that a relatively modest social faction like the fascists had come to control such a large and diverse society as Italy in the 1920s? This kind of question remains at the heart of our work today. Though hegemony is often used to try to understand how settled situations of power work, it is also invaluable to thinking through moments where the existing power structures begin to fall apart. Once all of the 'local laws' of power begin to fail, we must return to general principles, and it is hegemony that gives us a suitable method to understand the mechanics of power in their broadest dimensions

But what in fact even is power? Simply put, power is the capacity to influence. From this perspective, politics is *the operation of power and nothing else*. Politics is above all a practical business of the construction, transformation, and contestation of systems of power. Arguably, there can be no such thing as a theory of power in itself. This is because power is never merely concerned with itself, because power is that thing which is manipulatively involved in the relations, dynamics, and configurations of other things. Everything is *not* political, at least not a priori. Yet anything *can be* political should politics become concerned with its arrangement, whether as a matter of policy or through less intentional or explicit effects. Power, the sole concern of politics, must of necessity itself always be found within another substance. Power is that hungry thing that consumes all and is at once everywhere and nowhere.

It is this liquid, mercurial entity that hegemony best describes. Yet because power in itself must always be present in some other kind of substance, this raises for us the brute fact that we are writing today almost one hundred years since Gramsci's key prison writings. Our world is very different to that of the 1920s and '30s. The very existence of neoliberalism, a reactionary movement to route around all the efforts to restrain capital that were developed in the early twentieth century, attests to this, let alone the emergence of digital technology platforms, global finance, or disaggregated supply chains. For these reasons we need to update and upgrade Gramsci's account (and those of his most notable successors). This book therefore presents a number of developments on the modern and postmodern theories of hegemony.

This book is arranged in three main sections. We encourage our readers to tackle them in any order but would draw attention to the fact that most of the social history is concentrated in part I, the political theory in part II, and the political strategy in part III. We have also included a glossary of key terms for reference.

Power in the Twenty-First Century

Power can only be effectively measured with reference to processes of change and stasis. The way to determine who has the majority of power and who does not is to examine what the dynamics of relative change and stasis are, and to consider which interests are being served in the process, and which intentions are being realised. Given this, which of the competing social, political, economic and cultural agendas of the last great period of global political upheaval, the 1970s and '80s, have acquired the most force and social authority? Of all of the competing social groups to emerge during this period – from the New Right to the New Left – who actually got the world that they wanted? There is a clear answer to this question: the people who got the world that they wanted were the tech entrepreneurs of Silicon Valley and those sections of finance capital closely aligned with them. The precise combination of social liberalisation, anti-egalitarianism, globalisation, deregulation of markets, financialisation of assets and digitisation of media and information that has characterised the leading tendencies of global culture (and we do mean global) can be seen as more or less direct expressions of the interests and values of this particular coalition of class fractions.

It is the success of these forces in establishing a leading position in global society that is the key reason for a widely-remarked-upon sense of cultural stasis in those regions where they are most prevalent and from which they exercise power. This is ultimately symptomatic of an era during which there was no significant political challenge to the social leadership exercised by this grouping of interests, which fully established itself during the administrations of Bill Clinton and Tony Blair in the 1990s. The 'long 1990s', as we set out, is a cultural, political, and economic phenomenon which describes a situation, running up until 2016, where despite intensive technological innovation, social and political relations remained remarkably stable (while still following a distinct trajectory). This is one way we can understand hegemony. Contrary to mystificatory and obfuscatory accounts of 'hegemony' in much of the existing literature, what 'hegemony' means is precisely the capacity to organise social change to the advantage of particular social groups, as exhibited by the elite class fractions.

What are the precise mechanisms by which the power of these hegemonic class fractions has been established and maintained? One way to understand the hegemony of neoliberalism is by asserting the empirical specificity of 'actual existing neoliberalism': a configuration of ideological narratives, governmental techniques, technological adaptations and organisational procedures. These ought to be distinguished from any simple application of classical neoliberal *theory*, which characteristically tends to conceal its real operations.

There are three key aspects of actually existing neoliberalism as we understand it. First, there is the didactic and symbolic elements of neoliberal ideology, which can easily be discerned within much of contemporary culture: a set of entrepreneurial, competitive, individualist norms that are explicitly encouraged across a range of social sites, from schools to reality television shows and internet influencer culture. Second, there are the infrastructural, technological, and organisational aspects of this process, which are the ways in which neoliberal assumptions are institutionalised by practices of government and even by the specific deployment of new technologies. These elements must be understood as just as significant as the symbolic ones. Third, neoliberalism in practice has always been enabled and supported by authoritarian, racist, and outright antidemocratic practices of government that, despite the libertarian rhetoric, in no way run contrary to its persistent immanent logics.

Hegemony Now

How does this analysis of our political conjuncture require us to change the way we think about hegemonic power? How is it that particular political projects, such as neoliberalism, have been able to establish and maintain positions of hegemony? We have devised three major conceptual developments necessary to properly answer this question: a theory of passive consent, an analysis of material political interests, and a model of platforms and infrastructures. Each of these pushes the basic framework offered by Gramsci and his successors in new directions.

Different publics have participated in hegemonic relations in many distinct ways. 'Consent' to hegemonic rule by non-hegemonic groups is complex and takes many differing forms in practice. It becomes clear by analysing the history of political consent that the crude assumption that 'hegemony' can only be achieved through majority active consent to particular sets of governing norms is simply untrue.

Hegemony is best understood as a form of leadership where particular groups acquire the ability to determine the general direction of travel of a given social formation, while other groups must only be fully recruited to the views and outlooks of the hegemonic when it is strategically necessary. A good example of the latter situation is the recruitment of senior institutional managers to explicitly or implicitly neoliberal perspectives, even in situations wherein almost all other functionaries of those institutions explicitly reject such perspectives. In such a situation, the prevalence of a complex, multifaceted 'structure of feeling' is what helps to secure general participation in a specific hegemonic project, rather than simple active support for that project on the part of all concerned. 'Structure of feeling' is a term that we derive from the work of Raymond Williams, and refers to the idea that in any given society, at any historical moment, certain social groups will share particular sentiments, world-views and default responses to situations. For Williams, and for us, structures of feeling are always characterised by particular orientations towards hegemonic norms and interests, whether their orientation be one of general acceptance, enthusiastic endorsement, outright opposition or a complex combination of all three. For example, as we will argue in more detail later, for much of the past few decades, probably the most widespread structure of feeling in which citizens of the US or the UK have participated has been one that neither fully embraces nor fully rejects the individualistic, money-driven norms of a society ruled by corporate interests. This prevalent structure of feeling has combined a cynical resignation at the lack of political agency enjoyed by most citizens with a conscious but ineffectual critique of capitalist selfishness and an embrace of the everyday pleasures of an advanced consumer society. This exemplifies the ways in which the great continuum of possible reactions to hegemonic power that lie somewhere between active consent and active dissent can all be understood as varieties of passive consent. Contemporary forms of hegemony often focus on cultivating just this range of responses.

In recent years, the social agents who have established such a system of hegemony are the class fractions of Wall Street and

Silicon Valley. We can best consider them primarily as confluences of objective material interests. Contemporary radical theory desperately needs a coherent model of politics as primarily a contest between interests, in order to escape from the debilitating limitations of theoretical models which assume that 'identities' or 'values' are the real objects and subjects of contemporary political struggle. While the post-Marxist impulse to move away from class reductionism was a necessary and correct response to the growing complexity of modern and postmodern societies, the consequent abandonment of any understanding of politics as centrally concerned with the expression of material interests has been analytically and strategically disastrous. To put it simply: it is true that not all interests can be understood simply or primarily as class interests, but it is also true that what holds together political collectives – such as feminist movements, anti-racist protest groups or movements for transgender rights – is not primarily a shared 'identity' so much as a common set of material interests (which may or may not be signified in terms of a shared symbolic identity). Simultaneously, the prioritisation of social 'values' or 'recognition' as primary political processes always risks complicity with a liberal and idealist conception of politics. Instead, hegemony must always be understood as a crystallisation and ongoing expression of particular social interests.

In order to fully understand the role of passive consent and material interests we must look towards a third dimension of modern hegemonic power: platforms, the structural mode of hegemony. Here we can observe the key technical mechanisms by which the alliance of finance capital and big tech have established their hegemony within contemporary global politics. We consider the political means by which finance capital – greatly assisted by emergent digital technologies – re-established pre-eminence within the capitalist class and across wider society in the 1980s and '90s: a position that it had lost after the Great Crash of 1929. Alongside that, we can identify the methods that digital technology corporations such as Apple, Facebook and Google used to establish virtual monopolies both on the distribution of information and on key infrastructures of everyday life, communication, and entertainment. It is the platform that is today a key mechanism of infrastructural power, and it is through their control of finance and technology platforms that these groups have come to predominate. Platforms can be understood as instantiations of hegemonic social relations, enabling a range of forms of participation, while always setting subtle limits to the freedom of action enjoyed by their participants.

The Future War of Position

Given our present situation of crisis, what can be done, and by whom? In order to answer that, we need a detailed account of the social composition of the contemporary political moment. Who are the key social and cultural constituencies, who can be regarded as significant collective political actors, and what are the most significant emergent and residual tendencies defining the general directions of travel?

The implications of such an analysis establish the context in which strategies can be constructed for progressive politics in the near future. This concerns questions such as what specific class alliances and other types of social coalitions might plausibly have the potential to cohere and challenge both the hegemony of the techno-financial elite and the emerging power of the nationalist authoritarian alternative; what type of substantial programme might such coalitions coalesce around; and what types of technical and institutional infrastructures would they need to build in order to realise their political potential?

There is a necessarily socialist character to our strategy, which has both populist and democratic dimensions. Populist, because it must articulate the interests of the people, within the maximal possible political horizon. Democratic, because it must take a basic defence of liberal institutions of democracy and go further, to build new practices of democracy throughout society. Only a left political strategy that can productively combine populist and democratic aspects might have the capacity to supplant the hegemony of technology and finance sectors, and present a credible bulwark against the nationalist authoritarians rising to take their place.

PART I:

POWER IN THE TWENTY-FIRST CENTURY

1

WHO WON THE TWENTIETH CENTURY?

Something ended in 2016. Donald Trump won the presidency. Britain voted for Brexit.[1] Jeremy Corbyn won a second election for the Labour leadership in as many years.[2] A self-declared democratic socialist became, briefly, a plausible candidate for the US presidency.[3] None of this was supposed to be possible, and nobody was sure what it meant.

Commentators from the worlds of political journalism and political science alike declared that politics had simply become incomprehensible.[4] The apparently immutable laws of the political world had broken down, replaced with something monstrous and unintelligible. It was clear that something had changed and that something had ended, even if it was not clear yet what might be beginning.

What had ended was a period of certainty during which, if nothing else, such outcomes could be relied upon to remain unthinkable. All of these occurrences were signs that, to the right and to the left, a certain kind of consensus had broken down. That consensus maintained that there was really only one way to run a contemporary society. The basic elements of this ubiquitous governing agenda are familiar to us all: free market economics, a growth model based on ever-expanding consumption (enabled by ever-expanding private and sometimes public debt), a perpetual drive to privatise public services, a general tendency towards social liberalisation and multiculturalism, the official embrace of individualistic, entrepreneurial norms within every social and cultural sphere.[5] All meaningful political debate was supposed to take place within the parameters defined by this agenda. There could be disagreement, for example, over what form the privatisation of public services should take, or how far it should go; but there could be no question of reversing that process, or even severely limiting it.[6] Those who wished to break with this consensus were restricted to ineffectual forms of protest[7] and were told that their views were shared by an insignificant minority of the population.[8]

This neoliberal consensus had only fully consolidated in the 1990s. The 'New Right' of Margaret Thatcher and Ronald Reagan had paved the way for it. They had done this in part by simply beating into submission those populations who had the most to lose from the contraction of the public sector and the defeat of post-war progressivism: urban minorities,[9] organised labour,[10] and the legatees of the counterculture.[11] They had also won over sufficient sections of working-class constituencies by making promises that they could never keep: to defend 'traditional family values'[12] and to reverse the rise of multiculturalism.[13]

Their version of neoliberalism, however, was violently coercive and self-contradictory: it pledged to free the market but still somehow restrict the free movement of people, to liberate the individual entrepreneur but somehow protect the nuclear family.[14] It could never have lasted for long. What emerged in response in the 1990s was apparently a far more stable and plausible social model, embracing neoliberal economics but marrying it with forms of (limited) social liberalism and a kind of cosmopolitan aesthetic.[15] This was the politics of the 'Third Way' embraced by Bill Clinton, Tony Blair, and more or less every Western government at some juncture during this period.[16] Even the George W. Bush administration did not go far in departing from it domestically, despite the influence of the neoconservatives and their deadly foreign policy. In the UK, the persistence of the consensus was marked by the fact that David Cameron, Conservative prime minister from 2010 to 2016, proudly (and accurately) declared himself 'the heir to Blair'.[17]

What happened in 2016 is difficult to define with absolute precision. There was certainly no emergence of a clear alternative consensus, no smooth replacement of one order with another.[18] There was no public declaration from any government that the neoliberal epoch was over. In the US, the leadership of the Democratic Party remained doggedly committed to the 1990s *doxa*, even while opinion polls showed that this was going to cost them the election.[19] But something had shifted. The capacity of that consensus to define the terms of debate, to command the political stage unchallenged, had clearly entered some kind of terminal phase. Neoliberalism, if not yet dead, was *dying*.

What Ended?

'Consensus' is a lazy word for what went into decline here. It is a term that often finds its most frequent use in the idea of the 'post-war consensus', that general commitment to industrial consumer capitalism, an expanding welfare state, full employment and rising wages that was shared by governments left and right in the capitalist world from roughly 1945 to 1975, also variously termed 'social democracy' in Europe and 'embedded liberalism' in the United States.[20] But it is debatable whether neoliberalism ever achieved such a consensual status, in the sense of being able to command the explicit assent of a significant proportion of the governed population in any country.[21] The general assumption of most historians and commentators, from which we see no reason to depart, is that during the post-war period there was explicitly articulated majority support for the basic terms of this settlement.[22] This has never been the case during the neoliberal epoch. Opinion polls and surveys of public attitudes have consistently shown that to the contrary, there has never been widespread assent to the assumption that competitive individualism and the drive to privatise public services are desirable orienting values of public policy.[23] As we will explain further later on, general consent to the neoliberal project has been maintained by means other than mere persuasion of the public that it was a good idea. Some have been convinced that no viable alternative has existed or that the only viable alternatives would be worse; most have simply accepted the pleasures offered by life in an advanced consumer society as adequate compensation for the loss of those democratic and welfare rights enjoyed by citizens of the mid-twentieth century. To say that what ended was a 'consensus' is, therefore, not precisely accurate.

What ended was, more specifically, the capacity of a particular social group to convince the rest of the population to defer to that consensus, whether they explicitly agreed with it or not. This social group consists of professional politicians, journalists and media workers at various institutional scales, as well as the managers of public institutions and corporations. This includes many of the so-called political class that emerged as a distinctive group over the course of the 1980s, as the declining efficacy of liberal democracy gave rise to a new set of relationships between citizens and their representatives.[24] To refer to this grouping as a 'class' is clearly not accurate in any properly sociological or Marxian sense: we can think of them as a class fraction, a specific subgroup, or even a defined network of individuals, of the general class of senior managers and ideological professionals that usually does not exercise any direct command over capital but derives its authority from it. Its role since the 1980s has been to manage the general implementation of the neoliberal programme, while interfacing between the wider population and the interests that they ultimately serve (primarily those of finance capital).[25] Politically, its ongoing task is to push neoliberalisation as far as it can go without provoking too much concerted hostile reaction in any given local context, while determining what democratic or egalitarian concessions may be offered to the general population without in any way compromising the profitability of finance. The political class's main claim to public legitimacy always lies in its supposed 'competence'. Sometimes 'competence' is understood strictly as 'economic competence', which is registered by the public almost exclusively in terms of how far and for how long particular regimes are able to guarantee their ongoing and increasing capacity for private consumption.[26] Sometimes competence is understood in terms of a general capacity for effective administrative and ideological management. The political class's ideal mode of operation is as an explicitly technocratic elite claiming to be above politics, merely exercising the necessary judgement to manage a social and economic system that only fools would ever try to change.[27] Of course, this is not unique to this group or this time – to some extent, every social group that has ever exercised any form of social leadership has tried to pass itself off as doing the only things that could reasonably be done, and to mask the fact that it is always serving some interests more than others.

The 2008 financial crisis and its long-term aftermath had already compromised the political class's claims to economic competence in many countries. What 2016 marked was the almost complete loss of its political and ideological efficacy in the UK and the US. It is important not to exaggerate the scale or ubiquity of this crisis. Elsewhere in Europe, the period from 2015 to 2017 saw the European Union exert full authority over the Syriza regime in Greece – forcing it to abandon its social democratic programme and accept a neoliberal austerity package[28] and the election of Emmanuel Macron as France's most explicitly technocratic and neoliberal president.[29] This also came shortly after a period when the EU had effectively installed by fiat the government of Mario Monti in Italy in 2011–13, an administration of unelected technocrats.[30]

7

Apparently, within the institutional confines of the eurozone, the technocratic neoliberal political class remained in full control of the situation.[31] Even in the Anglosphere, neoliberalism remained so embedded, in so many key social institutions on so many scales of time and space, that it was difficult to imagine its effects ever being reversed. The Conservative government elected in the UK in 2015 had pursued the further neoliberalisation of those institutions that have remained relatively protected until now and that command no popular support from swing voters (most notably universities).[32] By 2017, elements of explicit neoliberal ideology still remained central to the discourse of the prime minister: Theresa May's first speeches in that role repeated the most clichéd and least plausible of all neoliberal promises: the construction of an authentic 'meritocracy'.[33]

However, these speeches also marked a shift in Conservative rhetoric, decrying social inequality and promising to address the concerns of working-class communities abandoned by thirty years of de-industrialisation. Labour radically improved its electoral position at the 2017 election, the first under Jeremy Corbyn's leadership (when almost every professional commentator and pollster had predicted an electoral disaster for Labour) despite the unprecedented hostility of the liberal as well as the conservative media, including the supposedly neutral BBC.[34] This success was widely credited to Labour's adoption of an explicitly anti-austerity, anti-neoliberal social democratic programme.[35] Just two years previously, media had accused the previous Labour leader, Ed Miliband, of revolutionary Marxism simply for advocating some regulation of the energy market,[36] attacks which appeared to have seriously affected his popularity. Between 2015 and 2017, something had changed.

This change can best be understood in terms of the political class's loss of control of the political situation. This in turn raises serious questions about the status of the overall neoliberal project, which has always depended upon them for its implementation and as a mediator between the demands of various elements of capital and national populations. The situation today bears many of the marks of what is known as a 'hegemonic crisis' or 'organic crisis':[37] a situation in which some relatively stable order of social relations and political priorities has broken down, and a new one has not yet emerged. But there would be a potential problem with confidently asserting that we are in such a situation today. The political class may have been crucial to the implementation of neoliberalism, but it is also clear that neoliberalism was never simply their project. Certainly all of their wealth and social authority depended upon its success. But they were never the principle or sole beneficiaries of the social and political arrangements that emerged in the 1980s and '90s. The question to address now, then, is: who were the main beneficiaries of those arrangements, and are their interests and intentions in any way compromised by the current 'crisis'?

Our answer, which will be central to much of our argument in this book, is that the real fundamental agents and beneficiaries of neoliberalism, as an actually enacted governmental project since the late 1970s, were specific sections of the capitalist class associated with the financial and technology sectors. As many existing arguments contend, this required the efforts of agents such as a reconstituted political class and neoliberalism's characteristic forward guard of think-tanks. However, it was ultimately the interests and values of these two groups – information technology and finance – which were most clearly crystallised through neoliberalism, and which simultaneously constructed the infrastructures which worked most to embed it within everyday life. Before considering the current and future state of neoliberalism, however, we must explain why we take this view, and how this group was able to take power.

Winning the Twentieth Century

Where is power today? Put another way, who or what has power in the world? How is it exercised, and how do we recognise it when we see it? Perhaps the simplest, crudest, way to answer this question is to ask: Who is able to get what they want? What individuals or institutions are able to produce outcomes that seem to be in line with their intentions, interests and preferences?

An interesting way to approach the question of who exercises or has exercised power today is therefore to consider this simple question: who is getting the world that they want? Of course, right now, as at any other moment in history, the active term here would be 'getting': we could probably never say that anyone has definitely 'got' the world that they want. So a useful question we can ask is 'Who seems to have come out best from recent conflicts over the question of what kind of world we should live in?'

At any one moment, it may be possible to take a kind of snapshot of existing power relationships on various scales. Globally, nationally, locally, even within a particular household, we can identify *who* has power in relation to *whom*. But any such static picture will always be misleading, because power is never something that anybody simply possesses or does not possess.[38] Power only exists to the extent that it is exercised – that is to say, power is an act, an action, a process. Power is exercised in particular situations in order to produce effects or to resist the production of effects. That is why when asking where power lies in any given situation, it is always necessary to consider that situation historically, asking what is *changing* and why. Power is dynamic because it is always trying to change something (or to prevent something from changing). This is the core of politics itself.

On the face of it, the answer to this question of who is getting the world they want appears to be very clear. It is the super-rich, the great financial institutions, the most prominent corporations and the international supra-governmental bodies (the International Monetary Fund, the World Bank, the World Trade Organisation, and the European Union) that seem most able to dictate terms to the rest of the planet, and most able to influence the direction of change.[39] We will not attempt to challenge this ordinary assumption. Nor will we offer any shocking revelations when it comes to the question of *who* or *what* exercises power in the world today. Instead, we will try to explain *how* they have been able to hold this power, which is a more complicated and interesting story, and one which is important for what it tells us about the nature of power itself.

At least since the early 1990s, we have been living through a period when there were few effective challenges to the worldwide extension of a particular economic system and the assumptions that animate it.[40] In global terms, the last such period of struggle ended with the defeat of Soviet Communism and the decision by the Chinese Communist Party to take its country on a 'capitalist road'.[41] In Latin America there have been periods of genuine popular resistance to neoliberalism that have crystallised for a time in the programmes of genuinely radical socialist governments;[42] but at the time of writing this book, almost all of those programmes have been terminated. In the Middle East and elsewhere, forms of religious conservatism have emerged in opposition to the cultural norms most closely associated with Western neoliberalism, but they have seldom posed a serious threat to its core economic agenda.[43]

Culture Wars

Western Europe and North America will necessarily be our main area of focus in this book, while most of our claims could be extended to Australia and New Zealand (where experiments in neoliberal governance arguably predated their equivalents in the US and the UK). In these regions, the last period of really sustained social conflict was that stretching from the moment of the break-up of the so-called post-war consensus to the crystallisation of a socially liberal, cosmopolitan, neoliberal consensus in the early 1990s. 'Culture wars' emerged as a key term of political debate in the early 1990s,[44] describing what was arguably the final phase of this period, after the global political defeat of the organised left had put fundamental economic questions out of contention, and before it had become clear that a socially and culturally conservative form of neoliberalism would prove both too unpopular and too internally contradictory to be sustainable. The phrase has been used by commentators to refer to the set of intense political conflicts – over 'social' issues such as reproductive rights, the legal status of LGBTQ people and their relationships, attempts by public institutions to combat institutionalised racism, and so on – that defined much political debate at that time in the United States, and (to a lesser extent) other countries such as the UK.

This term has remained memorable because it captures, succinctly and evocatively, the sense of an existential conflict between competing visions of the world. It seems clear enough in retrospect that the 'cultural' issues at its heart aroused such strong feelings partly because this was merely the terminal phase of a longer and more wide-ranging conflict. Indeed, in that larger struggle, almost everything had been at stake. The questions of what kind of world, what kind of economy, what kind of society, what distribution of power would replace the post-war order had all been on the table. This was all prior to the final collapse of the Soviet experiment in 1991, the election of Bill Clinton in 1992 and the creation of the World Trade Organization in 1995 (the express purpose of which was always to enforce American-led neoliberalism on a global scale).[45] Before all that, the final victory of cosmopolitan neoliberalism had looked far less inevitable than it would eventually seem.

To really understand the nature of what had been at stake, we must shift our historical gaze to the most intense phase of that longer conflict. This is the moment whose turbulent spirit is exemplified by the political events of 1968, but that really stretches over a much longer period: the May 1968 uprisings in France, the Prague Spring and its suppression, and the protest at the Democratic National Convention in Chicago[46] are merely one very widely remembered cluster of occurrences in a sequence that stretched out over almost two decades, in various spatial contexts, sometimes referred to in their broadest sense as 'antisystemic movements'.[47] Exactly when 'the long 1968' begins is open to interpretation; plausible starting points include the Montgomery bus boycott of 1955–56, Nikita Khrushchev's secret denunciation of Joseph Stalin (or the Soviet invasion of Hungary) in 1956, the Cuban Revolution of 1959, the formation of Students for a Democratic Society in 1962,[48] or the Algerian war of independence that ended that same year,[49] among many other events. This period's end point is more clearly demarcated, even if it evidently stretched out over a number of years, and was punctuated differently in different places. The decade 1979–89 saw the election of Thatcher and Reagan and the total defeat of the labour movement in each of their countries; in France, the jettison of François Mitterrand's radical left programme within one term of his presidential administration; and the storming of the Berlin Wall, followed by the final disintegration of the Soviet Union.[50]

The key moment in this long history is the one initiated by the events of 1968, culminating in the early 1970s. Of all the 1968 events, perhaps the most symbolically pivotal was the assassination of Martin Luther King Jr. in April, marking as it did the apparent end of the dream of peaceful civic reform leading to harmonious racial integration within the United

States. The Black Panther Party for Self-Defense, though almost two years old by this point, only became a major pole of attraction for black politics during the period of mass radicalisation that followed King's death.[51] If anything came to evidence the genuine threat posed to the American socio-political system by the global radical wave of that time, it was the reaction of the US security state to the Black Panthers and their movement – a reaction that only intensified once the Panthers switched their focus from paramilitary grandstanding to highly effective community organising.[52] The cold-blooded summary execution by police of a large number of activists and leaders, many of whose killers faced no criminal charges, and the recorded assertions by FBI founder and director J. Edgar Hoover that the Panthers represented the single greatest threat to national security bear witness to the fact that this was a moment when a real possibility of radical social change appeared to be manifest and immediate.[53] The fear of Hoover and the interests that he served was not simply that black militancy would get out of hand and threaten public order, but that it might develop the political and cultural capacity to inspire and lead revolutionary forces among many different sections of the population.[54] Notoriously, in 1975 the Trilateral Commission – an intergovernmental think-tank comprising representatives of American, European and Japanese governments – reported that liberal democracies were becoming ungovernable as a consequence of an 'excess of democracy' that was overtaking their societies and their institutions.[55]

The Trilateral Commission was not mistaken. A desire for more democracy than could be offered by the established institutions of representation was widespread and took many forms. It constituted a key point of resonance between many of the movements and struggles emerging at that time, and was arguably the overriding demand that they had in common. From women's liberation[56] to the nascent environmental movement,[57] from the communes of the counterculture[58] to the movements for workers' control in industry,[59] what they shared was a desire to make private issues public, to socialise and decentralise decision-making, and to redistribute resources and respect.

This may have been the shared aim and desire of a range of radical constituencies at that moment. But they were far from being the only actors on the political stage. The breakdown of the post-war consensus was apparent on the right as well as on the radical left. In the US, the conservative reaction against the legacy and agenda of the New Deal was already well underway. Republican senator Barry Goldwater's disastrous 1964 presidential campaign showed that the public was not yet ready to break with the progressive consensus; however, the same public would elect Richard Nixon four years later. While Nixon's attacks on the New Deal legacy met with limited success, they initiated a legislative programme of 'reform' that would be carried on by all of his successors up to the present.[60]

In the UK, 1968 saw a wave of student occupations and anti-war protests that were mild by international standards. The most significant political event of that year was the notorious speech given by Conservative member of Parliament Enoch Powell. Generally referred to as the 'Rivers of Blood' speech (although that precise phrase wasn't used in it), Powell's oration expressed an explicitly racist abhorrence of non-white immigrants while predicting that their presence in British communities would inevitably result in a race war. Powell's conservatism chimed with that of many of his American counterparts[61] as well as that of French reactionaries: whatever localised differences may have existed between them, they all shared a profound nostalgia for the untroubled white supremacy of the colonial and imperial era, and a desire to reverse the trend towards ethnically diverse societies. In the UK and the US, new organisations committed to the defence of public decency arose in order to curtail the growing permissiveness of media culture and wider society.[62]

By the early 1970s, it was clear that a new conservative 'structure of feeling' was crystallising in response to changing social and cultural conditions.[63] Combining an individualist rejection of corporatism and welfarism with an authoritarian social conservatism, this structure of feeling had not yet clearly attached itself to the ideas and policies of the explicitly 'neoliberal' tradition. In countries such as the UK, it was emerging as a largely endogenous reaction to the breakdown of the post-war consensus, as commentaries by sociologist Stuart Hall and others would note before the decade was out.[64] Its final political realisation would come with the electoral triumph of the New Right with Thatcher's election in 1979 and Reagan's in 1980.

A small part of the right-wing coalition that would emerge in the 1970s may have been made up of entrepreneurial individuals frustrated by the bureaucratic state – the key constituency whom Reagan and Thatcher would later claim to represent. However, a far larger part of that coalition seems to have been always motivated by hostility to the social liberalisation of the time and by white supremacist reaction. Indeed, opposition to the bureaucratic state was a position that tended to be identified with the New Left more than with the political right until the 1980s. What the new conservatives wanted was to check the tendencies that were transforming their social world: feminism, youth culture, anti-racism, and gay liberation. In this, they had very little success at all. The world that emerged in the 1980s and 1990s may have been one in which the very possibility of socialism or communism seemed to have been consigned to the past. However, it was also one in which, by 1995, a restoration of 'traditional' (i.e., 1920s–1950s) gender roles or a reversal of multiculturalism would come to be widely seen as implausible. Indeed, if anyone emerged from the turbulence of the

1970s to get exactly the world that they had wanted, it wasn't the social conservatives.

But it wasn't the radicals either. The 'new social movements' of the period achieved some of their objectives,[65] but only on the very limited terms made possible by the advance of neoliberalism. Liberal feminism became part of the normative ideology of the capitalist world, but of the various demands of the women's movement, only those compatible with neoliberal norms were realised, except in countries that had strong residual social democratic institutions.[66] In the US, for example, women were enabled and encouraged to compete with men in the labour market, but not to expect social support for childcare. As for the aims of the anti-racist movements: a black man could become president, provided he'd been to Harvard, but the rate of incarceration of black males continued to climb to historically unprecedented levels.[67]

As such, it became fashionable from 1978 onwards to claim that the radicalism of the '68 moment had all been superficial, an outburst of hedonistic individualism that would find expression in the consumerist culture of the 1980s.[68] In fact, no close attention to the demands and desires expressed in that moment can support that conclusion. It is clear that a powerful critique of liberal individualism and the limitations of consumer culture were central to the discourses of the counterculture, the New left, Black Power, women's liberation and gay liberation.[69] By the same token, however, it is clear that the world that emerged under Thatcher and her successors was a far cry from the one they had wanted.

The Winners

It would be naive to imagine that any constituency ever gets *exactly* what they think they want, or even that they have a fully verifiable notion of what that might be. Actual historic outcomes are almost always complex, incomplete and inconclusive. 'The world' at any given moment is the product of the dense interaction of multiple forces, and the outcomes of contests and struggles are an effect of the relative strength of the contending forces over time. Accordingly, it seems safe to say that the real culture wars of the 1970s were not won by either of the most obvious contending sides: the radicals or the conservatives. However, that doesn't mean that there are never winners at all. This raises an interesting analytical question: might there have been other allied or emergent constituencies, visible in the same moment of intense conflict in the early 1970s who might be worth considering in these terms, and who might have come closer to getting exactly the world that they were after?

The early 1970s marked a critical moment in the emergence and formation of Silicon Valley. Both Bill Gates – founder of Microsoft – and Steve Jobs – founder and long-serving CEO of Apple – began their activities in the area at this time, as members of the same small network of personal computer hobbyists and entrepreneurs. Those activities are now extremely well documented, and it is not difficult to extrapolate from their record, and from the subsequent development of Silicon Valley, a clear sense of the ideological priorities and material interests that animated them. A certain commitment to the expansion of computing for its own sake – its reach, power and application – has always been a key element.[70] It is easy enough to see that this represents simultaneously an ideological commitment and the expression of a basic material interest: the more computers are used, the more wealth and influence software developers, computer engineers and manufacturers accumulate. A commitment to entrepreneurial freedom and, concomitantly, a generally libertarian social outlook have been a clear feature of the culture of this formation throughout its existence. A distaste for both corporate and governmental bureaucracy, tending as it always will to limit both entrepreneurial freedom and the capacity of enthusiasts to engage in unregulated technical experimentation, has been discernible throughout that time. By the same token, a certain disavowal of the American computer industry's debts to the military-industrial complex has been a persistent element of its formation. This always went alongside a general sympathy for countercultural attitudes and tastes that was rarely accompanied by a serious commitment to political or social radicalism.[71]

Within even the very early culture of Silicon Valley, a distinctive tension could be discerned between the 'hacker ethic' – with its commitment to entirely free and open information, born as it was in a university laboratory – and the entrepreneurial drive to protect intellectual property.[72] This was not a superficial short-term contradiction, but a defining productive tension that continues to animate the entire domain of networked and computer-driven social and economic relationships. This tension is in part related to the complex class status of the individuals and companies that have made up the tech sector from the moment of its commercial inception. To the extent that they are engaged in activities whose long-term objective is capital accumulation, there is always a need to protect property and profits; to the extent that they are engaged in a social project to extend human capacities through the advance of computer technology, there is a certain drive to share information irrespective of profits. At the same time, even within the processes of accumulation, there are paradoxical imperatives to both protect property and to disseminate it. Hardware manufacturers, for instance, have an interest in the free distribution of software, while platform capitalists need to attract users to be able to sell their data to advertisers, to the point that it is in their interests to make entry costs to the platforms themselves as low as possible. These are the principal reasons why the behaviour and ideological priorities of Silicon Valley actors are, and always have been, in certain senses typical of those of capitalists in general, while in others they remain unique.

Taken all together, these features amount to a very distinctive cluster of interests and preferences. Moreover, it is difficult to discern any significant way in which the general direction of social change and public policy has failed to serve them since the 1980s. The general tendency towards social liberalisation has been effected by means of a general individualisation and privatisation of culture[73] that clearly expresses the priorities of Silicon Valley libertarianism far more fully than it conforms to the forms of collectivist liberation once dreamed of by the counterculture and the New Left. We live today in a world in which the vast bulk of the manufacturing industry once based in the Western economies has now relocated to China, and other centres across South-east Asia. Was this the dream of Nixon when he opened diplomatic negotiations with China, and of Thatcher when she undertook her assault on the British labour movement and the manufacturing sector that was its base? Of course not. Indeed, it is hard to see who on the planet (apart, arguably, from certain Chinese elites), has ultimately benefitted from this shift more than the US technology industry.[74] At the same time, the social and political influence of that industry has hardly been used to defend the traditional forms of authority and morality to which both Nixon and Thatcher were committed. It is true that the great geopolitical objective of the American military-industrial complex – total victory over the Soviet Union – was achieved. Therefore, one could argue that the military state should be understood as one of those actors on the political stage of the early 1970s that finally achieved the world it was looking for. However, it is hard to believe that any key figure in the US security state of the early '70s would have rested easy in the knowledge that the ultimate destiny of the US was to win the Cold War, only to find itself with a historically unprecedented trade and debt deficit to China.

Even the extraordinary success of the Chinese Communist Party itself has been bought at the expense of a complete reversal of many of the Maoist precepts to which its cadres were clearly still committed in the aftermath of the Cultural Revolution. This has been to the advantage, no doubt, of many Chinese capitalists. But above all it has been to the advantage of Silicon Valley, which would be entirely unable to function as profitably as it does without the low-cost manufacturing of computer and communications hardware in China. It is this that enabled the spread of computing, and its ubiquitous penetration of everyday life that is the single most striking historical change of the period. Indeed, as we will explain shortly, a good case can be made that all other forms of cultural and social innovation have been largely subordinated to the objective of maximal computerisation, with many deleterious consequences. Taking all of these factors into consideration, it is clear enough who won the twentieth century. It was Silicon Valley.

Of course, like any section of the capitalist class, or of the petite bourgeoisie, the tech sector is never fully independent of capital in general – and the power and priorities of finance, in particular. Indeed, until recently, it was the ascendancy of finance capital that appeared to be the real story of global politics in the late twentieth and early twenty-first centuries. The restoration of Wall Street and the rise of Silicon Valley have been deeply intertwined, it is true; but the two cannot be regarded as a simple, self-sufficient continuity. Before examining their relationship, however, it is worth rehearsing the key role that finance capital played in the transformation of the world since the early 1970s.

In Marxist theory, the distinction between financial capital and industrial capital is an important but contentious one. Put simply, this distinction differentiates between capital that is invested in manufacturing production, and capital that is used merely for speculation and lending (including being lent to manufacturers). There is a tendency, especially in the Keynesian and social democratic traditions, to understand finance as parasitic and unproductive, but to see industry as productive and progressive (sometimes expressed in distinctions between the 'real economy' of manufacturing and the 'financial economy'). It is also routine for orthodox Marxists to dismiss this perspective for its failure to understand the extent to which finance capital is historically prior to industrial capital (i.e., that there were banks before there were factories) and that industrial capital is almost always politically, economically and socially subordinate to finance capital. Whatever Marx's digressions on the 'fictitious' nature of financial capital,[75] for capitalism such fictions are necessary ones.

The 1971–73 dissolution of the Bretton Woods system of global monetary management marked a pivotal moment in the global crisis of post-war capitalism. There is little question that this marked the beginning of the restoration of finance capital, culminating with the major deregulations of the financial industries undertaken by Thatcher and Reagan in the second half of the 1980s. But it is also precisely the moment when the ascendancy of Silicon Valley really begins. The high-tech industry has been present in the Bay Area and the regions to its south since the early twentieth century,[76] and all of the key technologies that would drive the computer revolution (the computer, the microprocessor, networking, the mouse, the personal terminal, etc.) had been developed, mainly by military-funded university labs, by the end of the 1960s. But the beginnings of the personal computer industry as such, and a massive escalation in the use of computers by government and corporations, can be dated to exactly this historical moment.[77] Our simple contention is that these two developments – the rise of Silicon Valley and the restoration of Wall Street – must be understood as deeply intertwined and to a large extent mutually dependent. For example, without the introduction of electronic, computerised credit card payment authorisation systems from 1973, the general development of a consumer economy based on routinised personal debt, rather than on savings and perpetually rising wages, would not have been materially possible. The substitution of the one for the other was central to the entire shift towards a 'post-Fordist' economy based on very high levels of private consumption, and to the ascendancy of lenders (banks and other purveyors of personal finance) to their position of economic dominance by the 1990s.

A central episode of this story occurred in 1986. At a single stroke, a host of financial regulations governing the trade in stocks, securities, currency and debt were swept away by the Thatcher government; at precisely the same moment, the London Stock Exchange underwent full computerisation.[78] Still referred to as 'the big bang', this was simultaneously the moment of full financial deregulation and the moment of computerisation. This marks a crucial turning point not only in the story of the relationship between finance and the tech sector, but also in the history of the implementation of neoliberalism in the UK. As we will argue in the next chapter, it marked the moment when the authoritarian phase of that implementation, focussed on eliminating potential sources of opposition to neoliberalism (trade unionists, left-wing municipal activists, etc.), began to give way to a new phase focussed on the full restoration of finance capital to its position of glorious authority, and when neoliberal governments increasingly abandoned any commitment to social conservatism, instead embracing an ethic and aesthetic of globalising cosmopolitan liberalism. The year 1986 also saw the launch of the Macintosh Plus: Apple's longest-lived model of personal computer, remaining in production for half a decade.

By the time the Apple Plus ceased its record-breaking production run, the world had changed in other significant ways. The year 1991 saw the final dissolution of the Soviet Union, two years after the fall of the Berlin Wall and the effective exit of most of the 'Eastern Bloc' countries from the sphere of Soviet influence. At the same time, it had become clear during the same period that the liberalisation of the Chinese economy, underway since 1979 (the year of Thatcher's election as UK prime minister), was not going to be accompanied by any form of political liberalisation equivalent to that which had been undertaken by the regime of Mikhail Gorbachev in the Soviet Union. The military suppression of student protests demanding liberal democratic reforms was widely understood in the West a sign that the Chinese leadership had not yet grasped the inevitable truth: that progress into industrial modernity could only take the form of liberal democracy, married to a Western-style market economy.[79] In retrospect, it looks instead to be the moment when the Chinese leadership asserted their commitment to a different path for Chinese development: a path that, as it turned out, led to the most successful modernisation project in the history of humanity (if success is measured not in moral terms, but in simple terms of the number of people moved out of rural poverty and into relative urban comfort).[80] Without the success of this project, China would not have become the global centre for low-cost manufacturing. Without that occurrence, Apple would have found it very difficult to produce Macintosh computers, and eventually iPods and iPhones, in the quantities and at the price levels that enabled it, in August 2018, to become the world's first trillion-dollar company by market capitalisation. We do not mean to argue that Apple is somehow responsible for or complicit with the repressive regime in China. But if it is,[81] then so are many of us (these words are being typed on a MacBook).

Finally, alongside finance capital, big tech and the Chinese Communist Party, we should identify a fourth group of actors who succeeded in continuing to exert extraordinary influence over the direction of economic policy, geopolitical power and material culture. These are the interests accumulated around carbon-intensive energy industries, who have for decades successfully promoted fossil fuel use and ubiquitous motoring,[82] despite all the evidence of their social and material costs. Since the 1970s, oil companies have formed deliberate alliances with the far right of the US Republican Party as well as the most reactionary elements of evangelical Christianity, largely to help them pursue a strategy of climate denial to preserve their industry's business model.[83] While the cultural interests this nexus pursued have remained highly contentious across the whole dominant period of neoliberalism, the basic interest of carbon extractivism as usual has effectively been achieved through the continuous promotion of motoring and the extraordinary tolerance for flagrant human rights violations by the Gulf oil states on the part of supposedly liberal democratic governments.[84] It is only at the present historical moment that we can observe the development of serious opposition to the oil and gas industries' business model. However, this sector has been on the defensive since the 1970s: forced to ally itself with reactionary and residual[85] socio-cultural forces, it has been unable to exercise the same kind of persistent and ubiquitous cultural influence that the tech and finance fractions have.

Our point in elucidating all of this history is simply that this whole complex web of historical events, transitions and transformative processes can be seen by the 1990s to have produced some very clear winners: most notably the tech and finance sectors. But what exactly did they win?

The Prize

What these sectors won was a certain position of strategic superiority in the whole complex assemblage of global society. This is the position from which the tech sector, more than any other, has been able to exert an influence on the general direction of travel for culture, economics, and politics. This influence is most obviously registered at the level of material culture. What more evident transformation in the physical and corporeal texture of everyday life has there been in recent years, for almost all humans, than the ubiquitous spread of liquid crystal display (LCD) and organic light-emitting diode (OLED) screens? What more obvious change in lived culture has there been than the shift of huge quantities of specialised and general communicative activity onto the World Wide Web? (In either case, one could argue that the recent majority urbanisation of the planet has actually been the most dramatic such shift,[86] but this is more obviously the outcome of processes initiated decades and centuries previously). At the same time, it is hard to think of any social sector that has enjoyed more obvious deference from government than tech. The almost complete lack of regulation of social media platforms by the US government speaks volumes in itself.[87] It is no accident that 2016 saw the development of an urgent conversation across the developed world about the need to regulate the platform economy.[88]

At the same time, the tech sector, from this position of strategic superiority, has exercised all kinds of direct and indirect influence over the culture of the contemporary world, on many levels and with many regional variations. Simply by being the companies which more people aspire to work for than any others, they exert considerable influence as global populations of aspiring employees adjust their behaviour and public personae to accord with the perceived priorities and corporate culture of these companies. If a certain combination of cosmopolitan liberalism, entrepreneurial individualism and networked collegiality has become the common culture of global elites, then it has been through this mechanism more than any other. It is surely no accident that it was during the ascendancy of tech as the most globally influential fraction of capital that the professional political class became almost uniformly committed to this combination of values and attitudes as the ones that they sought to embody, exemplify and propagate.

At the same time, the tech sector has surely exercised a decisive influence over the nature and content of culture as such. Popular music is a key example. Arguably since the beginning of the recorded music industry, and certainly since the 1960s, the global complex of popular commercial music, centred on the US, had been a site of remarkable creative innovation. New forms, even recognisably new genres, had appeared with remarkable regularity, especially in the international space of the 'black Atlantic'[89] (the US, the UK, Africa and the Caribbean islands), from rhythm and blues to dubstep and grime. With the dawn of the millennium, however, this long period of intense innovation ground to an almost complete halt. There was no question that high-quality music continued to be made. But the experience of routinely hearing music that would have been practically unimaginable a decade earlier began to recede into memory as the new century wore on. This shift was observed by expert critics and commentators, but it wasn't just a matter of casual impression. It could surely be demonstrated with simple formal musical analysis that between 2001 and 2016, there was simply no structural innovation in popular music as significant as those that had marked the emergences of new stylistic forms such as hip-hop, drum and bass, and so on up until the end of the twentieth century.[90] What innovations that came were above all technical, relating to the storage and delivery of music: from downloading to streaming.

The Long 1990s

This was also precisely the moment when the economic and socio-technical conditions of music culture and the music industry underwent arguably their most dramatic shift since the invention of phonography. The popularisation of the MP3 file format, and the spread of broadband connectivity, made it possible for audio files to be reproduced and transmitted at effectively zero cost to most users.[91] For a relatively brief period, it seemed as if this might entirely undermine the capacity of anyone to continue accumulating profit by selling music. Although the first highly visible file-sharing site, Napster, was quickly shut down by the US courts, the rise of Myspace as the first global social media platform was fuelled largely by the way in which it became, for two or three years, one of the main loci of global music culture, as everyone from Madonna to adolescent garage bands began using it as one of the principal vehicles through which to communicate with their audiences.[92]

But Napster and Myspace only represented an intermediary phase. By 2015, it would become clear that those who were deriving the most profit from this new situation were the great aggregators – Apple and Spotify – who could sell access to huge streamable catalogues.[93] At the same time, the real losers were not the traditional major record labels, whose profits had begun to recover as they negotiated arrangements with the aggregators, especially for access to their back catalogues.[94] The losers were artists, who simply no longer had the option that the most creative of them had sought to exercise throughout the late twentieth century: to seek income by selling recordings directly to moderately sized audiences through smaller and independent record labels. Audiences benefitted to the extent that they had access to far more music far more cheaply than in the past. But to the extent that they might have hoped for new music or for musical experiences less sonically or socially impoverished than those made available by personal MP3 playback devices (that deliver poor-quality audio to isolated individuals, rather than the kind of shared and corporeal experience of music made available by traditional hi-fi or even by cheap portable stereos), they too would be disappointed.

We would say that the best characterisation of this condition would be to see both culture and institutional politics from the late 1980s onwards – after the global defeat of the left by neoliberal forces – as entering a 'long 1990s'. During this period, the increasingly unchallengeable ascendancy of particular class fractions and their specific socio-cultural agenda resulted in a gradual narrowing of the scope for either cultural or political innovation. Of course, everything changed during this time: the single most dramatic shift in human socio-technical arrangements since the industrial revolution took place, as we fully entered the information age. Yet at another level, nothing changed: the same people stayed in charge, the same political agendas were implemented, and the music all sounded the same as it had ten years previously. To be clear, 'the long 1990s' didn't have a clearly demarcated beginning, middle and end. Their characteristic structures of feeling became apparent in the 1980s, and their characteristic political agenda was consolidated in the early nineties, but the sense of an endless, ahistorical present didn't extend across popular culture until the end of that decade. What is important to understand is that none of this happened by accident, or as the result of some fundamental shift in the nature of human culture (as some theorists of 'postmodernity' seemed to posit).[95] This sense of social and cultural stasis was the normal outcome of a situation in which a particular configuration of power relations has been fully stabilised and seems to be unchallengeable. Above all, it was the unshakeable ascendancy of the tech sector that produced this overall condition.

Of course, in producing all of these effects, big tech has never acted alone (at least, as we will suggest, until very recently). It is only through its alliance with the financial sector that it has been able to achieve global reach, just as finance was only able to restore its power by deploying new digital technologies. Many of the values, agendas and policy commitments that achieved global influence during this time were ones that had historically been typical of finance capital during periods of socio-political ascendancy. Faced with historical crises, of course, finance has been prepared to make alliances with the worst fascists (who could not have committed their atrocities without its support).[96] But outside of such periods, when facing no immediate threat from the workers' movement or from governments intent on regulation, finance in its pomp, as during the fin de siècle,[97] has tended to favour a relatively cosmopolitan and socially liberalising culture: one suited to a world of frictionless international flows of people, money and products.[98] The long 1990s were as much the ultimate epoch of global finance capital as they were the period of Silicon Valley's ascendancy. This fact is attested in the relentless spread of 'financialisation' to so many areas of social life.[99] This term designates the ways in which many types of activity, service and commodity have become objects of speculation and have become fundable only through the creation and propagation of new forms of debt and indebtedness. The fact that so much of families' and individuals' consumption is today funded by borrowing is the most obvious example of this process in action, and benefits lenders (which is what finance capitalists primarily are) more than anyone else.

Post-Fordism and the Political Class

This analysis raises a crucial question: how did this coalition of class fractions (Wall Street and Silicon Valley) achieve its position of social, cultural, political and economic superiority? In part, the answer is self-evident. The tech sector has had primary access to the most advanced technologies of our, or any, age. It has used them to establish a commanding position in relation to other social sectors. Finance capital typically occupies a privileged place in any capitalist order, one that it loses only when subject to very determined and co-ordinated opposition from a sufficiently robust coalition of countervailing forces. The crisis of the 1970s undid the coalition that had held it in check since 1940, and its alliance with the tech sector enabled its swift restoration. To tell this story in any more detail would be to go into the whole history of the rise of neoliberalism – something which will have to wait for the next chapter. A key factor to consider here, however, is that neither of these class fractions, nor the coalition that they have formed, would have been able simply to impose their will by force. Both have had to offer material concessions to many other social groups in order to persuade them to acquiesce to their agendas. Most obviously, they have done this by facilitating an enormous expansion of private consumption for the majority populations of the 'developed' world.[100] But they have also had to take advantage of changes in the composition and class cultures of those populations, and it is worth briefly considering some of those changes.

We have already referred to the emergence, over the course of the 1980s and '90s, of a 'political class'. Of course, there has arguably been some kind of 'political class' in every hierarchical society. In the Roman Republic it was the social group represented by the Senate. In early modern European kingdoms, it was the aristocracy and the court. In these cases, however, it was simply the case that only specific and legally designated socio-economic groups were permitted to play any part whatsoever in the ordinary business of government. To some extent this situation obtained right up until the beginning of the era of mass suffrage, after which a distinct political class arguably began to crystallise as soon as there had been time for an entire generation of politicians to grow up under those conditions.

In the UK, for example, we can already see that the major figures of the 1960s Labour government comprised more professional politicians with elite university backgrounds, and fewer senior ministers with an organic base in the labour movement or municipal government, than had been the case for the Labour government of the 1940s.[101] But even up until the end of the 1970s, when working-class trade unionist Jim Callaghan was prime minister, it was clear that most Labour politicians saw themselves as at least partially accountable to the labour movement itself. By the time the next Labour government was elected in 1997, this idea had not only dissipated; it had been actively and vociferously rejected by Tony Blair and other leaders of New Labour.[102] Over the course of the intervening decades, the Labour leadership and most Labour members of Parliament had come more and more to resemble other members of that emergent class of managers, media workers and entrepreneurs that sociologists have often struggled to name successfully, even though everyone can see that it exists.

The emergence of what has been called the 'techno-managerial elite'[103] is only one feature of a general recomposition, during this time, of the 'middle' strata of society, between the manual working class and the capitalist class proper. Other key features include the expansion and increasing radicalisation of public sector professions, who expanded in numbers during this time while also finding their pay, conditions of work and social privileges under almost constant attack from the

1970s onwards; and, perhaps most importantly, the unexpected revival and expansion of the petite bourgeoisie. It is an often-neglected feature of Marx's thought, and of social theory proceeding from it in the twentieth-century, that it confidently predicted the long-term decline and historical irrelevance of the class of small, semi-independent business owners and employers, as capital concentrated in the hands of the capitalist class and the ranks of the proletariat swelled. Since the 1970s, we have instead seen a huge expansion of this class.[104]

Its growth has been due in part to the deliberate actions of neoliberal governments, acting on behalf of capital, who realised that they needed to engineer a recovery of the petite bourgeoisie to act as a bulwark between themselves and the working class – especially as university-educated professionals in the public sector were becoming increasingly militant and 'proletarianised' (a tendency that clearly confirmed some of Marx's predictive assumptions). But the expansion of this class is also the outcome of a new cycle of accumulation that began in the 1970s, creating new opportunities for entrepreneurs and small businesses, especially in the media and technology sectors. In the 1980s, some radical economists hoped that new types of co-operative and democratic enterprise might become the dominant form within these emerging sectors: hence the progressive hopes invested by some in the possibilities of so-called post-Fordism.[105] For these hopes to be realised, sympathetic and active governments would have had to be in place – the dearth of which is reflected in the dismal returns of radical politics at the state level in the ensuing decades.

However, those commentators were not wrong to detect a certain progressive potential in these new economic sectors. In terms of political and social outlook, the types of entrepreneurs who came to prominence within them were often very different from their predecessors among the classic petite bourgeoisie. The latter had been typically the most socially conservative section of the entire populace – the social base for fascism and, in France, the reactionary right-wing populism of Pierre Poujade,[106] whose class culture was defined by hatred of the proletariat and of any form of bohemian intellectualism.[107] But this 'new petite bourgeoisie' has been quite different: socially liberal, culturally adventurous, cosmopolitan, and hedonistic, they have typically been sympathetic to the social liberalism of the counterculture and to the demands of minorities for full participation in society.[108] They also, crucially, have no obvious home among the political parties that consolidated in the mid-twentieth century, belonging neither to the conservative right nor the socialist left. As such, they have tended to be 'up for grabs' more than any comparable social constituency,[109] and their support has been necessary to almost every government of the 'right' or 'left', at least in the US and the UK, since the 1970s (although the vagaries of the US Electoral College have enabled the Republicans to win the presidency twice without it: in 2000 and in 2015).

And Finally, Hegemony

This analysis paints a picture of a particular coalition of social force that has operated effectively as the leading power in capitalist societies since the 1980s. It is now time to finally bring in some technical terminology. Such a process of leadership, diffuse and complex in form, is what we broadly refer to when we use the term 'hegemony'. Hegemony is the process by which discrete groups or networks come to guide the development of society as a whole, in the service of a set of interests. The type of coalition of 'class fractions'[110] that we have been describing is precisely what Antonio Gramsci termed as constituting 'social blocs'.[111] We will use the term 'systemic hegemony' when referring to a situation where a social bloc of aligned class fractions builds a society-wide hegemony. A good example of a social bloc that acquired systemic hegemony is the coalition between trade unions and manufacturers that was able, from the 1930s to the 1970s, to pressure governments into pursuing growth-led economic strategies that favoured manufacturing and full employment.[112]

A Gramscian social bloc is normally thought of as operating within the confines of a specific national polity. Our use differs slightly, but we see it merely as a direct extension of the concept that is appropriate to contemporary conditions. On the one hand, the tech-finance historic bloc is mainly an alliance of different sections of the capitalist class; on the other hand, it clearly includes members of the intermediary managerial class and members of the new petite bourgeoisie (notably small-scale tech and media entrepreneurs). This coalition of groups has worked together to transform the world into one which enforces their values and pursues their interests through a variety of mechanisms, from those operating at the level of ideology through to the infrastructure that operates as a platform for everyday life and society at large. It is clearly global in its reach and international in nature; yet it also has a particular local political base in the United States, where both Silicon Valley and Wall Street are located.

A great deal has been written about the concept of hegemony in recent decades, and it is widely encountered in popular political commentary as well as within academic writing. There is a widespread misconception that the term can be used as simply synonymous with 'domination'. This is closer to how it is used in the field of international relations, where 'hegemony' can refer to the complete authority exercised by one national state over another, or within a specific region.[113] But in the Gramscian sense, 'hegemony' is better understood as a strategic position of 'leadership', conferring on the hegemonic force the capacity to determine the general direction of travel of a given social formation. The maintenance of that capacity depends on many factors: the co-operation of other 'subaltern' groups, the resources at the disposal of the hegemonic force, and so on. It depends to some extent on the consent of those subaltern groups. However, contrary to the simplified assumptions of many commentators, 'consent' need not take the form of straightforward, enthusiastic endorsement of the authority and aims of the hegemonic; it is often largely passive in nature,[114] a matter of compliance and casual participation rather than explicit support. Hegemonic leadership is therefore always complex in nature, including domination and consent, and the great grey expanse in between.

We will explore many of the conceptual issues raised by these formulations later in the book. For now, the point is simply this: the kinds of power that we have been describing the tech-finance bloc as exercising are absolutely typical of hegemonic power and exemplify the ways that hegemony operates in the twenty-first century. Much of the rest of this book is devoted to an exploration of existing and new ways of theorising hegemony. First, however, it is necessary to examine in more detail the specific form that the hegemony of tech-finance has taken since the 1970s: the strategic and ideological project of neoliberalism.

2

ACTUALLY EXISTING NEOLIBERALISM

One major system of power has dominated the late twentieth and early twenty-first centuries: neoliberalism. Though its grip is now slipping, any understanding of how power works today has to reckon with what this system of power actually is – a task which is anything but straightforward in nature. 'Neoliberalism' is a term that can be used to designate a number of interrelated phenomena.[1] Most commonly in academic literature it refers to a set of *ideas* that derive more or less directly from the work of a group of mid-twentieth-century right-wing thinkers, the central figure of which was the economist and political philosopher Friedrich Hayek (1899–1992). These ideas advocate for markets and market competition as the ideal mechanism for the processing of information and the allocation of resources within society, as opposed to any central planner. They constituted one of the most significant poles of anti-communist and anti-socialist thought in the mid-twentieth century. As has been detailed in multiple historical accounts,[2] such ideas were propagated through international networks of think-tanks, corporations and political organisations for several decades, remaining largely on the political fringes until the great political and economic crises of the 1970s created an opportunity for them to present themselves to governments, corporate leaders and politicians as offering the solution to those crises. Neoliberalism is in this sense a body of theoretical knowledge, an ideology capable of informing policy makers.

An earlier approach to the thorny matter of what neoliberalism is took a different approach, however, by basically ignoring this specific genealogy of explicitly neoliberal ideas and instead focussing on instances in which governments implemented programmes that seemed to be informed by them.[3] Such histories of what we might call 'actually existing neoliberalism' begin with the US-backed coup against Salvador Allende's democratic socialist government in Chile in 1973, which saw the CIA install, at the heart of Augusto Pinochet's military government, a team of economists trained in neoliberal ideas at the University of Chicago. A major chapter in this narrative of neoliberalism in practice is the Chinese Communist Party leadership's adoption of pro-market reforms – that is, policies designed to promote economic development, the partial deregulation of markets and the growth of a capitalist class. As in the West, the processes by which academic theory has been translated into actual public policy have been complex, uneven, and driven by many factors other than the sheer persuasiveness of those ideas.[4] It is important to note here that there is a significant difference between what we might call theoretical neoliberalism – the ideas of Hayek, along with those of Ludwig von Mises, Milton Friedman and their followers – and the programmes that governments since the 1970s have actually implemented, which were at least partially influenced by those ideas or by similar assumptions. In the case of China, it is notable that theoretical neoliberalism seems to have played at best a minor role in promoting its shift in policy direction, although an intensive and wide-ranging engagement between Chinese economists and their foreign counterparts was actively encouraged by reformist leaders from the late 1970s, playing a crucial role in China's subsequent evolution.[5] It is remarkable that the programme followed by China, while somewhat similar to that followed by its Western counterparts, could be explained simply by virtue of the Chinese leadership's conclusion that their historic task was to create conditions for capital accumulation as quickly and efficiently as possible. Hypothetically, this is a position that they could have come to, on the basis of their own training in classical Marxism, and the realisation that the Maoist attempt to bypass an inevitable period of capitalist-led industrial development had failed. But whether implemented by the government of Margaret Thatcher (who famously brought copies of Hayek's works into cabinet meetings) or by Deng Xiaoping (who did not), actually existing neoliberalism has seen some very similar policies enacted, often with similar effects.

At a certain level of concreteness, then, actually existing neoliberalism exists anywhere its hallmark policies take hold. These policies, now familiar the world over, include the privatisation of public assets by a range of means; reductions in overall taxation, and progressive taxation in particular; legal restrictions on trade union organising; reductions in spending on core public services such as health, education and social care; reductions and restrictions affecting entitlement to all kinds of welfare; and the remodelling of public services in order to create internal markets, competition between workers and between institutions, and the general promotion of institutional ideologies borrowed from the corporate sector.[6] Of course, this core policy agenda can be implemented in many different ways and can be accompanied by a range of attendant social and cultural policies. It can take the form of a brutal full-frontal assault on the organised working class and all of its allies, including the socially liberal sections of the middles class; this is what happened in Chile in the early 1970s and in the early days of Thatcherism in the UK, a decade later. Or it can be accompanied by a (relatively) liberal and supposedly meritocratic social agenda, encouraging cultural diversity while taking steps to enable individuals disadvantaged by poverty, racism or other forms of prejudice to compete more 'fairly' with others in the labour market.[7] This was the basic programme of Bill Clinton's and Tony

Blair's 'Third Way' in the 1990s, and it is the programme implicitly favoured by most of the giants of Silicon Valley.[8]

As we have already argued in chapter 1, over the long term the particular version of neoliberalism that has actually been implemented, at least in the developed Global North, has been one that more clearly conforms to the interests and desires of particular leading sections of capital (tech and finance) more than it does to any theoretical programme, in the pages of the neoliberal classics or even in the writings of 'Third Way' ideologues such as Anthony Giddens.[9] This is not to say that theoretical neoliberalism has not been a crucial resource in providing languages, conceptual frameworks and moral justifications for actually existing neoliberalism and its agencies. No doubt reading Hayek gave Thatcher a confidence and a clarity when confronting her class enemies that she otherwise might have lacked.[10] It is also important to observe here that the kind of individualistic, anti-egalitarian ideas that European commentators tend to attribute directly to the influence of figures such as Hayek and von Mises[11] have a specific genealogy in the United States that is probably at least as important in explaining their appeal to certain American elites as any influence that may have radiated out from the University of Chicago. It is neither Hayek nor his acolyte Friedman who is frequently cited as the greatest influence on Federal Reserve chairman Alan Greenspan, (whose tenure spanned from 1987 to 2006), but the American fiction writer and pseudo-philosopher Ayn Rand. The persistence of Randian ideas among both financial and technological elites in the US is well attested[12] and has afforded a certain degree of resonance between the organic ideology of those groups, theoretical neoliberalism as conventionally understood, and actually existing neoliberalism as an enacted programme. But this observation merely expands our conception of theoretical neoliberalism to include a wider canon of ideas than those proceeding directly from Hayek and his associates. Even if we accept this observation as valid, it remains the case that any relationship between theoretical neoliberalism and actually existing neoliberalism is complicated– and that, generally speaking, theoretical neoliberalism has only even been influential to the extent that it has provided a rationale for a set of programmes whose ultimate aim was the propagation of the interests of specific social groups.[13]

However, this observation leaves open a profound political question. If it is not simply the case that neoliberalism was implemented because Thatcher read Hayek, while Greenspan read Rand, then how was it that the programme of actually existing neoliberalism could be implemented so comprehensively, consistently and to such devastating effect? After all, the epoch of actually existing neoliberalism marks the end of a long period of egalitarian social reform dating back to the nineteenth century and arguably coterminous with the era of modern democratic politics.[14] This era has seen a reversal of the tendency towards social equality that was a marked feature of the post-war period,[15] to the overall detriment of more people than have benefitted.[16] Given that all of the institutions of representative democracy have remained in place throughout the relevant period – that in fact liberal democracy spread across the globe following the collapse of the Soviet Union – how is it that populations in apparently democratic polities have been persuaded to accept the neoliberal programme, and even to keep voting for parties that insist on its implementation? This might be described as *the enigma of neoliberalism*: how can a political-economic system whose key policies are near-universally unpopular be maintained for decades in an apparently democratic political system?

We will try to answer this question by examining several main levels at which the neoliberal programme has been enacted and legitimated. But it is important to appreciate from the beginning that the conceptual separation of these 'levels' is a useful heuristic device, rather than a claim about the actual separability of a range of deeply interconnected phenomena.[17] Actually existing neoliberalism has only been enactable through a complex array of technological innovation, institutional reform, ideological warfare and physical coercion. However, for the sake of a clear analysis, we will begin by identifying these different aspects separately. We will start with the most obvious way in which the neoliberal programme has been pursued and legitimated: through the propagation of neoliberal ideology.

The Ruling Ideas

Within the Marxian tradition, 'ideology' has most often been used to designate those systematic sets of ideas that are promoted and deployed by powerful elites that happen to serve the purpose of legitimating their power, while encouraging behaviours in others that are likely to be conducive to maintaining and enhancing that power. At times, 'ideology' is understood in the deceptively simplistic form of 'false consciousness': as distorting the true nature of a social reality that Marxist theory is presumed to understand in some more accurate or 'scientific' way.[18] Critics of this perspective have rightly pointed to the problematic epistemological claims that it implies, particularly the claim of a privileged knowledge of social relations that can never be absolutely justified or verified.[19] One response to this observation is for theorists of ideology to align themselves with a view that distinguishes between different ideologies as expressing the interests of different social groups (including the working class), rather than between ideology and non-ideological truth.[20]

From our perspective, both of these approaches have some degree of utility. On the one hand, we would certainly assert, along with those who would commit themselves to an explicitly 'realist' theory of ideology,[21] that the bodies of theory that we find most persuasive (e.g., Marxism) are able to make predictions about social reality, and the outcomes of certain types of activity, that competing theories are not able to make. For example, the fact that neoliberal policies demonstrably do not lead to increases in 'social mobility', despite this often being claimed by advocates as their overriding political objective,[22] is clear evidence that neoliberal capitalism tends towards the concentration of wealth rather than its even or just dispersal across a population – as predicted by Marxist theory in its criticisms of liberal economics.[23]

On the other hand, it is also true that to simply denounce 'ideology' for its falsehoods would be to overlook a large proportion of its power. Not only that, but such an approach often appears highly unconvincing; indeed, for more than one hundred years, the presence of Marxist explanations of capitalist ideology has not been sufficient to overcome the ideology in practice. It is never enough to merely 'speak truth' to power, no matter how often pious elements of the left repeat that exhortation. We might identify plenty of contemporary examples wherein corporate, governmental or media discourse explicitly advocates for a specific – and clearly neoliberal – world-view, implicitly legitimating social inequality and exploitation of the most extreme kinds.[24] It is also important to note that it is not only through the masking of social reality, or the propagation of fantasies and falsehoods, that such discourse achieves its ends. The real purpose of ideology is not best registered at the level of truth or falsehood, but at the level of social effectiveness and the realisation of interests: what does the ideology *do*?[25] The upshot of this is that while it is certainly part of the function of ideology to create a 'false' picture of the world that some people will believe to their objective detriment, its main function is neither to be believed nor disbelieved, but to facilitate certain behaviours while constraining others. Sometimes this implies belief, but it need not do so.

The great theorist of ideology Louis Althusser was therefore not wrong when he said that ideology encourages those to whom it is addressed to 'misrecognise' their place in the social order (for example, leading workers to see themselves as isolated individuals rather than as members of a collectively exploited class). But he was also correct to note that ideology is not only inherent in representational discourse (books, speeches, tv programmes, art, film, etc.), but also in institutions that oblige their participants to behave in certain ways, irrespective of their conscious beliefs about the world.[26] For example, most educators in the Western world probably do not believe that competitive examination systems serve any useful purpose, because they do nothing to improve the actual quality of students' educational experience. Competitive examination systems define and categorise the effects of the essentially collaborative and creative experience of education as individual, ranking outputs. Their purpose is not to help students learn, but to sort students into categories so as to attribute differential value to them on the labour market.[27] Students and teachers may be perfectly aware of this and may object to the orientation of educational practises and institutions towards the demands of competitive examination system. But in most situations, noncompliance with those systems would be likely to cost both students and their teachers very dearly; therefore, they are obliged to behave in conformity with the competitive individualist ideology that informs the system, irrespective of any personal philosophical objections to it. In such a way, hegemony inscribes itself into the topology of everyday life, sculpting a landscape through which we largely must flow, irrespective of our personal beliefs in its animating ideology.

This is a useful example of the ways in which 'ruling' ideologies can be deferred to even when they are neither believed nor agreed with. Indeed, to command such deference must be understood as one of their key functions. Another important function of ideology is to maintain the morale, commitment and 'esprit de corps' of powerful elites themselves,[28] and to connect them with other social groups to which they might be particularly close. For example, the people who *do* believe that competitive examination systems are a fair, accurate and reasonable means by which to allocate certain social rewards are precisely the beneficiaries of those rewards.[29] Sociological research into the attitudes and beliefs of contemporary social elites finds consistently that they genuinely believe that modern societies allocate rewards fairly on the basis of merit, that they themselves work far harder than members of other social groups, and that their efforts benefit society as a whole – a set of beliefs that all empirical evidence contradicts. In the case of neoliberal ideology, then, it would seem to be necessary for the perpetuation of neoliberal capitalism that at least some members of the social elites who manage and profit from it genuinely believe in the great neoliberal story: that the best way to run a modern society is to impose competitive market relations on every possible social sphere, that the private pursuit of profit is the main driver of social progress, and that those who benefit the most from it deserve to do so.[30]

As such, the public (and sometimes explicit) propagation of such ideas is clearly an important part of the process by which the power of those elites is maintained. Of course, the explicit endorsement of neoliberal ideology is fairly rare in the public sphere. This is perhaps unsurprising, given that the basic presuppositions of neoliberalism amount to a rather ugly and brutal view of humans as inherently competitive and calculatingly self-serving.[31] Thus, as we will see in a moment, the most significant way in which this ideology is circulated and reproduced publicly is through the reproduction of norms and assumptions about the nature of social life that endorse it implicitly, rather than explicitly.

But the role of explicitly stated neoliberal propaganda cannot be overlooked either. Generally speaking, this is the work of what economic historian Philip Mirowski calls 'the neoliberal thought collective': that network of think-tanks, lobbyists and commentators that has sought to recruit key sections of the capitalist class proper, and the professional political class, to neoliberal ideas as such. For example, neoliberal think-tanks played a key role in persuading governments to adopt responses to the 2008 financial crisis that upheld neoliberal orthodoxy,[32] putting the machinery of the state at the service of finance capital to a new and unprecedented degree while opening the door to an austerity regime which has seen entire populations forced to pay the price for maintaining the position of the banks.[33] These think-tanks rarely if ever propose the ideology publicly – it is addressed to policy makers and politicians themselves.

Perhaps no prominent politician in the English-speaking world has come closer than Margaret Thatcher to explicit endorsement of a neoliberal programme and world-view. This perspective was formulated by Thatcher, along with her advisors and close allies in think-tanks such as the Centre for Policy Studies and the Adam Smith Institute – think-tanks that provided the templates upon which their contemporary equivalents, such as those discussed by political scientist Dieter Plehwe, are still modelled. An open advocate of Hayek's ideas, between 1975 and 1985, Thatcher claimed that 'the pursuit of equality . . . is a mirage. What's more desirable and more practicable . . . is the pursuit of equality of opportunity. And opportunity . . . includes the right to be unequal'.[34] She asserted that 'in our education system youngsters should be told that if you don't make a profit, you won't be in business very long';[35] called British trade unionists 'the enemy within';[36] and notoriously remarked, 'Who is society? There is no such thing! There are individual men and women and their families.'[37] Thatcher frequently alluded to the idea that British people were traditionally individualistic and entrepreneurial, asserting that their creative ingenuity and capacity for

self-reliance had been smothered by the cloying authoritarianism of 'socialism' and the welfare state. She promised
to lift that burden from them.[38]

Thatcher was the most right-wing leader of the Conservative Party since the nineteenth century. And yet a generation
later, in 2005, Tony Blair, prime minister and leader of the
Labour Party, would give a speech informed by a remarkably
similar set of presuppositions:

> I hear people say we have to stop and debate globalisation.
> You might as well debate whether autumn should follow
> summer . . . The character of this changing world is indiffer-
> ent to tradition. Unforgiving of frailty. No respecter of past
> reputations. It has no custom and practice. It is replete with
> opportunities, but they only go to those swift [enough] in the
> era of rapid globalisation, there is no mystery about what
> works: an open, liberal economy, prepared constantly to
> change to remain competitive.[39]

Certainly Blair's version of neoliberalism was different from
Thatcher's. It acknowledged a more direct role for the state in
adapting citizens to the demands of the global market, and it
appealed to a cosmopolitan vision of globalised modernity
rather than to assertions about the inherently individualistic
and entrepreneurial nature of the British character. But its
basic assumptions, its basic aims, and the type of person it
wanted to valorise were exactly the same. In both cases, the
hero of the story was the imaginary entrepreneur, bravely
adapting to the market in order to make themselves and their
country as competitive as possible; in both cases, the most
despised figure was the trade unionist or public sector worker
who clung to old-fashioned ideas about social equality, universal service provision and a world of social values not
dictated by the market. Both Thatcher and Blair actively
sought to promote the most basic claims of neoliberalism:

that competition between individuals is the default mode of human interaction, and that this is an unalterable and desirable fact of social existence.

Despite their deep ideological continuities, there were significant differences between the way that Blair and Thatcher thought about the neoliberal project – or indeed, in whether they thought about it at all. Thatcher may not have used the word 'neoliberalism', but she explicitly acknowledged that hers was a philosophy rooted in the ideas of Hayek and his fellow travellers, fusing some elements of modern conservatism with the core assumptions of classical liberalism.[40] She was also never in any doubt that she was involved in a historic political struggle: with socialism, with the Soviet Union, with trade unionism and with Fabian social democracy.

By contrast, Blair and his followers never even acknowledged that neoliberalism existed – as an ideology or a political project – or that theirs was a philosophy to which any plausible or viable alternatives might be proposed. The language of that 2005 speech makes this very clear. For Blair, neoliberalism was not an explicit ideology to be fought for against well-defined opponents; it was merely neutral knowledge, a pure reality principle – an understanding of how the world is, what works and what doesn't. Of course, Blair recognised that not everyone agreed. But he famously castigated everyone who didn't – from the left or the right – as representing 'the forces of conservatism'.[41] He did not think of them as political opponents, but as misguided vested interests, blocking the path towards progress and modernisation. What we call neoliberalism, he just called the way of the world.[42] One could go with the systemic motion of the universe, or go against it, but it could never be supplanted. In this sense, although Blair's speech was unusual for its frankness, it expressed a relationship to neoliberalism that is much more typical of contemporary neoliberal ideology than is the kind of explicit partisan advocacy exemplified by Thatcher. Blair didn't recognise neoliberalism as an ideology at all. To him, it was just common sense.

Common Sense

Thatcher herself had famously asserted that 'there really is no alternative' to monetarism and neoliberalism.[43] But at the time when she said it, everyone (including Thatcher) knew that her proposals were actually highly contentious and decidedly controversial; in fact they were roundly denounced by many professional economists.[44] By the time of Blair's 2005 Labour Party conference speech, however, a great deal had changed. Neoliberal assumptions had come to completely saturate the field of professional economics, as well as many other areas of social life and public culture, becoming norms that were taken for granted rather than recognised as just one ideology contending with others. Under these circumstances, Blair could literally claim in his speech that 'globalisation' – a process that had taken a great deal of political and institutional engineering over the preceding decades, through the agency of institutions such as the World Trade Organization – is as physically impervious to human agency as are meteorological phenomena. The neoliberal socio-economic model – nominally free markets, competitive social relations – is described not as something to be fought for (or against), but simply as 'what works.' One might go against the grain, but that would be simply to impede basic efficacy.

There could hardly be a more perfect example of neoliberal ideology functioning as 'common sense' – Antonio Gramsci's term for the often paradoxical and contradictory set of assumptions about the nature of social reality held by members of any given social group. For Gramsci, a key way in which hegemonic relations are maintained is through non-hegemonic, less powerful social groups' adoption of a world-view – a 'common sense' – that aligns with that of the hegemonic group, or at least militates against any organised opposition to the hegemonic on the part of the subaltern.[45] Gramsci's own key example of such 'common sense' serving hegemonic interests was the fatalistic world-view that characterised the traditional culture of many Italians in the early twentieth century (and for generations previously). The belief that personal destiny was predetermined and unalterable, Gramsci argued, served to prevent the discontents of the poor with their material situation from crystallising into political radicalism or any belief in the possibility of social change through collective struggle.[46]

It's worth reflecting for a moment here on the meaning of the English phrase 'common sense'. It is normally used in colloquial speech to refer to a kind of everyday rationality – combined with a tacit understanding of the way things work – that enables the possessor of 'common sense' to make sound judgements and wise decisions. However, there is another, less common usage for the phrase 'common sense', meaning simply a set of everyday assumptions or 'received wisdom' that does not necessarily correspond to good sense or objective reality. The Italian phrase *senso comune* that is normally translated as 'common sense' has only the latter meaning in normal Italian usage: it refers to a set of taken-for-granted assumptions about the world that might well be false and misleading. This has led some commentators to question whether 'common sense' is the right translation of *senso comune*, because the English 'common sense' carries too much of this implication of rational, but untheorised, good sense; whereas the Italian *senso comune* might be better translated by a phrase such as 'conventional wisdom'.[47] But we would suggest that the use of the English phrase 'common sense' to translate *senso comune* is in fact appropriate precisely because of this semantic slippage. 'Common sense' discourse presents itself as a neutral and unchallengeable description of the world – it is 'just common sense'. But it almost always carries along with that claimed neutrality a certain degree of implied approval for the situation that it describes. The fatalism of the traditional Italians was inseparable from their attachment to conservative Catholic theology and a belief that the world as it was had been ordered by God's will.

Blair's speech remains the perfect modern example. He claims to be merely telling us how the world is. But it clear from his poetic and emotive language that we are supposed to find the world that he describes attractive, in a bracing yet energising fashion. More importantly, perhaps, we know as a matter of historical record that Blair – along with most other members of the international political elite – did not actually accept the inevitability of globalisation as he described it; his government was always an active advocate for international free trade, labour market deregulation, and the partial privatisation of public services. Blair didn't merely wait for it to happen or seek to adapt the British labour force to meet its challenges; he and his government were constantly advocating and arguing for globalisation, actively making it happen, in every possible international forum.[48] As such, when Blair declared that globalisation was simply the way things were, there was always a dimension of his speech that went beyond mere neutral description; it always had a 'performative' element.

'Performative' is a term for types of speech that actively make things happen in the world, rather than simply describing them.[49] For example, to say 'I promise' is not merely to describe a situation, but to do something by saying something. J.L. Austin's famous study of the distinction between performative and 'constative' statements (that is, statements that only describe) ultimately concludes that there is really no such thing as a purely descriptive statement. Austin argues that in fact all statements, however minimally, possess a certain degree of 'illocutionary force':[50] that is, a certain capacity to make the world – or at least to define our perceptions of it and behaviour in it – as well as to describe it. This is an idea that has famously been taken up with great effect within gender theory by Judith Butler, who famously argues that all gender discourse is performative in nature.[51] Just think of the phrase 'I am a man'. Even if no value judgement at all is attached to the statement (and it is difficult to think of many social situations in which that would be the case), simply to utter the statement is to reiterate the basic assumption that adult humans can be simply classified as men or women. This is not to say that that assumption is necessarily incorrect; it is merely to note that the statement cannot be understood as a purely innocent act of description. To consider a less politically charged example, take the statement 'This is a cat'. This might be an *almost* entirely descriptive statement. But it remains the case that the very zoological taxonomy that designates one set of animals, and only that set of animals, as 'cats' is itself historically specific[52] and is dependent for its social authority not just on scientific discoveries, but on it repeated usage and constant reference to it by large communities of speakers. To utter the statement is to enact such a repetition.[53]

'Common sense' discourse always works through precisely such processes of reiteration, relying for its authority more on repetition and familiarity than on any necessary correspondence to objective reality. Neoliberal common sense is reproduced via the presentation of a picture of social reality that conforms to neoliberal assumptions, while framing it as natural, inevitable and at least partially desirable. We could draw many further examples from political speeches,[54] but perhaps more important is the way in which these assumptions are actively promoted within the broader field of popular media.

Consider the profound resonances between two apparently disparate domains of media culture: hip-hop and reality television. Since the early 1990s, commercial hip-hop has been dominated by a sequence of star performers (from Snoop Dogg and Dr Dre to Drake and Kanye West) who, although their styles and subject matter may have varied, share undeniable tendencies towards explicit narcissism and a competitive world-view in which their success is always dependent upon their own special merits and is at least partially contingent on the failure of others.[55] This marks a very clear break with earlier traditions of black American music culture that tended to express world-views characterised either by fatalistic resignation (in the case of the blues), or, far more frequently, optimistic evocations of community, solidarity and mutual empowerment (in the cases of gospel, soul, funk, disco, house, as well as in the mainstream of hip-hop immediately prior to the turn to 'gangster rap' in the early 1990s). Of course, these are enormous generalisations to which exceptions could always be found, but the fact that a fundamentally neoliberal common sense has been reproduced and promoted by the most successful hip-hop artists since the early 1990s, and that this marks a significant discontinuity with antecedent forms of black American music culture, is difficult to deny.

Much the same can be said of the most successful forms of commercial television during roughly the same historical period. Prior to the mid-1990s, the most popular types of television programme globally were various types of narrative fiction: 'soap operas' and situation comedies. Much has been written about the complex, variegated and ambivalent politics that characterised the implicit assumptions informing such programmes.[56] No doubt they reproduced conservative and bourgeois ideology, and still do. But from the second half of the 1990s onwards, these popular narrative forms were displaced as the dominant format for commercial mass-market television. What replaced them was a new genre: so-called 'reality television'.[57] Although the term initially referred most often to various 'docu-dramas', which borrowed narrative

tropes from soap opera and situation comedy while present-
ing the 'real' lives of some members of the public, it quickly
came to designate a new genre of competitive game show that
would somehow involve players' full immersion in the game
for the duration of the series, while inviting viewers to participate by regularly voting to exclude their least favourite
participants from the following rounds of the games. From
Big Brother to *Love Island*, reality TV formats do their best
to present a vision of human interaction as always and necessarily characterised by ruthless and self-interested competition;
and notoriously, when players threaten not to exhibit the
behaviours predicted by this assumption, the programme
producers have gone out of their way to introduce mechanisms to encourage or compel them.[58] In class terms, TV
producers generally occupy much the same social, cultural
and income niches as do more obvious members of the professional political class.[59] As such they are able to use their
considerable power to reproduce the neoliberal common sense
of their own class fraction, in forms that are consumed by
millions of enthusiastic viewers. 'Look', they say to us, 'this is
how life really is, this is reality: an endless, ruthless competition for status, popularity and fame with no higher purpose
than winning.'[60]

The fact that hip-hop tracks and videos – or any other kind
of popular entertainment – are themselves shaped and
informed by neoliberal ideology does not mean that they are
necessarily successful in persuading others to accept that ideology, or even to defer to it. This observation has been
commonplace in media studies since at least the 1970s. Most
studies since then have suggested that rather than merely passively absorbing the ideological content of media, audiences
are quite capable of rejecting the ideological assumptions of
TV producers or pop stars, provided they have some more or
less defined political perspective of their own from which to
make any such criticism.[61] On the other hand, most evidence

also suggests that in the absence of any such clearly defined alternative perspectives, media output plays a crucial role in shaping the implicit assumptions, general reference points and broad world-view of large numbers of people. Let us be clear: audiences for neoliberal media are not being converted into explicit and self-conscious followers of Hayek. Nevertheless, because they end up forming the basic materials of much of vernacular culture – the things that people talk about, consume together, argue over, use as reference points when thinking about their own lives – this kind of cultural output does contribute heavily to the ambient mood and assumed norms of the culture in which it is consumed.[62] If your everyday culture is built on the assumption that individualised competition is all that matters, then over time it becomes rational to believe that this is indeed 'the way of the world'. Hence, the implicit ideologies contained within cultural products will contribute to the reproduction of common sense.

Another quite different example of neoliberal common sense is the way that policy makers and institutional managers reproduce concepts and assumptions that derive from neoliberal sources – or sources with identical ideological orientations – but do so without explicitly endorsing neoliberal norms as such. Since the 1980s, the emergence of the 'new public management' as a paradigm for public service delivery, especially in the UK and Australia, has seen an ongoing, deliberate effort to model the management of public services on the practices and organisational techniques typical of profit-seeking private corporations.[63] This has taken place at exactly the same time that the 'financialisation'[64] of much business practice has seen a shift away from the idea that businesses should either seek to grow for the sake of growing, or should seek to serve any kind of public good. Instead, it has moved towards the idea that the maximisation of 'shareholder value' (the profits paid to shareholders and dividends plus the speculative gains available to shareholders as stock prices rise) should be the only and absolute objective of all business practice. Just as corporations were abandoning any notion that they might have a purpose other than the ruthless maximisation of profit, new public management advocates were encouraging public services to model themselves on corporations. The result has been the extraordinary obsession with targets, performance indicators and 'efficiency' that has characterised public sector management in much of the capitalist world in recent decades, as institutions that were historically intended to play an entirely different role to profit-seeking businesses were set the impossible task of modelling themselves on those very businesses.[65] Central to this process has been the insistence that the relationships between service users and service 'providers' (e.g., between teachers and students) be explicitly conceptualised as retailer–customer relationships – as if there were no fundamental difference between getting an education and buying a hamburger.

This is a crucial example of how hegemony works in practice. Ultimately, the effect of all of these changes has been to reinforce the power of finance capital not merely to control flows of wealth and labour, but also to set the terms and define the terrain upon which many different types of social activity take place. However, this shift has rarely been a matter of anyone consciously saying to themselves, 'Bankers and financial institutions now rule the world, therefore I must follow their ways.' New public management was presented to managers of public sector institutions as a way of surviving and prospering in a fiscal and ideological climate that had already become hostile to the very idea of public service as such. It also acquired legitimacy from an entire theory of economics and social relations upon which it was based: public choice theory.[66] Emerging in the 1970s, public choice theory is a school of economics that only rarely makes direct reference to classical neoliberal sources, but shares all of their fundamental assumptions. In the decades to follow, it would form a core piece of justificatory infrastructure for neoliberal governance. Key features of public choice theory include a general scepticism towards any form of collective action or large-scale public good, the assumption that public servants are motivated primarily by the desire to enrich themselves at the public expense, and the assumption that they must therefore be disciplined by governmental mechanisms such as the introduction of competitive and market-like mechanisms (e.g., for teachers, school league tables, standardised testing, student customer-satisfaction surveys, etc.) in order to compel them to offer the best possible service at the lowest possible rate. Public choice theory is extremely problematic from the perspective of any economist with the slightest interest in grounding their theoretical assumptions in actual sociological, historical and anthropological data.[67]

In other words: anyone who studies how human beings and their societies actually operate, with reference to a broad range of examples from different cultures and epochs, can see that the assumptions of public choice theorists are simply not sustainable. They do not represent a theory based on any kind of robust empirical observation.[68] In fact, the claim that human beings are never motivated by altruism, or by a sense of collective rather than private self-interest, is so demonstrably false that we can only reasonably conclude that public choice theory is merely the formalised expression of the common sense of the capitalist class. It has been reproduced by cohorts of economists that have been very tightly bound up with that class, in term of their material interests, social backgrounds and political orientations.[69] As such, they have been able to impose their norms on entire populations who may never have actively subscribed to them.

Good Sense

Before we leave off this discussion of the concept of common sense, there are two more crucial elements of it to consider. One is that, for Gramsci and for all of his followers, common sense must be understood as never simply given in any particular social situation. It is always shifting, always complex and paradoxical, always in contention and capable of being changed. In the UK, for example, plenty of respondents to political surveys seem capable of simultaneously accepting certain key tenets of neoliberalism (such as the idea that poor workers should not receive welfare benefits)[70] while also believing that the National Health Service must be preserved in the purely socialistic, universalist form that it was established in 1948.[71]

For Gramsci, common sense is always to be understood as a site of struggle; in fact, it is arguably the key site of struggle for modern politics. The whole point of political campaigning is to change the common sense of at least enough of the population to be able to recruit them into support for your political project. However, this is rarely just a matter of changing people's opinions; it is almost always also a question of changing their material circumstances, or at least their organisational capacities. Even when the main object of a campaign or intervention is simply to change some people's understanding of a situation, this cannot be a matter of simply telling them that their current understanding is incorrect. Instead, it is almost always necessary to engage with the complex multiplicity of beliefs that they currently hold, identifying those that are already closest to the ones that the campaigner would like them to hold, and offering incentives for those beliefs to be further emphasised, while the force of other less compatible beliefs is diminished.[72] Common sense, as well as being a site of struggle, is also always the result of struggles in other spheres and domains. A transformation of the material reality in which people live will change their propensity towards certain kinds of frameworks for understanding the world.

For example, arguably the crucial question of contemporary politics – very obviously in the US and the UK, but also in many other places – lies in how far the common sense of a particular social group can be oriented in a progressive direction. This is the constituency of a certain section of working-class citizens, often in former industrial regions, whose economic prospects have not only deteriorated since 2008; they have also never fully recovered from the de-industrialisation of the 1980s and subsequent decades,[73] as lifelong jobs in industry were replaced by precarious and often demanding work in the service and retail sectors.[74] A huge amount of ideological work has been done by right-wing media since the 1970s in order to convince this constituency that the main cause of their problems is excessive immigration, as poor workers from other countries drive down wage levels and put intolerable pressure on public services.[75] In the UK there is clear empirical evidence that citizens who have been heavily exposed to newspapers such as the *Daily Mail* and the *Sun* hold demonstrably erroneous beliefs as to the level of inward migration and its effects on wage levels, crime rates and the public finances,[76] and there is no question that large number of such citizens voted to leave the European Union in the 2016 referendum.

A crucial point to grasp here is that the reactionary and progressive narratives competing for voters' endorsements in this case do not tell *entirely* contradictory stories. Both acknowledge the validity of the grievances of those communities 'left behind' by forty years of globalisation and Atlantic de-industrialisation (although the reactionary story will tend, of necessity, to exclude the grievances of non-white peoples from their story). Both present strong and active intervention

by national governments as the route to redress of those grievances. Both even suggest that some interruption of global
flows must be part of the action taken by those governments.
The difference lies in what kind of flows must be interrupted
and what kind of action governments must take. For the
right, it is primarily flows of people (in other words, migrants)
that are the problem; for the left, it is flows of capital. And
behind this lies a difference in the understanding of which
interests government must oppose in order to defend or assist
working-class communities. For the right, it is the interests
of poor immigrants that cannot be reconciled with those of
native workers. For the left, it is the interests of capital.

In each case, however, the preferred narrative is responding
to the same set of experiences and to the same intuitions as to
their causes. The voters to whom they are addressed know
that major socio-economic and technological changes of
recent decades have been implemented largely to their detriment, that someone other than them is responsible, and that
the arrival of newcomers in their communities has not happened by accident or been organised for their benefit.
Immigration may be of benefit to them, enriching their local
culture and field of social experience and increasing the tax
base from which their public services and pensions will be
funded, but that is not the primary reason for it, which is to
provide cheap labour for local employers. Each of these competing narratives seeks to attach itself to these same basic
observations and provide the most plausible or attractive
explanation for them and response to them. And the basic
observations, importantly, are not wrong. They form the crucial kernel, or 'healthy nucleus', of 'good sense'[77] that Gramsci
sees embedded in all common sense.

This 'healthy nucleus', we suggest, always marks the point
at which people are able to more or less directly intuit something of their own material interests. It also marks the limit
point of what kinds of narratives and world-views people can

and cannot be persuaded to believe in, participate in or endorse. This is an important difference between our approach and that associated with the greatest post-Marxist theorists of hegemony, Ernesto Laclau and Chantal Mouffe. As we will see in later chapters, our ideas are in some senses indebted to those of Laclau and Mouffe. However, in some important ways we will diverge. Their approach to hegemony notoriously tends to the view that any set of political demands and any set of ideas about the world can be linked up with any other, in the attempt to constitute a hegemonic political project.[78] Our view is that there are always important limits to such a process of 'articulation' of different demands, ideas and assumptions, and that those limits are found at the points where there are real contradictions between specific sets of material interests. For example, in the case we are discussing, it is possible for the right to articulate a particular set of demands and discursive terms into what Laclau and Mouffe call a 'chain of equivalence'[79] by trying to create connections in public discourse between the demand for well-paid jobs, the demand for government to intervene to protect working communities, mistrust of immigrants and even mistrust of socially liberal policies on issues like abortion and gay marriage. The left can also articulate these basic demands into a chain of equivalence that includes hostility to unregulated finance capitalism, social liberalism and scepticism towards established social elites (including corporate and media elites). What is not possible under present conditions, however, is for neoliberal 'centrists' to construct a working chain of equivalence that links these core demands of working-class communities – for some kind of end to the period of unregulated financial globalisation, for example – to the neoliberal commitment to the endless extension of market relations and an unregulated financial sector. There is no potential point of resonance between the common sense of the cosmopolitan neoliberal elites and that of the 'left-behind' working class, because there is no place in the discourse of the centrists for the 'good sense' of those working-class constituencies: namely, their realisation that the projects of financial deregulation and economic globalisation have absolutely not been in their interests as workers or citizens. From this perspective, 'good sense' is precisely the point at which social reality intrudes into the world of political discourse, and it must be reckoned with by any attempt to maintain or transform existing forms of common sense.[80]

Institutional Hegemony

To make either ideology or common sense (and good sense) the central theme of a political analysis always carries with it a certain risk: that of assuming implicitly that politics is simply about the contest for 'public opinion'. Of course, that contest is always crucial.[81] But it is also important to understand that it is perfectly possible for large numbers of people to find themselves in clear disagreement with a hegemonic common sense, while simultaneously being forced to defer to it and comply with its norms, behaving to all intents and purposes as if they did believe in it. We have already given the example of teachers forced to work within and administer a formally competitive and individualistic system of schooling and assessment. Many workers in neoliberal institutions will recognise themselves to be in comparable situations.[82]

Now, on a certain level, it could be claimed that even to defer to and comply with neoliberal ideology in such a manner is in fact to share one of the basic presuppositions of its common sense: the assumption that it cannot be challenged. But this is a problematic formulation. Indeed, there is a difference between accepting an ideology as simply an ahistorical norm – a true 'common sense', no alternative to which can be imagined – and recognising it as undesirable and contingent, yet too powerful to escape or overthrow. Indeed, individuals and groups may often find themselves in situations in which they are forced to comply with a set of norms that they fundamentally and consciously disagree with.

Beyond common sense and ideology, there are all kinds of mechanisms through which such compliance can be secured. Today, one of the most important is simply the labour market itself. A key feature of neoliberal hegemony has been the deregulation of labour markets, the reduction of legal and political protections for workers (individually and collectively),[83] and the generalisation of 'precarity' across much of the workforce. Reductions in social spending and downward pressure on real wages have all contributed to a situation in which even in some of the richest countries in the world, there has been a marked decline in job security accompanied by a measurable rise in anxiety, pessimism and economic insecurity.[84] The deliberate production and management of inequalities and insecurity,[85] along with the proliferation of debt, has been a key feature of this epoch during which finance capital has been restored to a position of hegemonic authority. The consequence of this is that entire populations who might otherwise have resisted neoliberal hegemony have been politically demobilised, as every individual finds themselves compelled to pursue private strategies to survive: searching for work, managing their public profile so as to remain employable, working short-term contracts, and so on.

Of course, this is not a new predicament. In fact, the present conditions of labour-market insecurity are still less severe than those that were normal in capitalist economies from the beginning of the industrial revolution up to the 1930s.[86] What has been new in our present epoch is the deliberate engineering of this situation of precarity for a large population, following the unique period of relative prosperity and stability for working people that came after World War II in the Global North. There are many historical factors that explain the political and cultural turbulence of the 1960s and '70s. But one such factor is the fact that the generation growing up after the war was arguably the first in recorded history of which it can be said that a majority came to adulthood with no direct experience of scarcity, in a social environment characterised by rising wages, increasing leisure opportunities and an expanding welfare state.[87]

Under these circumstances, huge numbers of young people saw no reason why they should accept or tolerate any of the social and personal repression, authoritarian hierarchy or systematic exploitation that still characterised advanced industrial capitalist societies. Indeed, such acceptance on the part of previous generations had always been partially contingent on the fear of poverty or state repression. It is important not to exaggerate this phenomenon; the same generation produced the voters that eventually put Margaret Thatcher and Ronald Reagan in office. But there can be little question that this was an important dimension of the cultural upheavals that characterised the period: for a significant section of the population, the end of scarcity and precarity was the precondition for their radicalisation and for a critical widening of democratic demands.[88] It was this widening of demands – the notorious 'excess of democracy' diagnosed by right-wing mandarins in 1975 – that lay at the heart of the strategic challenge faced by capital and its governmental agents at that time.[89]

From this perspective it becomes possible to see the deliberate production of precarity as a key means by which capital and governing elites have responded to that challenge. Precarity is not an unfortunate and unexpected side effect of neoliberal economics; rather, neoliberal economics is a method for the production of precarity. Precarity, debt and a generalised increase in average hours worked per week have created a situation in which groups and individuals simply have far less time and opportunity than they once had to engage in political organisation, struggle or reflection.[90] None of this is accidental.

This is but one local example of a much more universal truth about the nature of hegemonic power relations and the means by which they are perpetuated: the acquiescence of less powerful groups to hegemony, and their acceptance of subordinate social roles for themselves, does not always depend on them being persuaded to accept the common sense of hegemonic elites. Sheer material and organisational circumstances often do that work just as well as any form of persuasion. For the fact is, the major preoccupation of most humans beings during most of the adult lives will be ensuring their own survival and the survival and well-being of their children. Under circumstances where this goal is difficult, yet achievable, its attainment will absorb most of their attention and energy, and they are therefore highly unlikely to devote a great deal to political organisation and agitation. Where it becomes unachievable, poverty and desperation will drive them to agitate for change.

What we learned in the 1960s is that the obverse is also true: where that goal becomes too easy to realise, many will also begin to question their subordination and organise against it. There can be little doubt that capital and its agencies learned this lesson from the upheavals of the 1960s and '70s: the goal of feeding one's children must be rendered sufficiently difficult, even if, in our age of hyper-consumerism 'feeding them' means keeping them in a style that would have appeared materially decadent to aristocrats of the fin-de-siècle. Without the difficult task of caring for their families occupying all of their time and attention, who knows what the masses might do? This argument owes something to a classic study by British sociologists Nicholas Abercrombie, Stephen Hill and Bryan S. Turner: *The Dominant Ideology Thesis*.[91] In this work, the authors point out that indeed, the acquiescence of workers to capitalist social relations is often not dependent in any way upon their actually having been convinced by the validity or veracity of bourgeois ideology, but on material circumstances that render resistance to capitalism extremely difficult, or impossible.[92]

Of course, we are not positing a situation in which capitalist elites engage in a self-conscious conspiracy to render the lives of workers less comfortable in order to prevent them revolting against their exploitation. But if we think about the language that such elites themselves use, then it is clear that in effect this is their obvious implication. We are told that the overriding goal of public policy for corporations in our countries, and ultimately the countries themselves, is to remain 'competitive'.[93] Competitiveness is measured directly in terms of how much profit those companies are able to accumulate in a given year. We are also told that in order to ensure that competitiveness (i.e., profitability) is maintained, workers must behave in ways that maximise it. We are told, in unambiguous terms, that such behaviour involves, for example, not engaging in collective organisation to improve their working conditions or raise their wages.[94] Governments will even deliberately intervene in the labour market in order to make it more difficult for workers to so organise, in order to maximise the competitiveness of corporations. Further, we are told that the best thing that workers and those who train them (i.e., the schools and education system) can do in order to benefit both workers and the overall economy is to maximise their own competitiveness. But the maximisation of competitiveness necessarily has costs. It has material costs because being 'competitive' in the labour market necessarily means being willing to undercut rivals as well as winning a high rate of pay when the opportunity arises. It also has psychosocial costs: it is self-evident, and well documented, that the obligation to adopt an attitude of permanent competitive rivalry with one's fellow workers generates high levels of stress and anxiety.[95] This is the reality of neoliberal work culture, carried to its logical conclusion, and we can see that to all intents and purposes it does indeed involve elites telling workers that they ought to voluntarily make themselves less comfortable and to refrain from collective political action, so as to ensure their own subordination and the ongoing ability of capitalists to accumulate capital.

In a classically Marxian vein, we can see that very often it is the logic of the labour market and broader economic circumstances that compels such compliance. But there are also many instances in which it is other sets of institutional arrangements that shape the behaviour of their participants according to hegemonic logics. In making these observations, we can draw an interesting line of continuity between the arguments of Abercrombie, Hill and Turner, and those of later theorists and commentators who have drawn directly on the ideas of the philosopher Michel Foucault. Throughout his oeuvre, Foucault was concerned with the ways in which institutional arrangements, and discourses carrying institutional authority, could shape behaviour and define perceptions of the world. Famous examples that he studied included institutions such as the clinic, the mental hospital and the prison.[96] Another was the ways in which 'sexuality' emerged as a concept and an object of investigation for medicine and the law at the end of the nineteenth century: for Foucault, there is no natural or spontaneous sexuality as such, and the multiple ways in which sexuality is talked about and responded to by social group and institutions will define our experience of it.[97] Although Foucault is a very popular reference point in contemporary thought, it is worth keeping in mind that in some ways, these claims of his are just one example of a general tendency in twentieth-century philosophy, social anthropology and interpretive sociology that stresses the significance of the specific vocabularies and behavioural repertoires of particular groups in 'constructing' their social worlds.[98]

More importantly for our purposes, one of Foucault's particular interests was the way in which the very idea of government emerged and developed in the modern period. From the end of the Middle Ages, the organisational and technological capacity of state institutions, the extent and speed of communications networks, and the accuracy of systems of observation and record keeping all vastly increased, and with them the possibilities for the management and direction of human behaviour. In the context of this history, Foucault's classic lectures on neoliberalism present early neoliberal thought of the mid-twentieth century as trying to develop a particular art of government, designed to encourage citizens to behave according to competitive, individualistic norms.[99]

Decades later, we have seen countless examples of efforts by neoliberal governments to institutionalise these norms in practice.[100] One classic instance is the reform of welfare systems since the 1980s, and the promotion of 'workfare' schemes as substitutes for older forms of social insurance. This shift has involved a move away from the idea that a certain baseline level of material subsistence was a moral right of all citizens, towards punitive and regulatory regimes aimed at managing the behaviour of claimants, compelling them to adopt entrepreneurial and self-promoting modes of behaviour in order to compete in the job market, or else lose the benefit.[101] We can compare this to the role of standardised testing in school education systems, which has markedly increased under neoliberal governments. Combined with measures such as the imposition of competitive school league tables in the UK, this has the clear effect of disciplining the behaviour of not only students but also teachers and school administrators in line with neoliberal norms, encouraging teachers to 'teach to the test' rather than according to more holistic or group-oriented notions of desirable education, promoting a narrowly instrumentalist view of education[102] – one wholly in line with the general neoliberal tendency to reduce the scope of all social activity to that which can be quantified, measured, and put at the service of capital accumulation.[103]

Both of these are examples of what theorists following Foucault have called 'neoliberal governmentality'.[104] Now, there is a tendency within most scholarly and polemical writing about neoliberalism either to focus on this dimension of neoliberalism – understanding it as a particular mode of government, derived from the intellectual lineage of Hayek and his followers at the University of Chicago[105] – or to focus on neoliberalism as essentially a class project, a set of contingent mechanisms deployed in order to restore the supreme authority of finance capital over individual national polities and the entire global order.[106] This sometimes leads to the view that these are two distinct and mutually incompatible ways of understanding neoliberalism. This is partly because some defenders of the Foucauldian approach to social analysis have in the past gone so far as to declare any concern with either class relations or the question of hegemony to be simply redundant: old-fashioned Marxism, no longer relevant to the complexities of contemporary power.[107] We view these dichotomies as quite false. In fact we think it impossible to understand how neoliberalism operates without understanding at one and the same time its distinctive governmental logics and the material interests in the service of which those logics are ultimately deployed. A hegemonic analysis of neoliberalism demands attention to both dimensions – and indeed beyond them.

Both of the examples of neoliberal governmentality that we have given originate in relatively early phases of neoliberalism's implementation and are directly concerned with the management of key public institutions. It is worth considering, then, how we might understand some more recent developments as operating according to comparable logics, in less obviously governmental domains. If any phenomenon defines the historical period since the beginning of the twenty-first century, on a global scale, it is the exponential spread of social media and its insertion into the everyday lives of billions of humans in less than two decades. Although in theory social media is thought to promote 'sharing', egalitarian relationships and decentralised modes of social organisation, several analysts have pointed out that existing social media platforms actually tend to encourage highly competitive, narcissistic and individualistic modes of self-monitoring, self-presentation and interaction, as users compete for visibility and popularity – much as they do on the reality TV shows mentioned above.[108]

Here we might draw a conceptual distinction between different modes of governmentality as described by Foucault and another theorist close to him. For Foucault, the development of government in the early modern period is characterised by the growth of 'disciplinary' institutions, operating according to a logic of supervision: all activity within the institution is monitored centrally, and deviation from set norms is punished. It is slightly unclear from Foucault's writing how far he considers that logic still to be prevalent in the power structures of the late twentieth century,[109] or how far he sees it as having been superseded by a new governmental logic that emerges in the modern period: a logic of regulation, the maintenance of 'security' and the practice of 'governmentality' through the management of whole populations. Certainly some of his most influential followers have thought that it was necessary, building on Foucault's analyses, to posit this different logic.[110]

One early contribution to this discussion was Gilles Deleuze's famous argument that a new, more cybernetic logic of 'control' was taking over from the older systems of disciplinary governmentality, as systems of power emerged that tended to anticipate and adapt to the behaviour of populations and individuals, rather than simply imposing norms upon them.[111] Social media platforms certainly exemplify this shift: they do not compel complicity with explicit norms; they do not (usually) punish deviance; they merely reward certain types of behaviour (posting popular content, in particular) while continually adapting (through showing different content in different feeds) to the changing behaviour of users, with the aim of continually encouraging them to generate marketable data. But the key point to take away here would be that, in the case of all our examples, neoliberalism and its norms remains the operative 'attractor'[112] towards which systems of governmental power are oriented, whether those systems take on a clearly 'disciplinary' character, or whether they work through subtler mechanisms of self-modulation and 'control'. Such is the nature of hegemony.

Brute Force and Organisation

We have looked at the role played by didactic discourse of various kinds in securing neoliberal hegemony. We have also looked at the role played by institutional and even technical systems in helping to reproduce that hegemony, by compelling participants to behave in accordance with its norms. Finally, however, it would be naive to ignore the role played by sheer repressive violence in the historic imposition of neoliberalism.

In the earliest phase of its implementation, there is no question that this role was decisive. The first neoliberal regime was the military dictatorship of Augusto Pinochet in Chile, established by a CIA-backed coup against the democratically elected government of Salvador Allende.[113] In the UK, the first six years of the Thatcher government were characterised by violent confrontations between the police (whose numbers and pay were rapidly expanding) and a range of dissident communities. Urban ethnic minority groups protesting police harassment, trade unionists engaged in a range of historic disputes, protesters against public sector cuts, 'new age travellers' on their way to the Stonehenge Free Festival: all were subject to historically unprecedented levels of police violence.[114] London's left-wing city government was summarily abolished for openly defying Thatcher's right-wing agenda.[115] Most commentators and historians would concede that it was the Falklands War – a giant, and militarily pointless, exercise in nostalgic, post-imperialist nationalism – that saved Thatcher's government at the 1983 general election.[116] In more recent times, it's clear that one of the major motivations for repeated Western military intervention in the Middle East has been the fact that Islamism of various kinds has stood out as the only major ideological rival to neoliberalism on the world stage to have any consistent political success since the 1970s. Although the Latin American left has had some sporadic success in throwing up viable political alternative to neoliberalism,[117] only Islamism has successfully driven entire national projects for decades in a wholly different direction to neoliberalism, especially in the case of Iran.[118] In all of these instances, on multiple scales, we can see that neoliberal hegemony has at times been won initially by the use of sheer brute force.

Of course, the question of the real relationship between violence and political legitimacy is as old as politics itself.[119] Arguably all authority is ultimately backed by the threat of violence and the capacity to exercise it.[120] By the same token, arguably all compliance amounts to the promise not to offer violent resistance to the exercise of that authority. Importantly, these are observations that would be consistent with both the radical and the conservative traditions of political thought – both of which would reject the liberal belief that social relations are founded by contractual agreements between rational individuals.[121] The theme of understanding social and political relations as always characterised by relations of struggle, conflict, and war is a crucial corrective to any understanding of existing social relations as either inherently

rational, or as given, natural and ahistorical.[122] It is this observation that lends such polemical force to Marx and Engel's
famous dictum that all history is the history of class struggle.

An important observation, we would add, is that even all-
out war is never just about the imposition of an outcome on a
population by pure force alone. It is also always about the
capacity of one side to organise a population to greater strategic effect than the other side, as well as the broader
organisational capacity to choose which of its military forces
fights, in what order, and under what circumstances.[123] This
is why it is not always the largest army that wins. In fact, we
could extend this observation to the understanding of all
forms of social power. All power is organisational power. The
power of capital, like the power of a general, is the power to
organise the activity of a vast population of otherwise-
disaggregated people towards coherent and determinate
ends. All power to resist – to resist capitalist exploitation, to
resist patriarchal domination, to resist military invasion – is
the power to organise effectively against the enemy.

On the other hand, organisational capacity can never be
simply separated from the basic issue of resources. It is the
fact that the capitalist class has access to huge material
resources that give it the material capacity to organise millions of workers, to communicate with vast audiences at a
time, to determine the relative rewards allocated to those
media operatives who do or don't reproduce its ideologies,
and so on and so forth. As such, the struggle either to maintain or to challenge existing hegemonic relations is always a
struggle over access to resources and a struggle to deploy
available resources as effectively as possible. This is exactly
what Gramsci means when he describes modern politics as a
'war of position'.[124] This metaphor compares politics to the
trench warfare of World War I: it is a matter of winning and
holding territory bit by bit, as contrasted with the 'war of
movement', which is simply a matter of capturing one key

outpost or locus of power (for example, achieving a majority in a national legislature, or storming an imperial palace). From this perspective, for example, a progressive party that wins legislative election in a country such as the UK cannot possibly hope to reverse the effects of decades of neo-liberalisation simply by passing legislation; such an objective would require a mass movement committed to building alternative media and challenging neoliberal common sense within existing media channels, an organised and militant labour movement committed to implementing its programme in workplaces and a mass political movement building up loci of institutional power in local government, the public services, the wider culture and civil society.

As we can see, and as promised at the beginning of the chapter, the conceptual separation of symbolic, institutional, economic, technological and even military power in all of these instances is analytically necessary; but it is ultimately artificial and arbitrary. Hegemonic power combines all of them in the service of particular political projects and the interests that they pursue. This observation poses an immediate question, which our analysis has implicitly raised but not yet begun to solve: how far is hegemonic power actually coercive, and how far does it rely on either active persuasion or on resigned acquiescence? Gramsci famously states that hegemony always depends upon a combination of coercion and consent:[125] subaltern groups are partly coerced into deferring to it, party persuaded to consent to it. But as we have begun to see, the line between these two aspects of hegemony is often quite difficult to draw, and there seems to be more than one kind of consent, and certainly more than one kind of coercion. In the next chapter we will explore this issue further with reference to some prior historical examples, and the more detailed history, and prehistory, of actually existing neoliberalism.

PART II:

HEGEMONY NOW

3

PERSUASION AND PASSIVITY

The project of actually existing neoliberalism has been enabled by a complex set of interrelated power mechanisms. It has involved the selective empowerment of particular social groups and the partial subjugation of others. It has required some groups to be actively persuaded of its value, others to be obliged to defer to it, others to be physically coerced into obedience. In fact, matters are even more complex than that. Neoliberal hegemony has deployed techniques that have not merely empowered some groups and disempowered others, but have also brought about divergent effects *within* given groups and persons, disempowering them in certain ways while empowering them in others. Most obviously, these policies have involved the empowerment of individuals as consumers, even while they were disempowered as workers or as democratic citizens.

In the UK, a classic example is the reforms to the National Health Service undertaken by the New Labour administration in the early 2000s. The rhetorical focus of these reforms was the idea of 'patient choice': the claim that what would deliver a better experience for service users would be the opportunity to exercise as much personal autonomy as possible in selecting from competing providers (i.e., doctors and hospitals) within the NHS framework.[1]

This was never a popular measure. It ran against the principle of the NHS as a universal service providing uniform standards of care, and most UK citizens understood that. They did not want to have to select their doctors or the hospitals at which they would be operated on: they wanted to attend the nearest clinic or hospital to their home and to be sure that they would receive excellent service. But the policy makers behind the reforms did not believe this to be possible. Their assumption was that under such circumstances, local doctors and hospitals would in effect constitute local monopolies and as such would inevitably follow their own interests as service 'producers', in delivering as little as they possibly could to patients without incurring sanctions. Only pseudo-market mechanisms, they believed, would have the simultaneous effect of empowering patients to realise their interests as 'users', while disciplining doctors and nurses into offering more competitive (and therefore better) services to their users, rather than maximising their 'producer interests' by doing as little work as possible. This was the logical implication of a perspective shaped by public choice theory.[2]

This policy agenda, and its controversial assumptions, have been discussed in many quarters.[3] What has been less widely reported is the fact that alongside this effort to empower patients as consumers, the same NHS reform programme saw the abolition of the Community Health Councils: local representative bodies elected by NHS users, established in the 1970s in response to demands for the democratisation of public service administration (one localised manifestation of the global wave of democratic demands that characterised the 1960s and '70s).[4] The councils were eradicated by the New Labour government, who regarded them as no longer appropriate to the new governance structures that it was introducing to the NHS, replacing them with consultative forums on which patients and other 'stakeholders' would be represented, but which had no direct democratic mandate.[5] Therefore, even as they were to be 'empowered' as consumers, whose collective power could only be exercised by the aggregatory mechanisms of a market, NHS users were to be disempowered as citizens, no longer able to actually make collective decisions about local NHS policy.

This is one example, but there are many others. To some extent the logic of this scenario exemplifies the basic pattern according to which neoliberal hegemony has been established and maintained since the 1970s: in return for giving up collective and democratic power, neoliberal subjects are offered historically unprecedented levels of private autonomy. Most of this chapter will be concerned with elaborating on this observation, while situating it in a global and historical context. In the process we will investigate an issue that is always central to any understanding, and any theorisation, of the mechanics of hegemony: the nature of 'consent'. Although Antonio Gramsci's famous formula, *hegemony = coercion + consent*, is often cited,[6] and sounds simple enough, it actually raises a profound conceptual difficulty about where to draw the line between consent and coercion. Indeed, as we will outline, the vast majority of hegemonic power rests somewhere within the morally grey interzone between the two.

As we mentioned in chapter 1, Gramsci himself hints at a possible way to complexify the concept of consent, remarking at one point in the *Prison Notebooks* that consent may be either passive or active in nature.[7] Although Gramsci does not dwell on this distinction, it remains crucial, partly because many critics of the idea of hegemony seem to assume that all hegemony necessarily involves the active consent of the subaltern, and look upon any situation in which active consent is not discernible as one in which hegemonic relations must not be in play. Alternatively, other misreadings will tend to see hegemony in the guise of totalising force and coercion. We have already described a number of ways in which passive consent can be seen to operate: in situations in which people find themselves obliged to defer to an ideology or system of government that they do not consciously endorse but see no benefit in trying to resist; and in situations where people are subject to governmental systems that order their behaviour whether or not they concur with the abstract principles or objectives informing them.

Consent can be passive or active to varying degrees, while hegemonic projects can have effects that are simultaneously empowering and disempowering in different ways for the same people. In order to map such complex situations, we need an appropriately rich conceptual vocabulary. We have already indicated some of the most important theoretical sources on which we could draw for that purpose: Marx, Gramsci, Althusser, Laclau, Mouffe, Foucault. But the most important resource on which we propose to draw, in addition to Gramsci himself, is the ideas of Gilles Deleuze and Félix Guattari.

Deleuze, Guattari, Gramsci

This pair of radical French philosophers is often regarded as among the most obtuse and inaccessible of a whole generation of avant-garde theorists at work in Paris in the 1960s and '70s. Because of the highly idiosyncratic range of earlier philosophical texts on which they draw – from epicureans to early twentieth-century vitalists – their texts present a particular challenge to the non-specialist reader. Their complexity is partly a function of their sheer intellectual ambition. In their two-volume work *Capitalism and Schizophrenia*, Deleuze and Guattari attempt to develop nothing less than a complete, and fully materialist, theory of the psychosocial. Most comparable theoretical exercises up to that point had attempted to bolt together Marxian social theory and economics with Freudian psychoanalysis – always a dubious exercise, given the arguably very different presuppositions informing those bodies of thought.[8] Deleuze and Guattari aim instead to radicalise both Marxism and psychoanalysis, understanding unconscious processes as social facts, and, conversely, capitalism as a process that is always imbricated with psychic and bodily dimensions of experience, on every level.

There is not space here for a full exposition of Deleuze and Guattari's thought, but we can elaborate some of their key terms that we will go on to use in our analyses. The first such term is 'assemblage'.[9] This term can designate more or less any ensemble of elements that have some kind of effect in the world: a single cell, a hand, a human body, a human body holding a cell phone, a school, a town, a planetary ecosystem, and so on could all be considered 'assemblages'.[10] However, the term is most often used to refer to specific social formations or institutions. In such terms, we can say that actually existing neoliberalism only ever functions through specific assemblages of social institutions, practices of government, technological apparatuses and class relations; and that this assemblage always facilitates particular kinds of change (e.g., the privatisation and commodification of public services) while retarding others (e.g., any form of social innovation tending towards egalitarian social relations).

As several commentators have suggested,[11] there is an interesting affinity between some of Deleuze and Guattari's key ideas and some of Gramsci's. In particular, we draw attention to the resonance between the concept of the assemblage and at least two key terms from Gramsci's *Prison Notebooks*. One is the concept of the social 'bloc', as we called it in chapter 1. This slightly elusive idea is used in two overlapping ways by Gramsci.[12] It is used, as we explained there, partly to refer to a kind of coalition of class fractions, usually united by their common participation in a particular economic sector. For example, trade unionists and manufacturers can have a common interest in the success of manufacturing industry, thereby constituting a bloc, under specific historical circumstances. At the same time, the term is used by Gramsci to refer to the fact that such clusters of interests and identities can be seen to cohere both at economic and at cultural, political and social levels.[13] For example, in the case that we've just described, the idea of a 'national interest' – defined primarily by the capacity of a national manufacturing sector to remain profitable enough to maintain high levels of local employment – can become a powerful ideological element of widely dispersed 'common sense', belief in which can take on a key role in general political debates and struggle. It is the fact that in such instances, the coherence of such sets of social groups can be identified on discursive and cultural as well as political and economic levels, which Gramsci sometimes emphasised by referring to them as blocs.

This idea of the 'national interest' was a central element of hegemonic political discourse in post-war Britain and the United States. It was also central to Donald Trump's appeals to economic nationalism during the 2016 presidential election.[14] In the latter case, we could say that the key to Trump's election was the successful incorporation of some elements of the blue-collar working class, and a long-standing desire to restore the manufacturing base of the United States, into his hegemonic bloc – one composed, in part, of alt-right meme culture,[15] Fox News and its infrastructural capacity to monopolise information flows to certain audiences, the broader network of right-wing media and popular television (such as the show that made Trump famous, *The Apprentice*),[16] residual and resurgent white supremacism, the Republican Party as a national institution, the Koch brothers' funding of far-right think-tanks and campaigns, and the remains of the Tea Party. A core element of this assemblage/bloc was what has been called 'the evangelical-capitalist resonance machine'.[17] This is those mutually-reinforcing networks of Christian evangelicals and extreme pro-capitalist forces that have been so central to the American right since the 1970s, networks linked by shared 'resonances' – sympathies born out of sharing the same enemies and cultural prejudices rather than of any rational ideological coherence. What Trump and his election campaign did was to plug this resonance machine into the powerful 'amplifiers' of celebrity culture, centred on reality television and the growing 'intellectual dark web'[18] world of the online 'alt-right', creating a 'basin of attraction'[19] that was able to incorporate these strategically crucial constituencies while attracting others. This is a classic contemporary example of an assemblage that necessarily incorporates social, economic, cultural, political and technological elements to serve a particular political project and a specific set of interests.

The other key Gramscian idea that can be compared with assemblage is 'conjuncture'. This term designates, as an object of study and analysis, the particular set of historic conditions and power relations at a precise moment in history, in a more or less specific spatial location. It most famously came into English-language political analysis via the work of Stuart Hall and his colleagues and students from the 1970s onwards, in their efforts to understand the social, cultural and political conditions under which the post-war social settlement broke down and the New Right were able to begin implementing neoliberalism in the UK.[20] The most highly developed theorisation of the idea of conjuncture is to be found in the work of one of Hall's most important students, Lawrence Grossberg, whose synthesis of Gramscian and Deleuzo-Guattarian approaches is a strong precursor to our own project in this book.[21] For Grossberg, understanding the specificity of conjunctures and assemblages is always about understanding the highly context-specific nature of social experience and political outcomes. One implication of this way of understanding political and social change is that the primary question we are concerned with in this chapter – what are the types of active and passive that enable projects such as actually existing neoliberalism to function hegemonically? – will simply have different answers in different historical situations.

Because there is no universal model of ideology and power that we can apply, we must look to the detailed specifics of given situations for answers.

Coalition and Multiplicity

For Gramsci, and his intellectual followers, all politics is coalition politics. Hegemony is the capacity to *lead* a coalition of different social forces and social groups; however, the coalition must be formed in order for hegemonic relations to obtain, and it is never simply willed into existence by the magical leadership of the hegemon. What is more, a coalition is never simply an aggregation of discrete parts that remain unchanged by their relationship to each other.

The latter is one of the crucial insights offered by Ernesto Laclau and Chantal Mouffe in their post-structuralist reworking of Gramsci's theory. They address this theme partly through their key concept of 'articulation'[22] (a term that they borrowed from Louis Althusser,[23] but that has since become closely associated both with their ideas, and with those of Stuart Hall).[24] Articulation is the process by which certain political demands, ideas, identities, constituencies, or discursive terms become linked together to form 'chains of equivalence'. But becoming part of such a chain of equivalence does not leave the social meaning of any such element unchanged. For example, consider the way in which the legal right to abortion has become a symbolic dividing issue within American politics. From a certain perspective it might seem logically perverse that the political right should have become so attached to the attempt to reverse this legal right, given their supposed commitment to individual property rights and the freedom of the individual.[25] Nonetheless, American political history since the 1970s has produced a situation in which there is now in effect a strong chain of equivalence linking opposition to public welfare programmes with opposition to gun controls with opposition to abortion rights for pregnant women. In the process, each of these has become an issue associated with the others and now seems to have a quite different social significance to what it might have had if it had remained merely a discrete civil liberties or medical issue.[26]

Similarly to Laclau and Mouffe, Deleuze and Guattari see all identities and phenomena as relational and mobile, always in a state of relative flux and always changing as other identities and phenomena change too. One distinctive term they use to describe this process is 'becoming': all phenomena are always in a state of becoming and are always entering into states of mutual becoming with other phenomena. From 2015 to 2020, the elements composing the Trump assemblage/bloc were all in a situation of mutually constitutive and mutually transformative becoming, changing as the bloc emerged and acquired new capacities (while losing others) as it constantly mutated. This is true of all social coalitions: they are always composed of elements which change as the coalition takes place, as particular potentialities that might have been latent in those elements are amplified and expressed while others are not.

This aspect of the process of coalition formation can only really be understood if we understand another key concept of Deleuze and Guattari's: 'multiplicity'.[27] This term designates the way in which every phenomenon, every object, every being, every entity, is always 'multiple' in nature, always composed of diverse elements with diverse immanent properties. Think of the molecules making up a piece of wood or the diverse biographical experiences marking the singular persons making up any social group, however apparently homogenous it may be. In the case of our chosen example, this is a concept that can help to illuminate one of the most perplexing feature of the Trump phenomena: the fact that a small constituency actually transferred their support to him from Obama, having gone from voting for the first black president to voting for one who more or less explicitly endorsed white supremacism.[28] This fact provoked a number of different responses when it first manifested itself, including a fatalistic sense that the 'real' racism of white Americans had now been given voice and expression, whereas previously it had somehow been masked.[29]

While perhaps true at the level of public discourse, this is an inadequate formulation. We can be sure that voters who had been absolutely irretrievably and self-consciously racist, for example self-professed white supremacists, would not have voted for Obama at all. It makes much more sense to say that what had been revealed by some voters switching from Obama to Trump was a persistent *potential* for the endorsement, toleration or active propagation of active, public white supremacism among voters who had *also* shown a genuine potential for – or at least toleration of – cosmopolitanism and cross-class solidarity. If we understand each of these voters, and all of the groups and communities to which they belong, as *multiplicities*, it becomes possible for us to understand all of these quite different potentialities as inhering in the same people and groups at the same time. From this perspective, we can say that the power of the Trump assemblage was to give expression to that racist potentiality while suppressing other, non-racist potentialities.

This might seem a rather banal set of observations, but we think it has crucial implications for the analysis and the practice of politics in the twenty-first century. The assumption that specific social constituencies have clearly defined views and political priorities, and that these cannot be changed under any circumstances, is actually endemic in much political commentary. For example, the fact that a large number of working-class voters voted Leave in the 2016 referendum on British membership of the European Union has become the central reference point of a widespread political discourse in the UK that posits working-class voters in general as having become incorrigibly defensive, socially conservative and politically reactionary.[30] This discourse assumes that for any political party – especially the Labour Party – to achieve electoral success, it must make some accommodation with these apparently fixed and unchangeable attitudes of the 'working class'.[31]

There are several problems with this view. One is that it is simply empirically wrong. Certain sets of opinions may be prevalent among voters of particular socio-economic groups, but all empirical evidence shows that there is no absolutely uniform distribution of opinions within any group, however narrowly defined in socio-economic terms.[32] The other is that such a view simply cannot explain political change; it cannot explain how it is that, periodically, political majorities clearly do emerge in support of projects that could not command such majorities a few years earlier (and we will look at some specific examples shortly). Consequently, this mainstream political perspective, in both journalistic and academic commentary, found it notoriously difficult to account for the relative success of Jeremy Corbyn's Labour Party at the 2017 UK general election, following the Brexit vote. As utterly commonplace as this sounds, much political commentary simply finds it very difficult to grasp the basic fact that people can, and sometimes do, change their minds. A concept like 'multiplicity', as abstract as it sounds, can be helpful in focusing analytical attention on the potential for such changes to occur, and the fact that they often do.

From our perspective, then, the role of political organisation and political leadership is always to constitute assemblages wherein certain potentialities of particular social groups are likely to be expressed, while others are not. This, in fact, is what leadership means, and this is the nature of hegemonic politics. Politics is always a matter of aggregating political demands and interests in such a way as to maximise their potentials in certain directions; that is to say, their potential for certain becomings. All political constituencies are multiplicities, and the task of radical politics is always to create material, organisational and cultural conditions under which the progressive potentialities of those constituencies will be expressed, while their reactionary potentialities will not. The war of position is a war over potentialities.

With a basic understanding of hegemony as a practice of power established, we will now examine in more detail some historical situations in which distinctive sets of hegemonic relations have emerged. In particular, we will consider the different and complex forms which 'consent' has taken in these different contexts, and try to understand the different terms upon which relatively stable social coalitions have been formed.

The Post-War Settlement

The classic example of a hegemonic 'settlement' in the modern period is the situation that established itself in the Western liberal democracies between the end of World War II and the crisis of the 1970s. In fact, when English-speaking commentators and political theorists first began to engage seriously with Gramsci's ideas, it was in an attempt to make sense of the passing of that post-war world. It may not have been clear entirely where things were headed, but it was obvious to many observers at that time, given the extraordinary social upheavals and widespread economic dislocation of the 1970s, that something was coming to an end. And it was those analysts who made direct reference to Gramsci, who in fact did see exactly where things were going. Stuart Hall and his colleagues at the Birmingham Centre for Contemporary Cultural Studies earned an unparalleled reputation for astute political analysis with their Gramscian study of the British political crisis of the 1970s, *Policing the Crisis*, that correctly identified the emergent politics of the New Right, with its distinctive combination of neoliberal economics and social conservatism, as the force that was in the process of establishing hegemony in Britain.[33]

At exactly the same moment, the economists of the French 'regulation school' first began to draw on Gramsci's work in order to theorise the way in which capitalist economies can pass through different phases, characterised by different sets of institutional and technological arrangements that they called 'regimes of accumulation'.[34] Again, this was because it appeared to them (correctly) that the regime of accumulation first identified by Gramsci as 'Fordism' was giving way to a distinctively different regime: 'post-Fordism'[35] or 'flexible accumulation',[36] characterised by the disaggregation of manufacturing processes, of firms, of communities and of the entire national economies. In both cases, it was the apparently stable, prosperous, forward-looking and egalitarian society that had emerged from the crises of the 1930s that was, by the end of the 1970s, finally giving way to something very different. And in both cases, Gramsci's basic ideas seemed to offer the most useful way to understand and account for the change.

The Fordist World

The post-war political culture of countries such as the UK, the US and France has seemed to many commentators to exemplify a social formation within which clearly defined hegemonic relations could be identified. According to the story that is usually told about this moment, a combination of historical factors converged to produce a situation in which most major social actors and political parties accepted a broad range of premises that would inform most government policy, as well as the political behaviour of capitalists and trade unions for a generation. All accepted a basically Keynesian economic model, according to which government would take a historically unprecedented level of responsibility for the management of industrial infrastructure and the provision of social services, and would take any measures necessary to maintain equally unprecedented rates of adult male employment. The steadily growing industrial economy would fund an expanding welfare state, as progressive taxation and rising wages contributed to a continual narrowing of social inequality. Full employment would guarantee that organised labour maintained considerable political and economic leverage, while the leadership of organised labour in turn would guarantee that political demands from workers never escalated to the point of threatening capitalist social relations, or of undermining public support for the Cold War against the Soviet bloc. Political parties of left and right would maintain different priorities and different degrees of emphasis: for example, in the UK, the question of whether the steel industry should be nationalised or privatised represented a limit point to consensus, with successive Labour and Conservative administrations implementing their preferred policy until the 1980s. But such minor modifications would not challenge the basic foundations and parameters of the 'post-war consensus'.[37]

In Gramscian terms, this post-war consensus has been seen as the political expression of an underlying social 'settlement': a kind of negotiated peace between the class fractions that had been at war during the turbulent inter-war decades. Although this is often referred to as the 'post-war settlement', in actuality its model and its key exemplary instance was the programme enacted by the US federal government led by Franklin D. Roosevelt between 1933 and 1936. The so-called New Deal was explicitly understood as representing a new compact between state, capital and labour, and would define the parameters of American federal policy until the 1970s.[38]

Gramsci analysed the emergence of this new form of state-assisted capitalism in his classic essay 'Americanism and Fordism'.[39] As the title suggests, Gramsci understands this emergent formation not primarily in terms of a new kind of statecraft, but in terms of a new way of organising industrial production. 'Fordism' refers partly to Henry Ford's pioneering use of assembly-line production and Frederick Taylor's techniques of heavily regulated 'scientific management' at his Detroit factories, and partly to Ford's policy of paying unusually high wages for highly alienating labour, to a workforce whose personal lives and moral probity he rigorously policed.

For Gramsci, Fordism was in the process of intensifying the gendered division of labour, because the physical and psychic demands on male assembly-line workers required women to take on a full-time role as domestic carers and housewives.[40] It's notable that although the low point for women's industrial employment had already passed in countries such as the UK, it was precisely the era of the Fordist factory that saw the strongest emphasis in public discourse on the idea of the housewife as the only legitimate role for the modern female adult.[41] In advertisements, in the pages of government policy documents, public information films, movies and magazines, this was the 'golden age' of the housewife as an identity to be aspired to by almost all women outside of the residual landed gentry (and the new aristocracy of Hollywood). At the same time, Gramsci saw the Fordist factory producing 'a new type of man': highly disciplined, technologically enabled, but intellectually and emotionally uninvested in his work.[42] Gramsci was optimistic about the revolutionary potential of this new kind of industrial worker, and the success of the labour movement in winning major reforms over subsequent decades suggests that this optimism wasn't entirely misplaced. At the same time, Gramsci's remarks on the highly repressive sexual culture of Fordism seemed to presage the emotional repression and sexual conformism of mainstream 1950s culture with astonishing prescience.[43]

A New Deal

A key feature of this settlement was the formation of a social bloc composed by the alliance of industrial workers with industrial capital (manufacturers), led and co-ordinated by the newly interventionist Keynesian developmental state. Consequently, finance capital was politically marginalised as speculators and lenders found themselves subject to historically unprecedented levels of regulation, both in their domestic national contexts and within the international system of currency exchange and financial trading. This produced a complex and unique socio-political situation in which finance capital undoubtedly retained a privileged structural position in the overall capitalist mode of production, but in which it had lost the position of cultural and political influence that it had enjoyed at least from the moment of the fin de siècle until the end of the 1920s.[44] Indeed, there was a widespread belief on the right and on the left that while manufacturers had acquired a new level of social authority, it was organised labour and its political representatives that were really leading the whole social formation – and leading it inexorably in the direction of socialism.[45]

Of course, matters were never that simple. There was never clear, widespread support for a distinctively socialist vision of a post-capitalist future, at least in the English-speaking world.[46] The organised working class was never simply in the driving seat. The direction taken by successive governments, and by the general social formations within which they were situated, was one which enriched capital (especially, but not exclusively, industrial capital) considerably, and which exacerbated the long-term tendency for governments to value citizens as potential consumers more than in any other terms, as domestic consumer spending became more and more important to the cycle of economic growth.[47] The direction of travel was not set by any one set of interests; rather, it was a vector plotted between several co-ordinates. The interests of labour, exercising more influence than they have at any other historic moment, were one set of those co-ordinates. But they were not the only one.

The claim that this set of arrangements amounted to a 'post-war consensus' has been contested by historians for various reasons. On the one hand, political historians have pointed to the ongoing conflicts and debates both within and between major political parties during this time, arguing that it is not possible to speak of 'consensus' when, for example, the Labour and Conservative Parties continued to take opposed positions on issues such as the nationalisation of the steel industry.[48] Frankly, we regard this argument as a prime example of the tendency to which we have just referred, of an analytical position that is apparently unable to grasp the multiple nature of social phenomena. The point here is very simple. Nobody has ever claimed that there was complete unanimity of purpose between social and political actors during the post-war period. That is not what 'consensus' means in the phrase 'post-war consensus'. The claim is rather that a broad set of political parameters, and a general set of tendencies (e.g., towards greater social equality), were accepted, and that it was only ineffectual fringe elements that tried to push beyond those parameters in pursuit of their objectives. In our terminology, the post-war consensus was the effect of the hegemony of a particular assemblage/bloc; but like all such assemblages, both the hegemonic historic bloc and the wider social formation wherein its was hegemonic were defined as much by their internal multiplicity as by any degree of uniformity or unanimity. In making a judgement as to the reality of the 'post-war consensus', what matters, isn't whether everyone, or even anyone, precisely agreed with the general direction of travel; what matters is that there was a direction, and that there seemed little chance of altering its course during a sustained period of about thirty years. To refer to a post-war consensus is not to assert that social relations or political processes were ever static or uniform during this time; it is rather to assert that the 'constellation of assemblages'[49] that made up the post-war national social formations in some countries achieved a certain level of 'metastability'. The term 'metastability', coined by another French philosopher, Gilbert Simondon, refers to the state of relative stability that individuated objects can achieve, even while the processes that individuate them are never completed, and even while their stability is only ever partial, relative and temporary.[50] Simondon's basic model is the formation of crystals in solution, but he argues that it can also be applied to the dynamic existence of living organisms and even the relative stability of social systems.[51] Thus, this is a useful term to describe situations like the 'post-war consensus', in which a certain level of relative stabilisation should not be read as expressing some underlying homogeneity or stasis.

The Limits of Consent

The other objection that is sometimes made to the idea of the post-war consensus comes from a classically Marxian perspective. It points to the sheer level of coercion required, in restraining the working-class militancy of the interwar period, to render the post-war consensus unchallengeable.[52] It is certainly true, especially during the early years of the Cold War, that direct repression of communism and other revolutionary tendencies within the workers' movement was a feature of American, British and Western European politics.[53] The witch hunts against communists in the media and the US federal government in the early 1950s are the best-known example to English-speaking audiences. The US security services also intervened directly to prevent the Italian Communist Party (which was at that moment busy turning Gramsci into a national martyr)[54] from forming a democratically elected government. This must stand as one of the most crucial episodes in the history of modern continental Europe,[55] for without that intervention, the party would very likely have formed a government with a genuine popular mandate to build socialism in the Western Mediterranean, and the entire balance of power on the continent would have been altered. Even in the UK, the post-war Labour government colluded in the harassment and monitoring of revolutionaries by state intelligence services (despite the now well-known infiltration of those services by aristocratic Soviet sympathisers).[56] In each country, this repression applied not only to middle-class communists, but also to militant organisers within the major industrial sectors.[57]

Given these observations, we accept that the idea of the post-war consensus should not be taken to imply some cosy set of wholly consensual relationships. But any claim that this violent repression of revolutionary tendencies was the key precondition for the post-war consensus would also be difficult to sustain, at least in the British and American cases. There was never widespread support for anything resembling revolutionary socialism in those countries, and certainly no realistic prospect of it spreading beyond specific social sectors. In the UK, even in the 1940s – the high-water mark of Labour's popularity and of its radicalism in office – there was no clear majority of public opinion favouring a radical and wholesale transition to non-capitalist social relations.[58] There is thus no evidence that socialist revolution was ever on the cards, with or without its violent suppression.

But if revolutionary politics never posed any real threat to the interests of state and capitalist forces, why did they bother to suppress it at all? This brings us to a crucial aspect of our Gramscian understanding of politics: even if there was no immediate threat of revolution, militancy certainly did threaten the interests of capital and its state agents: it could encourage workers on a larger scale to intensify their demands, could help to improve their levels of organisation, and could thus generally put more pressure on capital for significant material concessions than would otherwise have been applied. In other words, revolutionary militancy could be a significant factor in shifting the balance of the 'relations of force' obtaining at a given historic moment.[59]

This is Gramsci's term for the relations between different social constituencies and the extent to which they are able to pursue their own interests to the exclusion of all others, or, conversely, find themselves forced to compromise with other sets of interests and the political agendas that express them. From this perspective the post-war consensus, and the entire project of post-war social reform, were only ever expressions of the balance of forces obtaining in societies like Britain's during that period. In the UK, for example, the workers' movement was strong enough to extract significant concessions from the capitalist class and the state: a historically high share of the proceeds of growth, a generous welfare state, a commitment to full employment, government control over key industries and services, a health service. It was not strong enough to extract others, and we can think of many policies that could have been enacted, had the balance moved further in favour of the workers: for example, democratic workers' control over industries and services, an end to British support for American international anti-communism, and the abolition of the system of private schools that remains so central to the socialisation of the British elite to this day.

The question that these observations lead to is obvious. If this 'consensus' was always an expression of the relations of forces and an effect of the hegemony of a specific social bloc, then just how consensual was it? In other words, what forms of consent did it depend upon for its metastability, its functionality and its apparent legitimacy?

The Fordist Assemblage

Our core contention is that there was indeed more active consent to the settlement that obtained during this time, and for the general direction of travel that it entailed, than at any comparable historical moment before or since. This is not to say that were was no dissent, no variation in opinion or no basic coercion in evidence. No doubt any given citizen of (for example) the UK or US during this period would have preferred some variation on the actual programme that was enacted: a variation more perfectly aligned with their own specific interests and preferences. But precisely because the balance of forces was more favourable to labour than at any comparable historical moment, more active consent was clearly required for governing projects than at other times. To put this very simply, if an average citizen were asked in 1955, 'Do you think that the current programme of pursuing a mixed economy, gradually expanding the public sector, guaranteeing full employment and rising wages, protecting certain areas of social activity from market relations, redistributing wealth and income to reduce overall inequality, supporting "traditional" gender relations, family form and domestic arrangements, and so on is the right one for governments to pursue?', that average citizen would presumably have replied, 'Yes.' At the same time, irrespective of measurable public opinion, it is demonstrably the case that living standards rose by a larger amount for more people during this period than during any other on record, while the gap between the richest and the poorest shrank by a demonstrably greater degree.[60] This is as good evidence as we can ask for that governments and broader social arrangements acted in the interests of the majority during this time. No wonder the French refer to 1945–75 as *les trentes glorieuses* (the thirty glorious [years]).

There are many historical explanations given as to what made this unique situation possible. One, as we have seen, is simply that the overall balance of forces, especially in Western Europe, was highly favourable to organised labour. This itself was the result of multiple factors in play. World War II itself gave a huge boost to manufacturing economies that had suffered from the depression of the 1930s, making full employment almost a requisite from a capitalist as well as a democratic perspective. Large sections of the capitalist class – beginning with Ford himself – had come around to the understanding that, as the consumer economy continued to develop, it was no longer in their own interests to do everything in their power to suppress wages. The reason was that wages now returned to them, increasingly, in the form of consumer spending.[61] The international success of the Communist movement and the military strength of the Soviet Union (and later China) placed enormous pressure on capitalists and capitalist governments to make major political concessions to workers, in order to forestall any danger of radicalisation, or even weakening support for the Cold War. In the 1940s and '50s, the policy of liberal anti-communists in the American security establishment was to actively encourage the development of generous social democratic states in Western Europe, in the belief that this would constitute the most effective political buffer against the threat of Communism.[62]

Perhaps most importantly, as Gramsci had seen in the 1930s, and as the New Deal had exemplified, there were features of the broad Fordist techno-social assemblage that made it far easier than at other historical moments for centralised national governments to act at the behest of politically organised populations. Most of the key technologies of the 'second industrial revolution' – railways, telegraphy, electricity, broadcasting, cinema – required some form of central admin-istration to make their infrastructures operable, while giving enormous power to whoever controlled them centrally. This was the great era of the totalitarian state, during which national governments could exercise higher levels of control over populations and territories – and flows of information, labour and capital – than at any time before or since. At the same time, the development of the global consumer economy had reached a stage at which domestic mass markets took on a new importance in the overall cycles of capital accumulat-ion, whereas the technological conditions did not yet exist for the mass relocation of manufacturing to parts of the world in which labour costs were low. As such, populations of work-ers/consumers had to be offered major inducements both to work and to consume.[63]

Many of these conditions also made it easier for mass dem-ocratic organisation to take place than had historically been the case. The congregation of workers in large factories made labour organisation much easier, while the relative homoge-neity that characterised the lifestyles of many citizens encouraged collective participation in mass political organi-sations (political parties especially; in the UK, membership of both the Labour and Conservative Parties peaked in the early 1950s).[64] Mass parties, formal political democracy and highly potent centralised states added up to a situation in which gov-ernments, for better or for worse, were more able and more likely to enact policies that corresponded with the explicit desires of citizens than during any comparable era. However, clearly nothing in these conditions made any political out-comes inevitable. Those that actually materialised were the result of particular social blocs emerging and achieving hege-mony. This in turn was the outcome of particular historical actors pursuing specific political strategies that allowed them to take advantage of the opportunities the new conditions offered.

In the British case, the question of how the progressive and long-lasting reforms of the 1940s were won, and of what the political, social and cultural conditions were for them, has been a major preoccupation for the left ever since the great reforming Labour government, led by Clement Attlee between 1945 and 1951, left office. No Labour government since has come close to having the same level of undeniable impact. Unsurprisingly, every faction of the British labour movement has had its own account of exactly what happened and exactly what made it possible, from those who see the 1940s as a missed opportunity to implement full-blown socialism (or even significant democratic reform),[65] to those who claim that even in the 1940s, the British electorate was always hostile to socialism and only voted Labour because the party leadership appeared to be competent technocrats.[66] We would argue that a fully adequate account can accommodate all of these perspectives, as each of them discerns important aspects of an inherently complex situation.

The most popular explanation for the apparent radicalisation of the British electorate during the 1940s is that this was a direct reaction to the experience of total war. There is no denying the importance of this factor. Indeed, the war provided a unique historic opportunity for a centralised state to demonstrate its capacity to organise almost every aspect of national life, directly contradicting the laissez-faire ideology that had remained deeply entrenched as the common sense of the British political class for over a century.[67] This overcame one of the major ideological obstacles to socialism in Britain. At the same time – and this is almost always forgotten in popular accounts of the war – for a crucial period of the conflict, the UK's only military ally in this war against fascism was the Soviet Union. It's hardly surprising that precisely that period saw the most rapid growth in the history of the Communist Party of Great Britain,[68] or that this had a radicalising effect on sectors of the population beyond those who actually signed up as card-carrying Communists.[69] However, this cannot fully explain a set of political developments that had already been anticipated in the pre-war United States, and that had correlates over the 1930s, '40s and '50s in various countries with very different experiences of the period.[70]

While many historical explanations have been offered, there are two key aspects that we will dwell on here. One is simply the exhaustion of the existing hegemonic bloc and its political project. The key alliance animating that bloc was between finance capital and the petite bourgeoisie. These were the constituencies whose interests and agendas most directly dictated government policy, and they were expressed in a political ideology that stressed the sanctity of property, the primacy of business interests, the value of free trade, and an ideological resistance to active social reform inherited from nineteenth-century liberalism.[71] Under these circumstances, the professional classes retained their historic deference to the culture of the petite bourgeoisie, while the workers' movement, utterly demoralised by the failure of the 1926 general strike and the betrayals of the first Labour government, could not challenge the hegemony of this bloc or form meaningful alliances with other social groups.[72] The economic crisis following the 1929 stock market crash discredited the hegemonic liberal ideology in the United States for half a century, opening the way for a Fordist assemblage/bloc to drive forward the New Deal. In the UK, it took the further failure of the Conservative government's attempts to avoid war with Nazi Germany to finally provoke the effective disintegration of the hegemonic bloc and the conditions under which a new one could be composed.

The other key explanation for the emergence of a new hegemonic bloc in the 1940s involves the changing class dynamics of industrial capitalist societies. As they became more technologically advanced, both state and corporate institutions came to require more sophisticated and specialised layers of managerial expertise in order to function. As late as the 1920s, the traditional petite bourgeoisie had overwhelmingly shaped the culture of the middle classes, rendering it implacably hostile to the workers' movement and deferential to the capitalist class and the traditional aristocracy. By the 1930s, however, a new professional class of salaried managers, technicians, and bureaucrats was on the rise. Culturally, these highly educated technocrats shared nothing with the industrial working class, and in many cases their roles involved managing and disciplining them. But as employees, rather than employers and investors, and as professionals who increasingly relied on state contracts or direct state employment for remuneration, it became increasingly possible to align their economic interests with those of workers. At the same time, their status as the newest social group, reliant for their positions on expertise in the most modern technologies and organisational techniques, left them far less emotionally invested in traditional social forms, and more open to visions of a new and improved society.[73] All of these factors made this new professional class amenable to a technocratic, modernist, state-led version of socialism that was perfectly expressed by the tradition of the Fabian Society – an organisation that was one of the founding constituents of the Labour Party, had boasted among its membership such public luminaries as George Bernard Shaw and H.G. Wells, and had always been explicitly committed to a gradualist vision of socialism as the rule of benevolent technocrats.[74]

The fact that a typically Fabian, modernist, technocratic vision of socialism began to predominate in the public discourse of the Labour Party from the mid 1930s onwards – substituting for the communitarian ethical socialism that had been prevalent earlier in the decade – was surely one key strategic reason for its success in winning over this crucial constituency.[75] At the same time, this constituency became a crucial element of the social bloc that achieved hegemony over the course of the 1940s, precisely because of their technical expertise. This was the social group most able to put the new technologies of government at the service of whatever political project they were aligned with. They would ensure that the state took on an increasingly egalitarian and redistributive function as the war progressed, rather than simply working to protect the economic privileges of the traditional middle classes from wartime austerity, as the civil service seems to have been inclined to do during the early days of the war. They would staff the new ministries, administer the national health service and manage the industries that the 1945 Labour government had just nationalised.[76]

Of course, this was only one element of the bloc that emerged and achieved hegemony at this time. As we have already mentioned, another crucial element was manufacturing capital itself, which benefitted hugely from a vast increase in state investment in infrastructure and from governments' new willingness to reign in the speculative power of finance. At the same time, full employment, and the radicalising effects of the experience of poverty and political struggle during the inter-war period, had left certain sections of the labour movement both extremely militant and with a historically unprecedented capacity to make political demands on capital and state institutions. This tendency was personified in the figure of Aneurin Bevan, the Welsh Marxist and former coal miner who was minister for both health and housing during the second half of the 1940s. Bevan is generally credited with having established the National Health Service on fully socialist principles (full free access to health care for all, funded entirely from central taxation), against those more 'moderate' elements within the Labour government who would have preferred that it be established – like most of the post-war welfare settlement – on the basis of a contributory social-insurance model.[77]

Famously, Bevan's inspiration was the Tredegar Medical Aid Society, a mutually owned institution offering universal health care coverage to its members in return for contributions, located in the South Wales mining town where Bevan was raised. Bevan was a graduate of the Central Labour College in London, an autonomous, union-funded institute that was probably the only Higher Education institution teaching Marxist theory in the UK in the early twentieth century. Whatever his level of theoretical sophistication, however, he would almost certainly not have been able to press for this model of the NHS, had it not been for the fact that the social constituency that was his power base – the miners of the South Wales coalfields – was at the historic peak of its influence and militancy. Key architects and agitators of the Great General Strike of 1926,[78] the South Wales miners were one of the few sections of the British labour movement in which something like revolutionary class consciousness had become widespread. Indeed, no region of the UK sent as many volunteers to fight in the International Brigades during the Spanish Civil War.[79] Having suffered mass unemployment and appalling poverty during the depression of the 1930s, by the mid-1940s the miners found themselves in a completely different economic and political situation: unemployment had dropped to negligible proportions, and the British industrial economy was entirely dependent on domestic coal. As such, they were able to leverage enormous influence within the labour movement and the wider national polity. If any of these conditions had not obtained, it is unlikely that Bevan's insistence on a socialist NHS would have had the effective force that it did.

Bevanism only represented the radical wing of the British Labour movement; it was never able to capture the leadership of that movement, or to win wide-enough popular support outside the most militant industrial communities to become anything more than a radical wing. But it was clearly a crucial element of the historic assemblage that established hegemony in the 1940s, creating a set of institutions that would entrench a particular set of governmental priorities and tendencies for a generation. If there is a historic lesson to be drawn from this experience, it is that revolutionary militancy may well be a necessary component of any social coalition that has a chance of establishing truly lasting and significant reforms. But what is most striking about this specific instance, from our perspective, is that the assemblage under discussion included not only the most militant section of the working class, but also the most progressive section of the middle classes, and a specific section of the capitalist class. All of their interests and perspectives were more or less successfully co-ordinated for at least as long as it took to establish a significant set of reforming institutions. Under these circumstances, a general direction of travel was established that was able to command the active consent of a high proportion of the population.

Disciplinary Fordism

For all of this mass consensus we have outlined above, it is important to remember that there was always dissent, and there were considerable costs imposed on dissenters. Gramsci explicitly noted the high level of sexual repression demanded by Fordism, as well as the extension of disciplinary mechanisms into the everyday lives of workers outside the factories (such as attempts to regulate or even curtail the consumption of intoxicants).[80] We could say that this was the epoch during which disciplinary institutions reached their highest level of development, being deployed by both capitalist and socialist institutions to administer highly conformist normative cultures.[81] The most obvious price was paid by women – of almost all social classes – who did not want to accept their allotted social roles as housewives. While women's participation in higher education and the labour market continued to expand, the contradiction between this social reality and a hegemonic ideology that severely constrained women's participation in public culture produced widely shared (though by no means universal) experiences of frustration and dissatisfaction. These feelings would permeate some of the most memorable cultural output of the period.[82] At the same time, the legal persecution of LGBTQ people reached a historic peak in the 1950s[83] – a fact that must in part be attributed to the highly conformist climate of the times, especially in matters of sexuality and gendered identity.

The post-war period also saw the first major wave of immigration to the UK from the former colonies of South Asia and the Caribbean. From a contemporary vantage point, one of the most striking features of the experience of new immigrants is the extent to which, again, they were expected to conform to the norms and behaviours of the 'host' culture.[84] However, this is very much a present-day perspective; the right to cultural autonomy was seemingly not one that most immigrants initially aspired to, as the adoption of normative British behaviours (eating habits, dress codes, etc.) was itself often seen as a marker of social status within immigrant communities. It would be the children of these immigrants, and of their 'native' contemporaries, who would rebel against the conformism of post-war culture, and the deference towards both their elders and their class 'superiors' that it demanded of them.[85]

But while it lasted, the post-war consensus saw little active resistance from any of these dissenting constituencies. At the same time, its critics on the right railed against it impotently from the margins of the political mainstream.[86] It was at these various points of tensions that the hegemonic bloc of the post-war period would come unstuck. Until it did, however, we can still say that the level of active consent to its hegemony was unusually high.

The End of the Settlement

Active consent to the post-war settlement began to break
down in the 1960s. This was partly because a new generation
of both working-class and middle-class citizens, free from the
memory of austerity and hunger, saw no reason to subject
themselves to the forms of social discipline that the maintenance of its coherence had demanded. By 1970, it was under
intolerable strain due to demands for women's liberation, for
black political representation and cultural autonomy, for gay
liberation, and for more opportunities for personal freedom
and self-expression for young people.[87]

At the same time, workers who had little investment in any
of these cultural and social demands, but who remained
largely subject to the forms of workplace discipline and alienated labour that typified Fordist industrial processes, saw
wage growth slow and unemployment return to some sectors,
provoking immediate reactions and a rapid intensification of
labour militancy. At its height this intensification saw the most
widespread support for genuinely radical political measures at
least since the 1920s, as demands for greater worker participation in the management of industry became a noticeable
feature of the rhetoric of some rank-and-file trade unionists.[88]
But while these calls for industrial democratisation resonated
powerfully with the democratic and liberatory demands of
other social groups, they never represented anything like a
clear majority of working-class opinion. All of the available
evidence suggests that what the vast majority of working-class
and middle-class citizens wanted, right up to the 1990s, was a
simple restoration of the post-war social order, perhaps leav-
ened with some cautious moves towards social liberalisation
and the emancipation of women.[89]

The problem was that this was never going to be materially
possible. The economic conditions that had made Fordist

social democracy viable in the US, UK, and France were arguably over as soon as the West German and Japanese economies had recovered from World War II, creating far more intense international competition between firms that provoked a new wave of automation in the manufacturing sector,[90] undermining capitalist support for full-employment policies. The development of container shipping and, above all, of computer and telecommunications technologies, began to make it logistically viable for Western corporations to outsource manufacturing for domestic consumption to lower-cost regions in Asia and elsewhere, putting downward pressure on wages and upward pressure on unemployment in their domestic economies. From the late 1960s, the deregulation of financial markets and the adoption of computer technologies by the financial sector began to make possible a revival of the mobility and political potency of finance capital. At the same time, the demand for personal self-expression among youth and other social groups created an enormous opportunity for those sections of capital focussed on retail and the leisure and entertainment industries. People could be offered the self-expression that they craved, to the extent that they were willing to adopt social identities defined more by specialised modes of consumption than by occupation, locality or class: this was the basis for the emergence of 'youth culture' as a formation wherein consumption (of clothes and music, primarily) was for most participants the first and only mode of participation and self-expression.

This is a crucial point to understand. It is not to say that youth culture, consumer culture, or the liberation movements that promoted certain demands for self-expression were inherently capitalist in nature. It is rather to observe that they were all complex phenomena, characterised by inherent multiplicity. They possessed the immanent potential to inform utopian projects of social transformation; indeed, one of the key political objectives of the counterculture and the New

Left was to find ways to express that revolutionary potential, through new experiments in culture, lifestyle, leisure and social organisation.[91] At the same time, these social phenomena clearly did possess a certain potential to be expressed in individualist forms, as demands for personal autonomy and private satisfaction that could be satisfied by a vastly expanded selection of specialised consumer goods (from T-shirts to luxury cars to hair-care products to real estate) and the promise of access to them. This observation is central to our story, because our claim will be that ultimately, consent to the entire neoliberal project has been secured largely by persuading populations to accept private 'empowerment' as consumers as a substitute for the partial reversal of social democracy, and for the weakening of representative democracy itself, after its high point of effectiveness in the post-war period.

The next chapter of that story is well known and well documented. In the late 1960s and throughout the 1970s, a global wave of demands for democratisation weakened or broke consent for the social settlements that had been in place since the war, from Mexico to Czechoslovakia.[92] In the British case, the post-war industrial growth model ground to a near halt in the 1970s, due to the irreconcilability of demands for wage growth, for more globally competitive firms and for continued profitability of manufacturing.[93] At the same time, those working-class citizens who had not benefitted from the expansion of universities (still catering to a tiny minority of the population) were mostly not attracted to the radical social programme of the New Left, the counterculture and the liberation movements. Meanwhile, very significantly, key organs of the popular press began to embrace a reactionary populist agenda in response to the general sense of cultural dislocation and dissensus.[94]

Tipping Points

In the 1970s, radical culture saw significant and probably historically unprecedented working-class participation,[95] even if it never included a majority of workers. However, it is important not to exaggerate any of these tendencies, or their historical novelty. Working-class conservatism was nothing new; in fact, it had been a persistent feature of British political culture since at least the eighteenth century.[96] The Labour Party had never enjoyed support from an overwhelming majority of working-class voters[97] (if it had, the political history of the UK might have resembled that of Sweden),[98] and had only ever been able to sustain successful governing projects with the support of key sections of the middle classes. Imperialism, authoritarianism and reactionary populism had been features of the popular press throughout the same period; in the 1930s, the *Daily Mail* had notoriously supported fascist parties at home and abroad.[99] Overall then, the number of people in Britain who actually changed their political views or allegiances during this time was small. But, as Gramsci was one of the first to understand, in complex modern societies, only rarely do major moments of political and cultural change result from a change in entire populations' political orientations; they are far more often the effect of certain thresholds having been crossed – certain 'tipping points' having been reached – as specific social groups move in and out of coalition with each other, and particular social blocs are composed or decomposed.

In this instance, it was the shift in loyalty on the part of one or two quite narrowly defined constituencies that changed everything. White, male, married, highly skilled, socially conservative manual workers had been among those constituencies who had been the most unproblematically privileged by the post-war settlement. It was they, more than any other social group, who saw both their economic privileges and their privileged cultural status threatened by the end of that settlement – and by the demands of feminism, anti-racism and broader countercultural tendencies for a culture in which their way of life would no longer constitute a universal norm, from which deviation would be punished. At the same moment, one of the most popular newspapers with that same constituency – *The Sun* – was transitioned by its new owner, Rupert Murdoch, from support for the Labour Party to support for the Conservatives and advocacy for a broad authoritarian populist outlook.[100] Despite all of these factors, it was never the case that a majority of this constituency shifted from support for Labour to support for the Tories. Nevertheless, enough of them did to guarantee Margaret Thatcher an election victory in 1979.

The other key constituency that Thatcher supposedly won over was a floating population of voters who might well have aligned themselves with some of the countercultural demands of the 1960s, but whose only real interest lay in personal fulfilment and individual freedom. Accounts of the political success of Thatcherism often attribute significance to this supposed constituency, seeing them as having been attracted by her hostility to state bureaucracy, and to all forms of collectivism, as well by as her rhetorical championing of entrepreneurial freedom.[101] The same is often said of Ronald Reagan and his support base.[102] This is a difficult thesis to test, because this supposed constituency of new individualists is usually described in terms of their possession of a particular set of attitudes and aspirations, rather than by specific and measurable sociological co-ordinates. But on the basis both of available qualitative evidence[103] and of subsequent historical developments, it seems fair to posit that such accounts describe a real phenomenon.

As we mentioned already in chapter 1, the key long-term development here was a historic transformation of the culture of the middle classes. The cult of sobriety, self-control, emotional repression and deferred gratification had been in decline since the Victorian era.[104] Since the days of the Romantic movement, there had been an alternative repertoire of ideas and behaviour to draw on, at least for those with the appropriate education: the Romantic sensibility emphasised the value of personal self-expression and intensive private or intimate experience as giving meaning and value to existence.[105] As sociologist Colin Campbell has shown, this repertoire became increasingly central to the practices of consumer culture over the course of the twentieth century.[106] Moreover, this was happening just as non-essential consumption became increasingly central to the dynamics of capital accumulation. In the age of the 'permissive society', middle-class culture became increasingly hedonistic – not necessarily in the sense of celebrating debauchery, but simply in the importance that it attached to the pleasures of eating, drinking, holidaying, cinema, music, home decoration and other sensual pleasures. Many of the victims and partisans of Thatcherism experienced it primarily as an authoritarian attack on the enemies of 'law and order':[107] trade unionists, feminists, black people, hippies, and so on. By others, however, it was experienced as an incitement to individuals to enrich themselves without thought for any traditional, ethical or political constraints. As such, no doubt people from both working-class and middle-class backgrounds who wanted to do just that found it liberating and appealing, and no doubt a number who may have been attracted by the libertarian promise of the counterculture found that Thatcherism offered them a far less complicated and demanding route to personal gratification.[108]

The New Right Narrative

The 'New Right' of Thatcher and Reagan was always a complex assemblage, and one that still seems historically improbable when considered from certain perspectives. It combined a neoliberal celebration of individualism, entrepreneurialism and free markets with an authoritarian social conservatism.[109] Philosophically, this was never coherent, but it was not at the level of the New Right's philosophical presuppositions that its coherence was to be found. Rather, it was the interests that it served that were its consistent feature: it was, in the medium term, a project to restore the hegemonic power of finance capital and to neutralise potential opposition to that restoration from all significant constituencies.

To be sure, those skilled manual workers who switched from Labour to the Tories in 1979 were never going to vote for a programme whose explicit long-term objectives were the deregulation of the financial sector and the permanent suppression of wage growth. But some of them were persuaded by the promise of another programme: one that still included those features as long-term implications, but whose more explicit aim was to suppress the cultural constituencies from which they felt increasingly alienated, while promising immediate compensations for the things that they might lose. The seeds of Britain's long-term housing crisis were sown at precisely this moment, because it was exactly this constituency of relatively affluent workers that was offered the chance to purchase the municipal housing stock in which many of them lived, at rates well below market value, as the major material inducement to collaborate with Thatcher's programme.

We can see from this account both the shape of the assemblage/bloc that emerged as hegemonic in the early 1980s, and the emergent differences between the forms of consent upon which its hegemony would depend, compared with those of the post-war hegemonic bloc. Of course, there were significant continuities. Most importantly, the promise of material prosperity and the conviction that existing social arrangements could no longer deliver it were central to winning any kind of consent for both post-war social democracy and post-1970s neoliberalism. But the process of assembling a new bloc – and recruiting enough people into it to achieve hegemony – is never merely a question of dispassionately persuading them that one solution to the crisis is pragmatically preferable to others. Some kind of narrative or narratives always have to be constructed that both offer to realise specific material interests of all the constituents – allowing for the expression of certain of their potentialities – and make a persuasive account of the crisis and its possible resolution.

As Stuart Hall and his colleagues showed in the case of the UK, the emergent discourse of the New Right constructed such a narrative.[110] It told a story blaming the general sense of dislocation on a series of disruptive social forces, including black people, immigrants, feminists, hippies and militant trade unionists. It promised to use state power to discipline those elements, restoring social order. Part of the problem that it identified was a bloated and over-generous welfare state and an increasing failure of public sector professionals (teachers, social workers, etc.) to enforce traditional social codes and cultural norms.[111] In the process it constructed a 'chain of equivalence' that made neoliberal attacks on workers' rights and the social wage seem continuous with a cultural war on all of those constituencies who questioned the privileged status that Fordist culture had accorded to white male workers with submissive wives and children.[112] But what was it really offering?

In its earliest iteration, the discourse of the New Right offered to restore the sense of national pride, purpose and prosperity that had apparently deserted both the UK and the US over the course of the 1970s. Implicitly, it offered to reverse the cultural and social changes of the period, defending the 'traditional' family and limiting or reversing 'immigration' (a metonym for the emergence of genuinely multicultural societies). Once in power, however, that proved harder to do in practice. This remained the case even as both the Thatcher and Reagan administrations made some gestures towards genuine social conservatism, particularly in their hostility to gay rights.[113] Black communities came under attack, but largely in the form of savage cuts to urban welfare programmes and the broader public sector, as well as brutal semi-militarised policing, rather than in the actual reversal of trends towards multiculturalism and cultural pluralism. Absolutely nothing was done to reverse the trend towards women's full participation in the labour market.

This fact becomes more important when we consider that the core neoliberal economic programme was itself simply never popular with a broad majority of voters (at least in the UK). In both the UK and the US, the military adventures and Cold War belligerence of the regimes were popular for most of the 1980s, while restrictions on unions had some popular mandate in the very early years of the decade. But opinion poll after opinion poll, as well as more in-depth research into public opinion and attitudes, showed that the unravelling of the welfare state, privatisation of public assets, continuing attacks on labour, tax cuts on the rich and deregulation of finance were never popular policies.[114] The New Right governments of the 1980s failed to deliver on the promise of their cultural conservatism, and they implemented a programme that never enjoyed a clear mandate even from their own voters, never mind a majority of the electorate as a whole. So why did people keep voting for them?

One answer is that they didn't. In both the UK and the US, electoral participation rates went into steep decline during this period.[115] In the UK, it was arguably the baldly unrepresentative electoral system and the divisions within the opposition that kept Thatcher in government. (Thatcher's percent of the vote share was always in the low forties, while the programmes of the opposition parties were far more similar to each other than to hers.) But the electoral system alone was never to blame; indeed, those divisions were an expression of the fundamental inability of anti-neoliberal forces to construct an alternative social bloc to Thatcher's and win hegemony for it. In the US, no such constitutional explanation could suffice, and polls made clear what the answer was. Whatever they thought of his socio-economic agenda, voters associated Reagan with the relative return of prosperity in the 1980s, and Democrats with the steep decline of the 1970s.[116] Lacking any convincing alternative narrative, the Democrats and other oppositional forces were not able to prevent the emergence of a new bloc that largely mirrored the one emerging in the UK.

The core of this new bloc was the classic conservative coalition of finance capital and petite bourgeoisie. However, it also included significant sections of both the working classes and the professional classes, all of whom were recruited into it on the basis of the understanding that just one core element of the post-war settlement would remain in place: the continuing expansion of their capacity to consume. This expansion would be dependent upon the availability of credit rather than real-terms wage increases, and the overall share of gross domestic product devoted to wages would fall continually from the late 1970s onwards. But this would not be allowed to reduce most citizens' capacity actually to consume, as both debt and low overseas manufacturing costs made daily access to consumer goods easier than ever before. As manufacturing, shipping and extractive industries shed millions of jobs, new work was increasingly found in the retail, service and financial sectors. Even as workers, more and more became tied to the consumer economy and the debt economy. In these sectors, union density was far lower than in heavy industry, meaning the socio-political influence and institutional culture of the labour movement was far weaker. Workplace culture was therefore generally more individualistic, or more determined by the influence of the employers, the corporation and the career structure.[117]

Consumer Consent

What held together this new bloc, then, was not a common belief in 'the national interest', social progress or manufacturing industry (and certainly not any form of class consciousness, except among the capitalist elite). It was, overwhelmingly, the common participation of all members in a culture that revolved entirely around private consumption[118] as the activity that compensated for otherwise-unrewarding forms of labour, for the loss of local and workplace communities, for the end of social democratic progress, and for the erosion of representative democracy. When cultural theorists of the 1980s argued that consumer culture could be seen as a site at which people – especially young people and women – could find new forms of agency that had been denied to them in previous epochs, they were not wrong.[119] A key element of the emergent relations of hegemony was the fact that, indeed, individuals *were* granted increasing autonomy in the 'private' sphere, above all in the domains of leisure and personal consumption.[120] It was also true, as pointed out by feminist cultural historians, that to some extent this was an extension of a particular domain of freedom that had always been more available to women than had the worlds of work or politics – at least since the early twentieth century. Women had been 'allowed' to go shopping before they had been allowed to vote,[121] and to some extent this freedom to express themselves through consumption was now being both increased and elevated in status, as even middle-class men increasingly found that consumption, retail and lifestyle management offered them more chances to experience a degree of agency and self-determination than did the world of politics or work.[122] However, what made some of the more celebratory accounts of these developments problematic was the fact that this expansion of the domain of consumer agency did not accompany an expansion, or even a defence, of people's ability to organise themselves or influence the world as citizens, workers or members of any kind of effective collectivity. By the end of the 1980s, the shopping mall had indeed become a space of freedom; but for many people, it had become the only one left.

Our analytical objective here is not a denunciation or a celebration of consumer culture. It is rather to emphasise the extent to which, by the 1990s, public consent to the hegemonic neoliberal programme depended upon the ability of that programme to deliver a continuous expansion of the capacity of the citizenry to consume. Access to an ever-widening range of consumer goods became the key means by which citizens felt themselves to be rewarded for their complicity, and the key means by which participation in a broader culture took place at all. This development can explain an important feature of voter behaviour that has been observed by political scientists since the 1980s: the overriding importance apparently placed by 'floating' voters on the perceived 'economic competence' of different political parties. Numerous electoral studies since that time have concluded that elections have been largely won or lost on this basis, irrespective of how the parties were perceived to perform or stand in relation to a range of issues that voters on average claimed to consider more important (such as spending on health and education).[123] But 'economic competence' is itself a vague and indeterminate category that often simply serves as a proxy for voters' existing ideological commitments.[124] Among voters who lack strong ideological commitments (i.e., precisely the 'floating' voters who decide elections), it seems obvious enough that when they rate parties for their presumed 'economic competence', what they are primarily evaluating is how far they deem that party as likely to maintain, protect and extend the capacity of those voters themselves – and their immediate friends and family – to engage in private consumption.

Passive Consent in the Long 1990s

The 1980s were a crucial transitional decade, witnessing not just the political hegemony of the New Right but also the end of the Cold War and the disastrous denouement of the Soviet experiment. The New Right bloc was able to hold together and maintain hegemony only during this transitional phase. By the early 1990s, its contradictions and relatively narrow social base were weakening it fatally. Indeed, the bloc excluded too many social constituencies, the visible tendency of aggressive neoliberalism to generate massive social inequality was compromising its political legitimacy, and the 1990–91 recession had undermined the economic reputation of Republican and Conservative governments.[125] The socially conservative working-class constituency that had been crucial to the New Right was shrinking – partly because its members were ageing and dying, and partly because social attitudes across all generations were changing. As social liberalism became increasingly normative across the middle classes, they used their influence in the media and education sectors to normalise it across much of the population (e.g., story lines advocating for liberal positions on race relations, gay rights and feminism became predictable, if ultimately welcome, features of mainstream television during this period).[126] Most importantly, the success of neoliberalism and post-Fordism themselves undermined the social basis for conservatism, by destabilising the material bases for the kind of communities and 'traditional' family lives that Fordism and the post-war settlement had made possible.[127] It made far less sense to be a cultural conservative if you were a family who needed two incomes to survive, with parents working in the fast-changing retail sector, than if you were one in which a single breadwinner still worked a factory job while the other stayed at home.[128]

Perhaps more important than any of these factors in explaining the exhaustion of the New Right was the simple fact that by the end of the 1980s, all of the major political obstacles to the full implementation of neoliberalism in the US and Europe had been removed. The New Right had pursued a violent campaign against the ideological enemies of neoliberalism at home and abroad, and had required a nationalistic, militaristic, authoritarian populist discourse to justify that programme even to its own core constituencies (even if it had never succeeded in making that programme generally popular).[129]

Historically, when finance capital has felt itself to be sufficiently threatened by others, it has aligned itself with the most violent and nationalistic political forces: for instance, in the 1930s, fascist governments would not have been able to pursue their programmes without the collusion of bankers. Nevertheless, all other things being equal, the tendency of finance capital is to ally itself with liberalising and cosmopolitan tendencies.[130] This is natural enough, given that the long-term effects of financial speculation are always socially disruptive, while the scope of financial speculation is always tendentially international and global.[131] At the same time, by the early 1990s, it was clear that the cybernetic revolution was having, and would continue to have, major economic and social consequences. The technological aspect of that revolution was crucial for the restoration of finance capital's hegemonic position and for the implementation of actually existing neoliberalism. By the early 1990s the sheer economic importance of the emerging tech sector was obvious, as was the fact that it was characterised by a distinctive sectoral culture that placed a very high value on cosmopolitan social liberalism.[132]

The Third Way

As the last decade of the century got under way, a new assemblage/bloc began to crystallise under the leadership of finance capital. This bloc now excluded those residual conservative workers that had been so central to the success of the New Right, instead incorporating a large section of the socially liberal middle class – and most importantly, the key agents and institutions of the tech sector. The programme around which this bloc was organised was the ongoing implementation of neoliberalism, but this time accompanied by a project of social liberalisation, and an effort to include many of those constituencies excluded by the New Right – ethnic minorities, the urban poor, public sector workers – provided they were willing to defer and adapt to the extension of neoliberal norms into their workplaces, communities and cultures. This was the project of the so-called 'Third Way'. The name, used by advocates of Bill Clinton's administration and that of his followers (Tony Blair in the UK, Gerhard Shröder in Germany, etc.), was supposed to designate a moderate middle path between the violence of the New Right and the hopeless naivety of those who sought a return to traditional social democracy. This was never a useful characterisation of its political specificity. It would be more accurate to say that the Third Way constituted a new phase in the implementation of neoliberalism – one that aligned it with tendencies to social liberalisation and that was actually much more ambitious than the New Right in terms of its willingness to implement neoliberal norms across the social field.[133]

A key feature of the social and political milieu from which the Third Way emerged was the 'professionalisation' of politics. This was a widely remarked phenomenon from around the middle of the 1980s and was not always regarded as the dangerous and deplorable development that it is usually (correctly) seen as today. It is well understood that the emergence of networks of think-tanks was an institutional development central to the rise of the 'neoliberal thought collective' and the implementation of neoliberalism as such.[134] But this was never an isolated phenomenon. Think-tanks emerged in the late twentieth century, at the same time that political lobbying became a huge and organised industry, at the same time that corporate control of mass media outlets was becoming an object of increasing concern, and at the same time that the ability of national governments to enact the will of national polities rather than that of global corporate actors began to decline.[135] These interconnected institutions constituted a growing employment sector for affluent professionals whose job was either to govern, to influence governments, or to manage information flows between governments, corporations and the wider public.

Today, it has become a cliché to observe that those working in this sector seem to have more in common with each other than with any section of the public that they are supposed to serve. But on certain sections of the left in the late '80s and early '90s, the professionalisation of politics was seen as marking a welcome break with the supposed amateurism, disorganisation and poor or outdated communication practices that were assumed to characterise the 'traditional' left, and upon which its recent defeats could be conveniently blamed.[136] This self-serving account of recent history was popular with prominent members of the emergent professional political class, enabling them to claim that the intelligent deployment of their expertise would bring political success. However, their claims to technical expertise were never clearly demarcated from claims to political insight. By the mid 1990s they would carry this line of argument to its logical conclusion with their increasingly explicit claim that the very idea of 'the left' (or 'the right') was now outmoded: that contemporary politics was not a competition between competing power blocs representing conflicting interests, but merely an exercise in the expert deployment of technocratic solutions to discrete problems.[137] Of course, those solutions would turn out, overwhelmingly, to be informed by neoliberal, but socially liberal, assumptions. The Third Way was now the only way; and conveniently, it happened to be their way.

Of course this was not a new claim, on several levels. On the one hand, every hegemonic ideology that has reached a certain level of success begins to pass itself off as the only possible way of seeing the world. This is inherent to the process by which contending ideologies try to become 'common sense'. We saw, in our earlier discussion of common sense the way in which, for Tony Blair, neoliberalism had come to be seen as simply a natural physical phenomenon; and if any politician ever represented the ideology and outlook of the professional political class, it was Blair.

Neoliberalism became the common sense of the new political class in a way that it had not been for any other class fraction. As such, it, appeared to them to be not a political ideology at all, but simply the way that anyone with sufficient expertise would understand the world. As 'neoclassical' (i.e., neoliberal) ideas came to dominate the field of economics, and as economics came to displace the humanities and other social sciences as the intellectual paradigm in which members of the political class were most likely to be trained,[138] neoliberal assumptions came to seem to them simply as the true, neutral knowledge of the world that trained experts like them possessed. At the same time, the tradition of political liberalism has always tended to promote a view of politics and government as being (either actually or ideally) about the aggregation of personal preferences, rather than contention between irreconcilable sets of collective interests. There was therefore a long-established repertoire of habits, assumption and prejudices – within the middle classes and the bourgeoisie, especially in the English-speaking world – that members of the new political class could draw on. This reinforced their sense that it was normal and natural to see the social world in terms that the liberal tradition shared with neoliberalism: namely, by understanding it primarily as a domain of market relations between competing individuals, while ignoring any underlying sociological dynamics. Hence the ease with which public choice theory was taken up as an organising conceptual paradigm, despite its horrific political and ethical implications.[139]

The mechanism by which (neoclassical) economics became central to the intellectual culture of this emergent social group is not difficult to discern. Over the course of the 1980s and '90s, major financial corporations became the institutions that more graduates from elite universities wanted to work for than any other: they offered the highest salaries, and by far the most organised system of inducements to attract those who were already at the top of the competitive social hierarchy, even before graduating from university.[140] They preferred graduates with training in the kinds of economics, accounting and mathematics that would facilitate their roles as speculators and traders on Wall Street and in the City of London. The attractive force that these institutions were able to exert throughout society was significant and was by no means merely an effect of their ability to offer incomparable salaries. The phenomenon of 'globalisation' was widely perceived – rightly or wrongly – as having produced a situation wherein the power of national governments to act in any way contrary to the wishes and interests of global corporations, especially financial corporations, had been limited to the point of negligibility. In fact, this view was fundamental to the politics of the Third Way. Whatever philosophical justifications were

constructed for it, the Third Way was in effect a political programme that sought to manage social relations and social
change while starting from the premise that the hegemony of
finance capital was unchallengeable. Building good relationships with Wall Street and the City had been absolutely central
to the political project of both the Clinton Democrats and
New Labour.[141] In the UK, the historical episode that most
clearly presaged the emergence of New Labour and fore-
shadowed its entire record in office would be the notorious
charm offensive undertaken by serious Labour figures in the
first half of the 1990s, during which senior leaders in finance
were personally promised and assured that whatever a future
Labour government might do, it would in no way challenge
their interests and privileges.[142]

From a left perspective, the brilliance of the Third Way
strategy was to realise that once the unchallengeable hegemony of finance capital had been accepted, there was a
reasonable amount of scope for variation in public policy.
Since the nineteenth century, finance capital had been the
chief enemy of the left; even moderately social democratic
governments had treated it with suspicion.[143] Third Way strat-
egists realised that in fact, acceptance of the hegemony of
finance capital could still allow for both a liberal social programme and high level of investment in public services,
provided that public services were 'reformed' in line with neoliberal ideology – turning patients into customers and students
into industry-ready trainees. But such a political strategy was
always going to require a high level of mediation between
capital and the wider public, precisely because that wider
public was never convinced of the value or desirability of neoliberal reforms and the assumptions that informed them. And
this was the key task assigned to the professional political
class: their job became, primarily, to determine what type and
level of reform could be offered to the public without challenging the authority of finance, while also finding ways to

represent the interests of finance to that public (who would never have accepted corporate rule in a naked, unmediated form). As we have seen, the key mechanism through which public consent to neoliberalism would be secured would always be to address citizens as consumers, empowering them as such, expanding their capacities as such, while limiting almost every other capacity they might have had. As we have also seen, this often meant reinforcing and enabling their status as debtors.

Of course, it also meant keeping people in work: those with no wages can neither borrow nor spend without costing the taxpayer money. This is why fury at the idea of welfare recipients being allowed to consume at all has been part of popular neoliberal discourse since the 1970s[144]: the 'welfare queen' has been a hate-figure for exactly that reason. As de-industrialisation progressed in the 1970s and '80s (a process that has carried on in the US and the UK up to the present day), work had to be found for a clear majority of the population, even if the full employment of the early '60s could never be allowed to return. Thus, as we have already seen, a key element of neoliberal hegemony has been the maintenance of a precarious labour market, with the retail and finance sectors taking unprecedented importance. Again, a key task of the professional political class became the maintenance of a social order wherein people could find work, but could not organise as workers; wherein people could consume, and would increasingly come to experience consumption as their only meaningful form of agency and self-expression; wherein people would borrow, and would remain trapped in cycles of debt and expenditure over the course of their entire lives. And this is exactly what finance capital wants people to be: consumers, debtors and (non-organised) workers.[145]

The hegemony of actually existing neoliberalism was therefore always dependent upon the activity of this professional political class. Of course, this was never a wholly new development, as we saw in chapter 1. Critical sociologists long ago pointed out that in advanced capitalists societies, one of the key social roles taken on by middle-class professionals had been to mediate between the interests of the capitalist ruling class and the wider public of workers and citizens: teachers, social workers and public administrators had all been seen in this way, as well as corporate managers.[146] But during the post-war period, the professional middle classes had acted as key elements of a hegemonic social bloc that, as we have seen, enjoyed the active support of a majority of the population, while themselves enjoying a huge amount of professional autonomy and an ever-expanding social role as the main agents of the welfare state. They were never going to willingly abandon that autonomy and expansive role in the service of neoliberalism, especially given neoliberalism's ideological hostility to the very existence of public services. Under these circumstances, they could not be expected to play the same mediating role that they once had. In fact, it was inevitable that they would prove mainly resistant and obstructive to the neoliberal programme. Disciplining them therefore became one of the main problems for the professional political class, and this became one of the key aims of neoliberal public sector reform. For example, a principle aim of the intensification of standardised testing and the introduction of public 'league tables' for schools in the UK was always the disciplining of teachers, who could not be otherwise expected to deliver a curriculum oriented to the instrumental demands of the neoliberal programme.

The Managerial State

This disciplining of the public sector could not be carried out by the political class proper alone. It required the creation of an entire new layer of managers within the public sector, who were increasingly trained to adopt corporate norms and culture in the management of public institutions. To the most astute commentators, it was already clear by the mid 1990s that a new 'managerial state'[147] was taking shape, wherein an entire layer of bureaucrats, modelling themselves as corporate executives,[148] sought to impose norms, targets and behaviours on a sector that had previously been treated as necessarily autonomous and distinct from the world of capitalist social relations. By the mid 2000s, for example, the budgets of British universities had become massively skewed in favour of a highly paid cadre of managers (at the expense of teachers, researchers and students),[149] whose internal culture had almost nothing in common with that of academics and students, and whose senior members were increasingly drawn directly from the corporate and financial sectors.

The politics of the Third Way in some ways represented the interests and spontaneous outlook of this social group of managers more than any other. It offered to resolve the contradiction between their roles as public sector workers and their status as corporate managers by encouraging the development of a technocratic ideology and a cultural common sense that could be shared by managers in both private and public sector, enabling them to believe in the progressive nature of their social role. This is one reason why the ideologies of 'diversity'[150] and corporate feminism[151] became so important to corporate culture during this time. Managers may have had to carry out an increasingly unpopular set of functions, actively dismantling the professional culture of public service that had characterised the post-war welfare state, intensifying the exploitation of labour in all sectors every year. But at least they could tell themselves that they were offering black people, women and gay people the opportunity to be so exploited, or even to join the ranks of the elites themselves, as previous generations would not have done.

However, we shouldn't dismiss the importance of the Third Way commitment to certain, very narrowly defined kinds of feminism and anti-racism. In fact, these were fundamental to its project, and especially to its ability to build a wider coalition – and hence a more potent assemblage/bloc – than the New Right had been capable of. Third Way neoliberalism was genuinely committed to the removal of traditional social obstacles to individuals becoming fully functional neoliberal subjects that compete in the labour market, borrow, and consume. Those obstacles against which it would set its legislative face included sexism, racism, and even those extremes of childhood poverty that could be seen self-evidently to prevent the poorest children from competing 'on a level playing field' with their more fortunate competitors.[152] Ideologically hostile to the collectivist, egalitarian attitudes of both the socialist traditions and the radical social movements of the 1970s, what it proposed instead was the building of a true 'meritocracy', in which the combination of talent and effort would enable each individual to rise to their deserved station in life, irrespective of social background.[153]

Of course, across the whole population, this was utter nonsense. 'Meritocracy' was a derogatory, satirical term first coined by socialists and social democrats in the 1950s, who believe that what it designated was a liberal fantasy.[154] Such thinkers assumed that the only way to make it easier for those who start life poor or disadvantaged to end their lives in a more privileged social bracket was simply to use the institutions of the welfare state to narrow the gap between the 'top' and the 'bottom'. They thought that it was nonsensical to believe that a society could be engineered in which overall inequality was maintained, or even increased, yet in which somehow social elites could be prevented from using their position to secure advantages for themselves and their children, ostensibly making it easier for individuals with 'talent' to climb the social ladder. And yet, just a few decades later, Third Way politicians explicitly and enthusiastically embraced precisely this idea of 'meritocracy' and set about implementing a policy agenda informed by its ideal. In particular, they did so by imposing competitive norms and rigid hierarchies within the education system,[155] wherever they could, encouraging parents and children to devote all of their energies to the pursuit of success at the 'best' schools and 'best' universities in order to secure the 'best' jobs (i.e., the highest paid, which would also bring the employee as close as possible within the socio-economic order to the domain of finance capital). To date, this project has indeed been proven to be a delusional fantasy. Both economic equality and social mobility declined from the late 1970s onwards, as every prediction made by the 1950s critics of 'meritocracy' was proven correct.[156] But of course, the project of Third Way 'meritocracy' was never intended to produce the kind of society that it claimed it would. Its purpose was merely to legitimate a social order in which finance capital reigned supreme, and to recruit as many people as possible into behaving in conformity with its hegemony.

And yet, none of this alters the fact that certain social groups did find their 'life chances' enhanced. Women of the professional class (or who managed to enter it), people of colour who managed to enter higher education, and gay people of most classes and ethnicities[157] experienced significant transformations in the opportunities and quality of life available to them. All had certain of their immanent potentialities enhanced and expressed to an unprecedented degree by their participation in the new assemblage/bloc that the Third Way crystallised.

The Beginning of the End

The 2008 financial crisis was the culmination of the economic strategies pursued by neoliberal governments and the political class since the 1980s. Deregulated financial markets, the proliferation of debt and speculative lending, deliberately overheated housing markets: all resulted in a series of major bankruptcies, near bankruptcies, and multibillion-dollar bailout packages for financial institutions deemed 'too big to fail'. This left governments such as the UK's shouldering massive debt burdens, inaugurating a long-term regime of austerity (i.e., low government spending and low wages) that carried on for over a decade.[158] It also forced governments and banks to introduce some regulation of lending.

This presented the professional political class with a problem. All of these measures reduced the capacity of citizens to consume, and that capacity had long since been established as the only basis for their consent to neoliberal hegemony. Various political responses were adopted. In the UK, the government of David Cameron warned of government insolvency and social breakdown if the harsh medicine of austerity were not applied,[159] while pursuing a far-weaker austerity regime than they had actually threatened.[160] In the US, Barack Obama's rhetoric promised a break with the years of rule by a venal and self-serving elite, while his policies offered nothing of the kind. Nevertheless, he did use the country's globally unique position as the home of the world's reserve currency to pursue mildly inflationary policies rather than make massive spending cuts or drive down wages. In both countries, consumer spending was supported mainly by cutting interest rates to historic lows, increasing the spending power of middle-class mortgage holders and encouraging continued inflation in housing prices. Within the eurozone, severe austerity was imposed on the populations of Greece, Spain,

Portugal and Ireland largely in order to prevent the banks or the population of the most powerful country – Germany – from suffering any serious consequences.[161] Few of these measures did much to improve the situation for the youngest or poorest citizens, however. Those whose communities had never recovered from de-industrialisation and those who were too young to have become property owners before prices became unaffordable, suffered from dramatic declines in wages and public spending, with little compensation offered.

Although the 2008 events seriously weakened the public moral authority of finance capital, nothing demonstrated the subservience of the professional political class to it better than the governmental response to the crisis. Almost without exception, governments in the most affected countries did everything they could to maintain the position of the banks, no matter what the cost to poor workers and taxpayers. But other changes were underway that would alter the power dynamics of global capitalism. Although the tech sector had been central to the neoliberal assemblage/bloc since at least 1990s, the emergence of the platform economy in the 2000s saw Silicon Valley firms (Google, Facebook, Amazon, YouTube, Apple) become the wealthiest and most culturally influential corporations on the planet during this time – all of them deploying the new technology of the internet platform to accumulate astronomical quantities of capital.[162]

As various commentators have already noted, 'platform capitalism' exhibits distinctive characteristics in comparison with post-Fordism. Where post-Fordism encouraged a pro-liferation of brands, styles and firms (while still allowing capital to concentrate at the commanding heights of the econ-omy), platform capitalism tends towards the massive aggregation of users onto single platforms and the congruent development of monopolies within specific sectors. In a 2015 interview, the radical economist Robin Murray, the person most responsible for popularising the ideas of the French 'regulation school' economists on the British left in the 1980s, argued that we were no longer living in the epoch of post-Fordism, but of platforms.[163] Although he did not use the term explicitly, Murray was clearly arguing that 'platform capitalism' constituted a distinct new regime of accumulation.

The emergence of any new regime of accumulation creates a whole series of challenges and opportunities for actors across the political spectrum. Fordism made possible the success of post-war social democracy; but it also enabled the rise of fascism.[164] Post-Fordism could have been the terrain on which a new, radical democratic left emerged;[165] instead it became the context for the achievement of neoliberal hegemony. While they have handed enormous power to a new generation of plutocrats, platform media have also enabled new forms of mass political mobilisation by significantly reducing the cost to users of communicating with each other in large numbers. Many political movements and parties around the world have emerged to challenge the authority of the professional political class since 2008: examples include the Five Star Movement in Italy, the Indignados movement and Podemos party in Spain, the campaigns to elect both Donald Trump and Bernie Sanders in the US, and the pro–Jeremy Corbyn movement in the UK. These are normally classified as populist formations, but this is a vague and often problematic designation. In fact, it would be more accurate to observe that what they all have in common, and what makes them historically distinctive, is the fact that all of them have made creative use of platform technologies to organise and communicate with their supporters, invariably outstripping their more established political rivals in their capacity to organise on this basis.[166]

Since 2008 a new situation has therefore begun to emerge, characterised by several historic features. In many places, the capacity of the professional political class to continue to administer neoliberalism, and to enable most of the population to participate in the consumer economy, has been fatally compromised. In response, numerous constituencies whose consent to neoliberalism was only ever relatively passive have entered into direct opposition to it. In many cases, especially on the right, that opposition takes the form of hostility to the professional political class and their perceived cultural norms of cosmopolitanism and liberal individualism, rather than opposition to neoliberalism as such or to any section of capital. In some other cases, especially on the left, it is the social effects of the recent austerity regime – and the political class associated with its implementation – that is the immediate object of hostility. In all of these instances, we can see that the professional political class that was crucial to the success of the second neoliberal assemblage/bloc is now unable to command any kind of consent, and so is no longer able to carry out its function.

As such, the internal relations that defined the neoliberal assemblage/bloc since the early 1990s are changing, possibly leading to the emergence of a distinctive new hegemonic social bloc. The fact that the majority of young people no longer feel themselves to be included even partially within the Third Way assemblage/bloc (into which their parents were incorporated, at least as consumers and homeowners) is a clear and crucial development.[167] Another is the fact that it is the tech sector, rather than finance capital, that is clearly the most powerful fraction of capital. The economic and cultural power of the platform giants has become increasingly visible over the past decade, with figures such as Mark Zuckerberg and Jeff Bezos increasingly functioning as the most widely known exemplars of the global capitalist class.[168] Although scandals over the misuse of data have led to growing public concern over the accountability of these monopolies, such panics have so far had no real political repercussions. It is also clear that the masters of Silicon Valley now see themselves, confidently, as the leading figures of their class.

It remains to be seen exactly what kinds of bloc may now emerge, what political projects they will pursue, and what kinds of consent they will require or be able to command. What is clear, however, is that they will all operate within the new techno-social paradigm of platform capitalism: the new regime of accumulation. We already have some sense of what that means. Arguably, one of the conditions for the submission of young people to the neoliberal regime since the early 1990s – even as their wages and share of overall disposable income shrank throughout the period – has been the growing availability of free media content and free access to software, platforms and other tools that enable them to participate in an advanced communications culture despite declining access to other resources. The unpredictable political implications of that access were seen in 2015 when a small number of Facebook groups became the main hubs around which crystallised the successful movement to elect Jeremy Corbyn as Labour Party leader.[169] Given the importance and complexity of the problems and potentials inherent in platform technology, we will not dwell on the subject here, but will dedicate chapter 5 of this book to its discussion.

Modes of Coercion and Consent

We will close this chapter by reflecting on the multiple modalities in which both 'consent' and 'coercion' may operate in highly complex societies. Consent on the part of non-hegemonic (or subaltern) groups may range from the most active and explicit endorsement of elite projects and ideologies, to reluctant acquiescence. The enthusiasm of post-war social democrats, or nationalist supporters of Donald Trump during his presidency, might exemplify the former. The highly passive consent conceded by typically 'disaffected'[170] citizens of neoliberal post-democracies might exemplify the latter. Forms of coercion, likewise, can range from the outright oppression of a totalitarian regime, to the complex forms of unfreedom experienced by precarious workers and debtors in a highly unstable labour market. This is a far more nuanced understanding of both coercion and consent than is often found in accounts of what 'hegemony' is supposed to mean. But one aspect of even those simplest understandings remains incontrovertibly valid: even the most minimal, passive and disaffected modes of consent cannot be secured or maintained without at least *some* of the interests of subaltern groups being at least partially realised.

This much is clear from our examination of the multiple forms and modes of consent in advanced capitalist societies since the 1930s. The assembling of social blocs, and the success of hegemonic projects, is always based on the aggregation and expression of material interests. Hegemony is always about assembling coalitions. Those coalitions may at times converge or be convened around shared identities or points of identification; they may coalesce around coherent narratives; they may be motivated by shared opposition to specific outsiders, oppressors or others. But this is never their fundamental basis. None of these phenomena will emerge where there is not a set of shared of compatible interests to be defended, extended or expressed. There is no consent – active, passive or otherwise – where all of the interests of the subaltern are being traduced. Before anything else, politics is about the aggregation of – and the conflict between – sets of material interests.

But what are 'interests'? How can they be recognised, identified or measured? The term has been widely used for almost two centuries. But in recent years, very little attention has been paid by political, social or culture theory to the question of interests: how to conceptualise them, how to recognise them, how to analyse them. Because this question is clearly central to the understanding of contemporary forms of power, it will be the topic of the next chapter.

4

THE NATURE OF INTERESTS

All politics involves contestation and negotiation between competing sets of interests. To some extent, this is a truism. But it is a truism worth exploring for several reasons. On the one hand, the liberal political class tends to reject any acknowledgement of this truth, preferring to present themselves as expert managers, as above all sectional competition, and as objectively serving some general good. Or else, they dissolve questions of conflicting interests in a purely discursive conflict of public debate within the liberal public sphere. This is why, politically and analytically, we regard it as crucial to stake out a position in support of this basic claim: that politics is about the contestation and negotiation of interests. There may well have been, and there may well be again, historical moments in which making this assertion would seem to be completely unnecessary, merely the expression of a banal truism. The primary reason that it is so urgent today is simply that it is implicitly denied, and actively occluded, by so much of contemporary public discourse, and even mainstream academic political science.

There is a further reason for concerning ourselves with the question of interests. Indeed, there is another history that coincides with the legacy of neoliberal hegemony to produce a situation in which we very much need to talk about interests. In the earliest days of political sociology, a number of key theorists understood 'interests' – conceived in appropriately expansive terms – as the central element of social and political life.[1] The assumption that 'class interests' are the central motivating force of historical action has been a key tenet of historical materialism since its inception. But the conceptualisation of 'interests' as such has not been a significant feature of radical political theory – at least in the English-speaking world – for many years. There has been very little attention paid to the concept of interests in recent years, and it is not an idea that features heavily in any branch of radical political theory, except when used in the most casual sense. In the radical tradition, this lack of discussion of interests is the legacy of an explicit rejection of the concept as an analytical category that took place within some of the most significant strands of Anglophone theory during the 1980s.

The Problem of Objective Interests

Broadly speaking, during this period, the category of interests came to be associated with crudely deterministic forms of Marxism that were seen as being necessarily superseded by the more complex, subtle, multidimensional and non-deterministic approaches associated with the turn to 'post-structuralism' and 'post-Marxism',[2] to post-industrial sociology and to the politics of the 'new social movements'.[3] Unlike many contemporary advocates of broadly historical materialist approaches, we do not dismiss the theoretical and analytical advances made during this period, or the contribution of thinkers such as Michel Foucault, Ernesto Laclau and Chantal Mouffe and their followers. On the other hand, we also regard the picture of Marxism that began to appear in much of the subsequent literature as itself a caricature, often derived from a rather simplistic reading of the work of thinkers such as Louis Althusser and Nicos Poulantzas, committed as they were to somewhat schematic and abstract versions of Marxist theory.[4] This 'structuralist' Marxism had itself emerged as a corrective to the rather romantic and voluntaristic tendencies of post-war Western European Marxism, at a

138

historical moment (the late 1950s and early 1960s) when the prospect of proletarian militancy seemed to be fading further with every prosperous year.[5] By the late 1970s, a new global wave of radicalism had risen and fallen, leaving in its wake a deep mistrust of official Marxism among those who had been disappointed by the lack of support for radical students, women's liberation or other new progressive causes shown by the communist parties of the Third International.

In this context, Marxism stood accused of various crimes. On the one hand, the lack of support for these new movements, which often had an integrally cultural dimension, was seen as exemplifying its incorrigible 'economism' or 'class essentialism',[6] and a concomitant blindness to cultural and social power dynamics that could not be reduced to class relations and economic struggles.[7] On the other hand, the long tradition of communist authoritarianism was seen as intimately connected with a certain tendency to determinism in Marxist thought. When it came to the question of 'interests', the Marxist claim to be able to determine what was or wasn't in the 'objective historical interests' of the workers, capital, or anyone else was seen as analogous to the claims of communist elites to constitute a historical vanguard with unique access to the truth of history: both claims deriving from the same position of epistemological arrogance. Scientific Marxism claimed to know things about the world that the people actually living in it didn't know, and this was a problem. Importantly, this accusation did not simply come from outside the Marxist tradition. For example, the British communist historian E.P. Thompson had waged a war against what he saw as this type of dogmatic, scientistic Marxism since the late 1950s. His classic study, *The Making of the English Working Class*, set out to show that the very concept of 'the working class' only emerged through the struggles and developing culture of industrial workers themselves, and that the working class could not be said in any meaningful sense to have existed 'objectively' prior to the development of a shared political consciousness among its members.[8]

In the most developed body of theory to emerge from this moment – the early work of Laclau and Mouffe – the concept of objective interests – outlined as being economic in nature – is subject to an unrelenting critique. But it is important to understand exactly what is being rejected here and why. The overall political objective of Laclau and Mouffe's classic *Hegemony and Socialist Strategy* is to convince its readers that the work of socialist coalition building must not start from any naive or ahistorical preconceptions as to which social groups can be brought into it, which groups must lead that coalition, and on what terms. What they write against is a particular conception of historical change that sees the industrial proletariat as being historically destined to bring about socialism, and as being the only social group capable of doing so. As such, what they reject is the idea that 'interests' pre-exist the political struggles and negotiations that enable particular conceptions of those interests to emerge in actual political discourse. Interests, they argue, only emerge as the outcomes of the political practices that cause them to be expressed and articulated. They assert that

> to deny economism . . . is to maintain that political and ideo-logical struggles cannot be conceived as the struggles of economic classes . . . class 'interests' are not given to politics and ideology by the economy. They arise within political practice, and they are determined as an effect of definite modes of political practice.[9]

In developing this model, Laclau and Mouffe became rather dismissive of any discussion of 'interests' at all, preferring to see political discourse as characterised by contestations between – and mutual articulations of – different sets of *demands*. In fact, in Laclau's later work, the 'demand' arguably take on the status of the basic unit of political activity.[10] It is demands that are linked together into 'chains of equivalence' by the articulatory work of politics. For example, during the months leading up to the UK's 2016 referendum on membership of the European Union, the Leave campaign made a crucial move by claiming that leaving the European Union would free up huge amounts of government expenditure that could be directed towards the cash-strapped National Health Service.[11] This attempt to articulate the demand to leave the EU with the demand for increased NHS funding was successful with at least some key groups of voters, creating for them an equivalence between leaving the EU, reducing net immigration to the UK and preserving the remnants of the welfare state. Of course, the claim made by the Leave campaign was entirely and demonstrably false: no one could show how leaving the EU would directly or even indirectly increase NHS funding.

Laclau and Mouffe's model does not necessarily deny that competing interests are at stake in such a scenario, or even that the discourse of class struggle may be one politically expedient way of articulating them with other interests in a broad chain of equivalence. Their point would be that the interests at stake here are those of NHS users, whose status as NHS users with a particular set of interests (*as NHS users*) has only emerged in the course of a specific history of political practices and discourses, and is not simply given objectively by the class position of the NHS users in question.

The problem with any such formulation is that it simply leaves out of the explanation of some factors that even most casual observers would regard as salient to understanding the situation.[12] The particular interest that NHS users have in securing funding for the service is not unrelated to the fact that most of them have no access to private health care, which is in turn not unrelated to the fact that their particular position in the relations of production affords them fewer opportunities to amass wealth than are available to their employers. More fundamentally, this interest clearly relates not just to the discursive status of service users *as service users*, but to their status as corporeal subjects who will find themselves more or less able to preserve (or even extend) their physical well-being, depending on how well funded the health care services to which they have access are. Finally, it is also clearly true that Britain leaving the EU was not going to contribute in any direct or indirect way to a significant increase in NHS funding, whereas the figures promoting the idea that it would clearly did stand to benefit financially and politically from Brexit.[13] In order to able to say something meaningful about such a situation, we need to be able to say something more about interests than that they simply emerge as discursive categories in the process of political contestation.

It would be easy at this point simply to accuse Laclau and Mouffe of philosophical idealism, dismissing their approach as recklessly denying the existence of extra-discursive social reality. But this would do a gross disservice to their complex philosophical position, which never denies the existence of 'the real world', but does suggest that, in an important sense, political ideas only become historically relevant when they appear in the field of political discourse. From our perspective, it is most useful to acknowledge the profound problems with certain formulations of the concept of interests raised by Laclau and Mouffe, while suggesting that more work can be done to elaborate a concept of interests that meets some of their objections, and while leaving us still able to deploy the concept meaningfully for political analysis.

In the case of our Brexit example, it is simply not acceptable to dismiss the validity of the basic intuition – that Leave voters voting in the belief that they were voting for increased NHS spending were in fact being deluded into voting *against their own interests* by powerful social agencies that were ruthlessly pursuing theirs. But the valid question raised by Laclau and Mouffe is simply this: in what sense are these 'interests' identifiable or verifiable phenomena, outside of the explicitly political discourses in which they might be articulated?

The Virtuality of Interests

To answer this question, we propose to make use of a conceptual dyad that has been explored in the work of philosophers such as Henri Bergson,[14] Gilles Deleuze,[15] and Manuel DeLanda:[16] the *virtual* and the *actual*. The 'virtual' designates a specific sense in which phenomena can be definitely *real*, without being physical incarnated as actual objects. A good example is mathematical concepts such as the number three. There can be little question that the number three has a certain objective reality; and yet there is clearly no actual number three existing anywhere in the physical universe. In a comparable sense, we suggest that 'interests' have a *certain kind* of objective reality irrespective of the subjective conceptions of the individuals or groups to whom they pertain. However, it is not the same kind of reality as that of political demands which are fully and consciously expressed by those subjects. From this perspective we can actually specify the relationship between interests and demands quite precisely: demands are interests that have been actualised on the plane of active political discourse. Interests that have not been so actualised can be identified, and even identified with a certain 'objectivity'; moreover, it can be recognised that part of the work of politics in any given moment is the practice of actualising certain interests as explicit political demands.

But does that mean we are simply back in the realm of 'objective historical interests' that theorists like Laclau and Mouffe identified as so problematic? Not exactly. The model to which such theorists objected was one in which the 'objective interests' of historical actors represented a kind of singular, essential truth, derived from a simplified structural economic analysis. If subjects failed to act in accordance with this truth, then they were failing to act in accordance with their true nature and historical destiny. Political leaders and intellectuals who sought to lead them in the pursuit of those interests could therefore claim to know the very nature of those they sought to lead, in ways that the led could not yet know it.

The Multiplicity of Interests

The implications of our model are very different. This is because, following the philosophy of Gilles Deleuze, the virtual is always a domain of irreducible *multiplicity*.[17] From this perspective, there is not just one set of objective interests pertaining to any given historical actor; in fact, there is a potentially infinite set of them. As such, interests are best understood as *potentialities*: as potential future states of being that could or could not become actual, depending on the precise outcomes of historical and political processes. In the case of our Brexit example, the issue at stake is which outcome would be more likely to lead to the realisation, on the plane of lived social reality, of the potential of voters to become citizens with access to adequate, well-funded health care. From this perspective, in fact, it would not be strictly accurate to say that this potential *could not possibly* be expressed and actualised through a political process that began with the UK leaving the EU, but merely that it was always far less likely to be so than through a process beginning with a defeat for the Leave campaign in the referendum. From this perspective, to say that Leave voters whose main political priority was NHS funding were voting 'against their interests' is not an absolute statement about their objective historical nature, but a 'strategic-relational'[18] statement about the most likely outcomes of a given political decision, given what is currently known about the overall historical situation in which it was taken. As such, a political activist seeking to persuade such voters to vote a different way in the referendum would not be seeking to bring their consciousness into accord with their 'true' nature, but merely to enhance their strategic sense of the balance of probabilities in a given historical situation.[19]

An important feature of the model that we are proposing is that it allows for – indeed, insists upon – the fact that given historical subjects can simultaneously have complex, contradictory and competing sets of interests. In the case of our Leave voters, any real attempt to explain their voting behaviour would have to take account of some of the other interests they might have had, in addition to their interests as NHS users. For example, the most notorious reason for Leave voters voting as they did was their desire to severely limit immigration to the UK from EU countries (especially in Eastern Europe).[20] Now, as we will see shortly, there are ways of explaining this behaviour which simply make no reference to any notion of interests, pointing out that when voters support anti-immigration policies, they are generally motivated by fantasies of cultural purity and stasis, and by entirely mistaken beliefs about the real causal relationships between immigration, poverty, crime and austerity. Such accounts do have considerable explanatory power. But they also leave out some uncomfortable, yet crucial, facts about such scenarios.

Rather than denying that the curtailment of immigration can *ever* serve the interests of poor and working-class people at all, in any way, it is more accurate and more useful to say that it may do so, but only on a very limited scale, only over the short term, and only to the extent that no other ways of expressing and realising those interests (such as significant increases in government spending) are assumed to be possible. From this perspective, different sets of interests can be seen to be operable, expressible and realisable at different temporal and spatial scales.[21]

Horizons of Realisability

There is a crucial difference between the qualitatively different sets of interests that can pertain virtually to given historical subjects. At the largest and most universal scale, it is clearly true, as the Marxist tradition has always insisted, that the long-term interests of workers (and almost all other people) would be best served by them forming relations of solidarity based on their most basic shared interests – their interests as workers, defined by their position in the overall relations of production – in opposition to the set of power relations that has the most far-reaching negative consequences: capitalism as such. It is within this 'communist horizon'[22] that the maximum possible potential of as many human beings as possible to become as physically and intellectually potent as possible could begin to be realised. However, under historical circumstances that make it seem unlikely to workers that the reconfiguration of social relations necessary to realise that potential (i.e., workers' revolution) is imminent, they may well look to some 'lower' horizon of potentiality in order to realise what interests they can. We might speak of a 'social democratic horizon', wherein it would be possible to realize those egalitarian reforms that could coexist with the continuation of the capitalist mode of production in some modified form; a 'liberal horizon', wherein freeing individuals from certain traditional constraints is the only way in which the maximisation of future potentials can be imagined; and even a 'conservative horizon', wherein the defence of existing privileges and resources is the only conceivable way of avoiding a continuous narrowing and reduction of such potentials, when threatened by various historical forces (such as a vicious pro-gramme of government austerity). From this perspective, workers who vote for immigration restrictions are acting against their interests when conceived within a liberal, com-munist, or even an expansively social democratic horizon, but not when conceived within a conservative horizon. What is it that defines the particular characteristics of the horizon within which interests are perceived, computed, and acted upon? In part it must be a question of the scale – in terms of space and time – of that horizon. When horizons of interest are operating at small scale, this will mean a focus on the hyperlocal (my immediate family) and the hyper-present (today and tomorrow and perhaps next year). What is reason-able within one horizon is unreasonable in another.

Of course, the political and analytical question in such a case is: how is it that particular sets of workers, citizens or voters are persuaded to operate within one horizon rather than another? The answer to this question is always nuanced and is always slightly different in every specific situation. This is why the detailed analysis of social, cultural and political conjunctures is such an important task for radical politics.[23] One important tradition of ideology critique has used psycho-analytic theory to argue that powerful ideological institutions encourage people to believe in fantasies (or at least to behave as if they believe in them) about the true nature of the social world and their place in it. The post-Marxism of Laclau and Mouffe constitutes an interesting development of this line of thinking, retaining a psychoanalytic account of the nature of political motivation, while abandoning any claim to be able to speak for wholly scientific or rational alternatives to the phantasmatic productions of bourgeois ideology. For Laclau and Mouffe, the left's task is to construct a 'radical democ-ratic imaginary'[24] with which to contest the authoritarian or liberal-individualist imaginaries of right-wing and liberal opponents.

Thinkers such as Nicholas Abercrombie, Stephen Hill and Bryan S. Turner have criticised all such models,[25] instead suggesting that (to use our terminology) workers and citizens may generally be making perfectly rational decisions about which 'horizon' to operate in, based on a realistic assessment of the current balance of social forces in a given conjuncture, and the likely risks and benefits of operating on a more or less radical scale. From this perspective, each *horizon of realisability* constitutes a genuine set of potentially realisable possibilities; but each such horizon is not equally realisable under given historical circumstances.

The Function of Ideology

While this is a very useful perspective, it leaves open the very basic question of how workers or others make such judgements and calculations, what their sources of information might be, and how far their sense of their own collective potency is derived from accurate scientific assessments and how far it is an effect of a range of cultural and psychosocial factors that can be manipulated for better and for worse. As such, it seems reasonable to assume that the kind of psycho-political factors posited by psychoanalytic versions of Marxist and post-Marxist ideology critique can coexist and interact with such rational factors, 'overdetermining'[26] historical outcomes – just as rational and irrational factors can drive human behaviour and decision-making at all times. Finally, it is always important to acknowledge the role played by pure propaganda in such situations. At times, populations of political actors may act in accordance with false beliefs not because they have any particular psychic 'investments'[27] in them, but simply because they mistakenly believe them to be true.

In all such cases, the function of analysis is to determine the role being played by a range of elements operating at different affective and discursive levels. Althusser's classic analysis of the function of ideology and 'ideological state apparatuses' remains useful here.[28] State institutions, work-places, social rituals, media outlets of many kinds: all work to offer the individual a specific sense of their place in the world – of the scope and limitations of their capacity to act – which at least partially distort the reality of their position in the universe of social relations. But we must also honour the impulse that led thinkers such as Foucault[29] as well as Deleuze and Guattari[30] to reject 'ideology' as an analytical category, because it seems to rely on too clear a distinction between objective, 'scientific' reality on the one hand and 'false consciousness' on the other. The correctness of this intuition lies in the realisation that, indeed, the citizen-worker who identi-fies with the symbols of patriotism, who obeys the cultural injunction to think of themselves primarily as a consumer rather than as a worker or citizen, is not simply expressing 'false consciousness'; rather, they are acting in accordance with a certain set of plausibly realisable interests. Conversely, the correctness of the communist intuition lies in the fact that the same citizen-worker does, in reality, have other interests that could be realised on a longer and more ambitious time-scale. Ideology therefore functions as a kind of sieve, filtering out certain sets of interests from the consciousness of sub-jects, creating conditions whereby only certain interests become cognisable or appear to be realisable. Ideology is a kind of filter mechanism, enabling certain interests rather than others to become politically salient, by actualising them as political demands.

This model poses, in particularly clear and stark terms, a question which is always implicit in theories of hegemony and which is never easy to answer. Subaltern social groups do not fail to engage in revolutionary or counter-hegemonic struggle simply because they are deluded as to the nature of reality. Often, their conservatism or quietism is grounded in an assessment that is relatively realistic, if intuitive (rather than fully conscious), as to the relative likelihood of success of radical political projects, and of the relative costs and benefits of participation in them. As such, how do counter-hegemonic forces create conditions under which this rational scepticism can be overcome, given that the best way to overcome it is already to wield a large-enough coalition of forces to make the success of the project seem likely?

There is no single formula with which to solve this problem, which can only be answered by careful analysis of any given conjuncture. In most situations, the answer will involve identifying those class fractions most likely to be radicalised most easily, and organising them into a coherent force before trying to mobilise other groups. The social groups easiest to radicalise will normally be either those with the most obvious interest in radical change, or those easiest for progressive forces to reach and to mobilise (or some combination of the two). Both elements of this description are crucial. Radicals often make the mistake of assuming that the social layers with the least to lose from revolution will automatically be the easiest to radicalise, without considering other social or ideological factors that may render their mobilisation extremely difficult. Conversely, many radical movements are never able to extend their reach beyond the constituencies they generally find easiest to reach: the young and highly educated. Frustration with these situations often leads critics to dismiss the political potential either of the 'lumpen' poor or of students and young professionals. Such dismissal is almost invariably symptomatic of the failure to recognise counter-hegemonic strategy as necessarily taking place within multiple temporalities.

Adventures in Brexitland

To further illustrate the relevance of our model, let us return to our consideration of the politics of Brexit. In their landmark study *Brexitland*, political scientists Maria Sobolewska and Robert Ford offer one account of the fracturing of British political opinion in relation to the Brexit question. For them, this development is the product of long-term demographic and cultural changes responding to waves of mass immigration to the UK and the expansion of higher education from the 1990s onwards.[31] According to this narrative, the growth of university education has expanded the proportion of the population that is socialised into becoming 'identity liberals', who, as a matter of principle, therefore strongly endorse liberal, cosmopolitan positions on matters such as race and immigration. At the same time, older and less well-educated voters have reacted against their perceived loss of social and cultural privilege in a world in which liberal, cosmopolitan norms have acquired more authority, while the economic status of non-graduate workers has declined. In particular, this reaction manifests as hostility to mass immigration and its perceived social, cultural and economic effects. These 'identity conservatives' adhere to 'ethnocentric' notions of political community which are incompatible with the liberal cosmopolitanism of the 'identity liberals', who themselves now form the core of the urban electorate and activist base for the political left in most countries. Sobolewska and Ford make a convincing argument that it is the confrontation between these sets of values among different portions of their political coalition that has caused such grave problems for centre-left parties such as the British Labour Party in recent years.

Sobolewska and Ford identify a third constituency as playing a key role in debates over immigration and its consequences:

immigrants themselves, along with their descendants, who are identified as rejecting the anti-immigration politics of the 'identity conservatives' not because they share the values of the 'identity liberals', but because it is in their direct 'interests' to oppose them. It is this latter qualification that is particularly intriguing, because only in the case of this third grouping are 'interests' as such named explicitly as a possible source of political motivation, contrasted starkly with the far less liberal social 'values' of the same sets of immigrant community voters. Sobolewska and Ford directly contrast this 'interested' motivation towards anti-racism with that of graduates, all of whom are assumed to be motivated by liberal 'values' rather than by any consciousness or expression of interests.[32] At the same time, however, the authors argue explicitly that 'identity conservatives' are not necessarily motivated by racism or xenophobia as such, but by a consciousness of their own waning sense of cultural status and influence.[33] Clearly, in this case, 'values' and 'interests' are difficult to disentangle, given that 'identity conservatives' are presented as *not* merely acting on or expressing an abstract principle, but as being motivated by a perceived shift in power relations which has directly disadvantaged them. And this observation raises a further problem. If it is the case that 'identity conservatives' are reacting directly to a reduction in status and influence on their part, this can only be because the kind of cosmopolitan norms against which they react have acquired a degree of social authority that they did not have before. But if that is the case, then why should we not assume that 'identity liberal' graduates learn to align themselves with such values at university *because* those values enjoy such authority, such that aligning themselves with them is in their social and economic interests?

In fact, this claim would seem to be entirely consistent with a more nuanced interpretation of the data on which Sobolewska and Ford rely. From this perspective, it is clearly inadequate to claim, or imply, that the experience of university education merely confers upon graduates a moral commitment to liberal 'values', according to some mysterious process of ethical socialisation. Indeed, it would be unfair to attribute such a simplistic account to Sobolewska and Ford, who are always careful to abjure any claim that their analysis is exhaustive, and who go very far in the direction of producing a comprehensive account of changes to British political culture that takes account of economic, sociological, ideological and institutional factors. But it is a clear limitation of some of their key sources that they treat 'liberal values' as moral norms into which graduates are socialised by some disinterested process of ethical education. It would be both more accurate and more analytically comprehensive to point out that there are at least two more consistent and plausible mechanisms according to which the alignment of graduates with liberal cosmopolitan norms may be understood.

The first such mechanism can be inferred from exactly the same historical phenomenon that Sobolewska and Ford see as explaining the growing resentment and sense of disempowerment experienced by white non-graduates: namely, the widespread sense that liberal cosmopolitan values have become socially normative and institutionally privileged at the expense of more 'traditional' social ideals. If that sense corresponds to any actual social reality, it can only be to the extent that powerful elites have themselves become committed to the propagation and normalisation of such values. This is hardly a new or controversial observation: from the early days of the 'Third Way',[34] political elites – from the left to the centre right – have increasingly tended to endorse certain versions of liberal, cosmopolitan, individualistic and 'multicultural' values, to the extent that they have proven compatible with neoliberal socio-economic objectives. Any graduate seeking gainful employment in the globalised knowledge economy who is unable to comport themselves in accordance with such norms, and to comply with their general social enforcement, is likely to experience severe setbacks.[35] Indeed, training students for employment in the globalised knowledge economy is increasingly understood by governments and university administrators to be the only purpose and function of university education. As such, it is easy enough to see that graduates acting in accordance with such norms are not necessarily doing so out of some purely disinterested commitment to them, or because they have been socialised into such norms as ends in themselves. Rather, they are acting in such a way as to express and realise a particular set of material interests, and those of the social elites with whom they are culturally and economically aligned.

On its own, this is an intellectually satisfying explanation. But it also flies in the face of the intuition on which the idea of the 'identity liberal' graduate rests: namely, the notion that graduates do, after all, acquire distinctive outlooks and capacities from their experience of education that enable them to conceptualise themselves in terms not limited by the ethnocentric communitarianism of the 'identity conservatives'. However, our model of interests as multiple, and expressible at different 'horizons of realisability', can in fact explain this phenomenon very easily. From this perspective, there may well be a qualitative difference in the social attitudes of graduates, compared to citizens with both little formal education and little access to sources of information outside the extremely conservative and philistine organs of the British press. (Indeed, it is notable that Sobolewska and Ford do not refer to the influence of the press at all, despite the fact that the right-wing control of the UK press coincides precisely with the historical period during which they identify the long rise of 'identity conservatism'.)[36] We would stress here that such liberal and cosmopolitan attitudes are not only typical of university graduates; historically, they have also been associated with workers who lack formal education but are heavily socialised by radical political traditions within the labour movement.[37] As such, we might well infer that the experience of university, in equipping students with greater factual knowledge and with a greater capacity to seek out and critically evaluate information sources, confers upon them a greater capacity to conceptualise their own material interests as potentially shared with others who do not share their social identities, and as realisable within a larger temporal frame. We would expect this greater capacity for complex and longer-range evaluation of their interests to express itself precisely as a commitment to anti-racist values as moral principles, but this does not mean that we have to interpret at face value in such naive terms. Our justification for this interpretation is nothing more or less than our own personal experience as members of a highly skilled class of graduate employees, committed to anti-racism as a moral principle, but able to reflect upon the extent to which that principle both aligns with certain contemporary hegemonic norms and constitutes a discursive-affective expression of our own material interest in a potential social future which any form of institutionalised or normalised racism can only obstruct.

So far we have presented our model of political behaviour and identification as motivated by the elective expression of material interests, with reference to social groups that others have theorised as motivated purely by a commitment to some form of political 'identity'. It's worth noting here that our response to Ford and Sobolewska could apply to other psychosocial models of political identification and motivation, including those which, like the work of Laclau and Mouffe, draw heavily on psychoanalysis. Laclau and Mouffe would understand 'identity liberals' and 'identity conservatives' as psychically invested in different political 'imaginaries' and as motivated by different sets of political demands. It is important to stress that our model would not invalidate any such claim, any more than it does the claims of Ford and

Sobolewska. Rather, we seek here to elaborate a key question of political motivation that neither account really sets out to address: namely, the material interests informing the expression of particular demands or the identification with particular imaginaries. While these other accounts largely only encounter this phenomenon via its traces in the domain of epiphenomena, we claim that we can identify its fundamental source at the level of interests.

When considering the politics of Brexit, there is one group of voters who have played a decisive role in UK elections since the 2016 referendum whose behaviour simply cannot be explained with reference to any focus on identity and identification. This is the set of voters – probably just under a million[38] – who voted Leave in the European Referendum, then voted for Jeremy Corbyn's Labour Party in 2017, but switched to the Conservative Party in 2019, once Labour was perceived to have back-tracked on its commitment to implement Brexit without a second referendum on the final shape of a Brexit treaty with the EU. These voters can't be assumed to have endorsed Brexit simply as an expression of 'identity conservatism', because it was already very clear by 2017 that Corbyn and the party that he led were aligned with liberal and cosmopolitan values.[39] Rather, it can logically be inferred that those voters were motivated primarily by an economic narrative according to which mass immigration *does* pose a direct threat to working-class economic interests – a threat that withdrawal from the EU would mitigate decisively. These may have been at least partially mistaken beliefs, but to the extent that they were sincerely held, and constituted a prime motivating factor for some voters, a certain consciousness of interest must be assumed to have taken precedence over any logic of political and cultural identification. A large part of the anti-immigration sentiment expressed by populations of voters in the period leading up to the referendum was expressed in terms of the perception that high levels of immigration posed a threat to wage levels, while putting intolerable pressure on public services. At least some of the voters motivated by these claims were also motivated by the promise of a radical social democratic programme of government, which they also saw as expressing their interests.

By 2019, this group of voters were presented with a choice between a Tory Party whose commitment to Brexit was unequivocal, and a Labour Party committed to a social democratic programme that remained largely desirable to them, but which two years of abject hostility from the media and from the right wing of the parliamentary Labour Party had made clear would face enormous opposition in practice. On some level, it would be hasty to interpret their choice as anything more than an economically rational decision, given the range of information available to those voters.

Arguably this episode demonstrates the limitations of radical politics constituted within a 'social democratic horizon' in the globalised world of the twenty-first century. The logical correlate of a political appeal to this precise constituency of voters who had voted Leave and then Labour was the 'Lexit' project of pursuing a 'left-wing Brexit' that would see Britain leave the EU while committing to a strong programme of 'social democracy in one country'. Whether this would involve the imposition of restrictions on immigration was not a matter on which advocates of the strategy agreed. Indeed, some seem to have believed that they could implement Brexit without draconian immigration restrictions. Nevertheless, the most influential supporters of the position explicitly argued that the free movement of workers across borders was simply not in the interests of labour.[40] Within the social democratic horizon, that may have been true, given that that horizon has always been defined by the possibilities for egalitarian social reform within a single nation-state administering a broadly capitalist economy.

The problem for advocates of this strategy was that too few of Labour's supporters and members actually agreed with it, or saw it as an adequate expression of their interests. Their reasons for opposing it, and for wanting to remain in the EU, were themselves complex and overdetermined. Many simply did not believe that 'Lexit' could deliver on its promises even within a social democratic horizon, given the damage to the UK economy (and consequently, the government's tax base) that would ensue. But many also felt that to leave the EU, despite its current institutional commitment to neoliberalism, was to give up on the long-term objective of using trans-national institutions such as the EU to weaken the power of capital and strengthen the power of citizens – an objective without the realisation of which no programme of social reform in individual countries could expect to meet with much success.[41]

Without doubt, complex questions of identification and culture played an important role in defining the allegiances of different social groups to different visions of a possible future relationship between the UK and the EU. But one of the most striking features of voting patterns in both the referendum and the 2017 and 2019 general elections *across all social classes* was the 'generation gap' that saw voters over the age of fifty overwhelmingly likely to vote Leave and Conservative, and those under fifty becoming progressively more likely, the younger they were at the time of voting, to vote Remain and Labour. This was broadly attributed to the cultural differences between older 'authoritarian', socially conservative voters and younger, 'libertarian', cosmopolitans;[42] it can also be understood in the terms set out by Sobolewska and Ford. However, these differences could equally be understood in terms of differences between different temporal horizons within which the realisation of particular sets of interests could be reasonably expected. The old increasingly saw no prospect of enhancing their wealth or social capacities and sought only to protect them from any potential external threat; the young voted according to the potential inherent in an implicit long-term project for reform of both the EU and the British state and society.[43]

The 'baby boomer' generation of retirees is today characterised by historically unprecedented levels of asset wealth, in the form of property and pensions, such that any objective assessment of their class status must recognise that for a high proportion, their basic economic interests are effectively aligned with those of finance capital (or at least some elements of it). Historically, perceived or actual alignment with the interests of the ruling class is the factor most likely to induce 'subaltern' social groups to identify with themes such as patriotism and general social conservatism. At the same time, as we have just suggested, the shortened temporal frame within which retirees may be expected to imagine their own interests is also likely to encourage a defensive orientation and a rejection of longer-term projects to benefit a range of social groups. And the argument that older voters' conservatism may be related to their specific relationship to the property market and the asset economy is not confined to speculative studies by radical theorists. A very tight statistical correlation has been demonstrated between voting Conservative, asset wealth, and age among the UK electorate, with Joe Chrisp and Nick Pearce arguing that

> while the turbulence of recent political events has created many 'supply side' explanations for political change – and opened up considerable space in which challenger parties can operate – the 'demand side' of voters' preferences has focussed too much on the cultural values of older voters and 'left behind' places, and not enough on the relative prosperity of the older population and the means by which they have secured their economic interests since the financial crisis.[44]

This stark analysis dovetails very neatly with our own.

Identities and Recognition

Brexit has been widely misunderstood as a contest about culture and values. But as we have demonstrated, it can better be thought of as a field of competing interests, and of competing attempts to orient a collective sense of possibility towards differing sets of interests, realisable at different temporal and spatial horizons. But is it really possible to separate considerations of 'interests' from considerations of 'culture' and 'identity' in a case such as this one? Clearly one cannot do so in an entirely clean fashion.

Our argument is not that issues of culture, identity, affect or value should be removed from the kind of analysis we have been undertaking here. Rather, our case is simply that culture, identity, recognition, and similar accounts of psychological political motivation can be better understood as ultimately a matter of material interests, once we have expanded what the word 'interests' actually denotes into an appropriately complex and multivalent conception.

Before we can do that, we need to acknowledge the scale of rejection that the concept of interests has received during the 1980s and '90s, and up to the present day. We can cite at least two key examples, one of which we have already referred to. In the work of Laclau and Mouffe, as in that of other theorists heavily influenced by the psychoanalytic theory of Jacques Lacan, the pursuit of coherent and stable identities (a pursuit that is always doomed to fail, according to the Lacanian model) at times comes close to being treated as the overriding objective and motivation of all politics as such. Within this framework, the very motivating factor in all politics and all political struggle is the desire to recover the 'absent fullness' (of both the self and society as such). The impossibility of doing so – the fact that there is always a gap between reality and fantasy, and that there are always antagonistic social relations that seem to block the final realisation of the fullness – comes to be seen as the motivator of all political action and discourse. Within such a schema, identification – understood as a process that is always ongoing and never successful –comes to play almost the same role that 'interests' does in others. For thinkers of identity, it is what politics is, why politics happens, and the object of all political striving.

A different but comparable model of modern politics is that put forward by the German political and social philosopher Axel Honneth. Honneth claims that modern social struggles are not primarily conflicts over access to physical resources, but 'struggles for recognition', in a concept that he derives mainly from the thought of Hegel. Put simply, Honneth's argument is another rejection of the idea that contests over material interests can be seen as the basis of all political struggles. In place of this view, Honneth argues that such struggles are often – if not always – as much about the competing demands of different groups and individuals to be recognised as deserving of dignity and autonomy within the moral economy of their societies. This assertion has unsurprisingly been subject to many criticisms and interlocutions, but it important not to caricature it. In fact, in his classic work *Struggles for Recognition*, Honneth explicitly distances himself from any view according to which social struggles can be presumed never to proceed from the pursuit of material interests.[45] However, even while Honneth makes this acknowledgement, and even while critics such as Nancy Fraser[46] have stressed that formations such as the women's movement are almost always engaged in struggles simultaneously for access to resources *and* for status, such debates are usually couched in terms which retain a clear distinction and demarcation between 'interests' and some other set of psychosocial factors: 'identity', 'values', 'respect' or 'recognition'.

Interests After All

We propose a different perspective, according to which these distinctions do not actually name different categories of political objective or motivation, but merely designate different *types* of interest and different *horizons* within which those interests may be expressed and calculated. Our logic here is very simple. The distinction between, on the one hand, 'values', 'identity', 'status' or 'recognition' and, on the other hand, 'interests' is artificial, and in fact is always based on a dualistic conception of the human: between the 'economic' body and the moral *psyche*. From a materialist, non-dualistic perspective, however, to be possessed of a certain social status, or to receive 'respect' and 'recognition', to have a secure and stable sense of identity (or, depending on the situation, to be liberated from any such thing), or to have government conducted in accordance with one's 'values' are all in fact realisations of specific and concrete *interests*.

This is not merely a semantic or rhetorical flourish. There is simply no conceivable situation in which the fulfilment of 'identity', 'values', 'status' or 'recognition' does not have direct implications for a person's, or a group's, capacities to act in the world, and on the world. Why, in so many towns and cities, do white people (above all, middle-aged, middle-class white men) fear the police less than black people?[47] Is it only because of the different levels of 'respect' which that institution accords them? Or is it because that 'respect' is a direct index of how likely either group is to receive either protection or injury at the policeman's hand?

The Materiality of Oppression

As we have already mentioned, the rejection of 'interests' as an analytical category, or the insistence on supplementing it with some other, has often been motivated by the perception that to reduce all political analysis to the question of interests is also to understand all social power relations merely as expressions and epiphenomena of *class* interests. This is not our position, as the above example should make clear. To take another, there is abundant evidence that while poor people are the most exposed to the institutionalised racism of white-dominated culture, black people of more privileged socio-economic groups are not insulated from it.[48] Black people have a shared interest in dismantling racist institutions that goes beyond that deriving from their class positions. At the same time, of course, white populations also share that interest on a certain temporal, spatial, and imaginative scale, except where the only interests they feel capable of realising are those expressible on a purely defensive scale.

This is a crucial point to underscore. It is inaccurate to posit the maintenance of white supremacy and its structures of oppression as being in the absolute interests of white people. It may be in *some* interests of *some* white people, and it may be in the interest of white people under circumstances where no better future than one guaranteed by the maintenance of white supremacy can be imagined. But to the extent that racism impedes the realisation of even relatively moderate social democratic goals, it obstructs the realisation of even quite basic material interests shared by vast majorities in most modern societies.

There is an even more fundamental sense in which white supremacism should be seen as obstructing the interests even of those who benefit from white privilege. 'Whiteness', as many commentators have pointed out, is neither a natural nor inviolable condition, but is itself a social construct: the product of a set of institutionalised power relations that serve to reinforce hierarchies within 'white' populations, as well as between them and the victims of racism. But as well as reinforcing and legitimating hierarchies *within* white populations, by imposing standards of 'whiteness' to which only the most privileged subjects can aspire, the criteria for whiteness almost invariably involve a set of constraints and regulations imposed upon even the most unambiguously 'white' subjects.[49]

For more than a century, commentators have recognised the attractive force that key elements of 'black' culture have for many 'white' audiences'.[50] Often this is treated as a curious but trivial feature of modern culture, or merely as a manifestation of racism as such – the white social tourist, culturally appropriating black culture for its exotic affective resources, but without bearing any of the risks that black identity carries in a white supremacist society. None of these accounts are entirely wrong, but they risk overlooking the phenomenon that most needs to be explained in this situation: why should the culture of a less privileged group exert any attractive force on the privileged?[51] This question could be answered in crudely psychological terms; after all, psychoanalytic theory can certainly explain why some people may desire, or identify with, subordinated and abject 'others'.[52] However, we would offer a somewhat different explanation, stressing the sheer range and innovative power of, for example, black music cultures in explaining their attractiveness to so many different audiences around the world. If black music does not possess a genuine capacity to offer certain forms of empowering self-transcendence to white subjects, then its persistent centrality to global commercial music culture since the early twentieth-century music culture is difficult to explain. And without there being some features of white culture and identity which some white subjects have some motivation to transcend, this key feature of modern global – and especially transatlantic[53] – culture makes little sense. We make all of these remarks merely to illustrate the extent to which, even at a personal and affective level, structures of white power can be understood as limitations which, at a certain horizon of realisability, even white subjects have an interest in breaking down. It is at precisely this horizon that 'the abolition of whiteness' may become realisable: a process that, in Spinozan terms,[54] must be understood entirely in terms of a maximisation of the 'joyful' capacities of even white subjects, rather than any form of loss to be suffered by them.

Of course, this horizon is often difficult to obtain, and it is challenging to operate in ways that are oriented effectively towards it. Still, this difficulty must not be mistaken for impossibility. An understanding of interests as multiple, and as realisable within differing temporal and spatial horizons, illuminates many of the problems that are frequently encountered by any effort of political coalition building.[55]

Consider, for example, the persistent tensions since the 1960s between advocates of liberal anti-racist and feminist reforms, on the one hand, and revolutionary socialists, on the other.[56] One reason for that tension is that members of social groups who lack access even to the full benefits of liberal citizenship have more to gain from a range of short-term reforms than do those who already have them. An educated white man may well intuit that few political outcomes short of full-scale revolution are likely to significantly enhance his already highly advantageous situation. A woman of colour, by contrast, may rightly feel that even very modest reforms will benefit her significantly. On the other hand, while such men may well experience even the short-term weakening of racist and misogynist power structures as liberating and empowering, they will clearly experience this on a different scale, within a different temporality to a woman of colour. The tendency towards suspicion and mutual recrimination – defensiveness and perplexity on the part of white men, exasperation on the part of those who do not enjoy their privileges – which so often typifies attempts to resolve such issues arguably proceeds from the absence of a conceptual framework with which interests can be understood as multiple, different, and yet not necessarily opposed. It is precisely this level of nuance and qualification which the complex process of building and sustaining counter-hegemonic coalitions requires. It is its absence that so often renders such coalition building apparently impossible.

We cannot claim access to a magic key, capable of unlocking issues that have proven so intractable over decades. Nevertheless, we offer this simple formulation as one potentially useful object of reflection: men *are* oppressed by patriarchy, but they are oppressed by it both less, and differently, than women, and are offered the benefits of 'male privilege' as compensation for the ways in which patriarchy oppresses them, where women are offered no such compensation. Therefore, men will very often be motivated only to express and pursue their short-term interests in defending that privilege rather than their longer-term interests in abandoning it. The same applies to all other dyads of oppression: white people and people of colour; queer people and straight people; trans people and cis people; able-bodied people and disabled people.

Interests and Hegemony

The conceptualisation of interests that we have developed here shares strong affinities with the thought of Frédéric Lordon, whose Spinozist-Marxist approach is highly compatible with our own.[57] Lordon does not discuss hegemony as such, but is interested in notions of command, consent, compulsion and servitude in the modern world of work. Lordon's core argument is that power in the modern capitalist economy involves certain mechanisms of 'co-linearisation', whereby the interests of workers come to be experienced as directly or partially aligned with those of their employers.[58] This is an excellent term for describing the relationships between hegemonic and subaltern (non-hegemonic) groups within any social bloc and on any given scale, and Lordon's specific example of the employer–employee relationship perfectly illustrates some of our general principles. To the extent that capital depends for profits on the maximal exploitation of labour, the interests of employers and employees are mutually antagonistic, as classical Marxism has always maintained. On the other hand, in a competitive market economy, on certain temporal scales, those interests are clearly aligned, to the extent that employees will suffer if the firm goes bankrupt.

We can compare this to a quite different example, which remains comparable at a certain level of abstraction. Why are there so many instances worldwide of women from certain social groups actively resisting feminist demands and their political implementation? Examples would include many of the women who participated in the Iranian Revolution, in the rise of organisations such as the Christian Fundamentalist Moral Majority in the US, and so on.[59] From our perspective, the answer to this question cannot be reduced to a psychological or psychoanalytic one. It must first be acknowledged that such positions are most commonly found among women who derive the most social privileges, status and material rewards from their fulfilment of 'traditional' feminine roles, and who have the least opportunity to benefit from the classic liberal feminist demand to open up access to education and the professional labour market for women.[60] It is, likewise, as an expression of those specific sets of interests that such groups of women have often been incorporated into the assemblage/blocs of the conservative right. Of their many potential, virtual interests, it is their interest in defending their traditional status that becomes actualised in line with the interests of more powerful groups, whose hegemony is thereby extended.

Furthermore, it is the expression of such sets of coherent interests that will tend to animate the production, circulation and success of particular forms of common sense. Fundamentally, what the traditionalist and reactionary common sense of such social groups expresses is precisely the co-linearity of certain of their interests with those of the group to which they are hegemonically subordinate. To be successful, any attempt to challenge that common sense at the political or cultural level must effectively express a *different* co-linearisation of a *different* set of potential interests with those of a different social group. For example, the success of liberal feminism in many contexts since the 1970s has been partly a function of the production of a new common sense that co-linearised the interests of many working women and housewives in the expansion and levelling of education and the labour market with those of radical campaigners seeking significant social change, as well as the interests of key sections of capital in expanding the pool of workers with very high communication, customer-interface and information-management skills.[61] This is an observation with crucial implications for progressive political strategy, which far too often seems to be conceived in terms of 'narratives', 'values' and 'frames',[62] without any attention being paid to the question of precisely which sets of interests any discursive interventions in prevailing common sense should be seeking both to actualise and to co-linearise.

From Interests to Platforms

From this perspective, what is an interest in itself? It is in fact nothing more than political motivation itself, expressed as virtual or actual force. Interests sit as internalised mental mediators between the world of structures (established forms of power exerting causal effects) and agents (individual and collective subjects capable of exerting force to transform their worlds). The objectivity or materiality of interests rests upon the fact that they are never merely arbitrary, causeless, or simply whims, but rather interests always arise in relation to the structures which configure the social, cultural, economic, and political environment of subjects. These structures cannot be considered merely in a simplified economic account, but must be understood rather as themselves complex and multiple in scope. Hegemony-as-leadership functions by using structural constraints to both generate interests and affect the expression of interests and the configuration of horizons in populations of subjects. Rather than naturalise political motivation into value, identity, or recognition, leaving us with a political force which cannot be contested, this non-essentialist model of political interests is ultimately a form of constructivism. It implies that while political motivations can be explained, they can also be changed. The entire edifice of political hegemony and the ability to transform it rests upon this fact.

Understanding interests and hegemony in these terms ultimately enables us to refine our understanding of what hegemony actually is. Hegemony is a process by which certain sets of interests are able to co-linearise with others, thereby determining the general direction of travel taken by the social formation within which they are situated. Of course, social formations are not self-enclosed and clearly bound entities, so different sets of hegemonic interests will exert different degrees of influence at each point in the vast and multiply overlapping networks of social relations which constitute the context for every action, agent or institution. Nonetheless, it is clearly possible to identify key nodes at which particular clusters of interests are able to be actualised, expressed and realised even on global scales. In the world of the twenty-first century, the most obvious examples are the centres of the technology industry and finance capital – and above all, the points at which their interests most obviously converge, co-linearise and become mutually reinforcing. In the next chapter we will consider in more detail a key mechanism through which the hegemonic power of the tech sector has been expanded and co-linearised with that of many others, with implications for understanding the power of each of these other major power-loci: the platform.

5

PLATFORM POWER

How does power leave lasting traces on the landscapes of the social? At its core, modern hegemonic politics is about building alliances of groups and their interests to construct socio-political change, imbuing a social system with a particular direction of travel. For neoliberal societies, this was a process of continual change towards market and market-like mechanisms backed by the coercive power of the state. At its extreme this can be described as constituting a kind of *platform power* – the crystallisation of the direction of political travel within the infrastructures of technology, the economy, energy, transport, management practices and everyday life. Once established, these infrastructures embody and reinforce a process of transformation, automating hegemonic influence into the very fabric of the social and technological world. As such they are a site of considerable political contention, albeit a contention which is often hidden from view.

Hegemonic Platforms

So far we have tried to theorise hegemony in the twenty-first century from a number of angles. But there is another dimension upon which we must expand in order to make sense of our modern world of power, and that is the domain of *platforms*. In a certain sense, we have already invoked them in other forms, particularly when outlining, in chapter 1, the class fractions who most managed to get what they wanted from the long 1990s. To talk of Silicon Valley or financial elites as having secured most of their interests requires us to think beyond many of the typical ways in which we understand politics, beyond governments and elections, beyond the surface layer of conventional politics. What these groups of people have in common, beyond certain particular interests, is their ability to design, influence, and control some of the key infrastructures which work to structure our contemporary world, from the economy, to social and cultural systems, and even to conventional politics itself.

A basic definition of platform power is this: the ability to use infrastructures to exert influence, directly or indirectly, intentionally or unintentionally, to secure goals related to a group's interests. Such an idea has always had some role to play within the Gramscian understanding of hegemonic power.[1] Indeed, one of the most interesting dimensions of his work on hegemony often goes relatively unremarked upon. This is his focus, beyond the politics of the state, upon the myriad modes within which power can work to embed itself in ways that are much more difficult to alter than through a vote or even a revolution. The cunning of hegemonic power rests in its obfuscation and erasure of itself, its secretion into the furniture of everyday existence that we merely 'take as natural'. It resides in a use of power to seed the grounds for its own continuation. It is therefore in the guise of the platform that we can observe hegemonic power operating in its most long-lasting and epochal modes.

The classic Gramscian example of this framework, alongside the world of production, is usually education. It is in education systems that we find a key social mechanism that effectively produces subjects, strongly influencing individual and collective world-views. Indeed, for Gramsci 'every relationship of "hegemony" is necessarily an educational one'.[2] These influences extend beyond that of just content, the knowledge or information that education imbues into its recipients. More important are the multifarious ways in which schooling creates frameworks through which content about the world is itself interpreted. The lengthy battles between different political orientations around the world (but especially sharply in an Anglo-American context) over the exact nature of education systems, from primary school to university, is indicative of the significance of educational infrastructures in cultural battles to secure a particular vision of the world as a common sense with widespread social influence.[3] In particular, we might consider conflicts over history teaching within the UK and US as important examples of the ways in which historical frameworks relating to the role of Britain, especially in relation to colonialism, tend to lead towards certain political world-views. In the US, the recent moral panic over 'critical race theory' as an imaginary hate-object for the right has focussed as much as anything on the question of what version of America's history can be taught in schools. In the UK, the Conservative Party's insistence on a Churchillian 'Island Story' of nationalist 'heroism' is more than merely an aesthetic preference.[4] It constitutes a structure of feeling for English conservatives: a lens through which the world is seen and interests discerned. By constructing a particular narrative and historical backdrop to the present, it proposes that both the present and future be seen differently. This lens will tend to generate a set of interests and a manner of perceiving them that focuses on the alleged positives of the British Empire and its legacy, distorting the violent and contested reality in favour of a jingoistic nationalism.[5] Thus a postcolonial melancholia sours rapidly into the delusory panacea of Brexit and rabid anti-immigrant rhetoric.[6]

Similarly, the emphasis on the corrupting influence of leftist lecturers on university students[7] consists of more than just a culture war, but indexes a significant worry for right-wing politics that elites and broader populations are being educated towards an understanding of their interests which is very distinct to what the former would prefer.[8] Thinking more systematically, particular forms of school structure and ownership, such as academies in the UK or charter schools in the United States, have the effect of shifting decisions around schooling out of the hands of those amenable to democratic influence and into those of the private sector, effectively insulating the school system from popular contention or control, enabling particular political or behavioural goals to more easily be developed – which is why they tend to be favoured by those on the right and feared by those on the left.[9]

In more contemporary accounts of hegemony, particularly those filtered through recent ideas such as framing theory,[10] it is the media that will occupy centre stage as the key nexus of engineering world-views and political consent. The media certainly constitute one system that is pivotal to any process of contending for power. Increasingly under pressure from digital forms over the last twenty years, traditional media have now retrenched and combine the curious features of being both largely unprofitable with a shrinking base of paying customers, while growing possibly more influential than ever. The function of the conventional mass media of television and print news in 'feeding' digital social media has effectively centralised even more the influence of editors to shape perceptions and govern the news cycle. As such, a crucial factor in the limited efficacy of left political tendencies in the post-2016 era has been the continued predominance of centre and right-wing world-views within conventional and traditional media infrastructures.

While we ought to be wary of overly simplistic conceptions of influence through mass media, we must not underestimate their ability to help shape the 'Overton window': the range of acceptable mainstream opinion (named for the American political scientist Joseph Overton). Their general ability to set the agenda for public debate is also very marked. It is worth distinguishing between these two different effects. The Overton window operates as an emergent effect of many smaller decisions, opinions, and institutional set-ups to constitute a window or span of political views which are deemed to be acceptable (or not) within the public sphere.[11] Much of the work of far-right or -left politics is to try to expand this ambit in certain directions. Understood in such a way, 'outrider' logics expand what more 'reasonable' operators can openly discuss. We can consider the Overton window as being something like the contemporary public media sphere's version of 'common sense'.

Agenda setting, on the other hand, is a primary method through which interests are manipulated by hegemonic politics, by influencing perceptions of the relative importance of different issues. This aims not so much to 'change people's minds' but instead to shift up or down the salience of a belief, issue, or problem.[12] The continuous presence of headlines on a given topic will tend to shift that interest higher in any internal order of priorities. We only have to think of the twenty-year campaign in the British media against immigration and its continual presence on the front pages. Not only does such agenda setting serve to shift saliency; it also works as a kind of intersubjective 'big other' – influencing what is deemed by society to be important. Even if I may not personally be concerned about an issue, the fact it is always being discussed in the mass media means I will at least consider it to be important to society in general. By modulating the saliency of existing interests over creating new ones, mass media tends to exert influence over political motivation and behaviour today.

Platforms Defined

When we use the term 'platform' here, rather than 'infrastructure' (or even more simply 'structure'), we are drawing upon the contemporary resonances of the term. It is now a relative commonplace to discuss 'the platform economy', 'platform design', or even 'platform capitalism' in relation to the expansion of a particular set of digital economic platforms.[13] They have also, in the period since 2016 – which we identify as one of the emergence of a structural crisis for neoliberalism – come under increased scrutiny for their social and political effects. However, our idea of platform power extends beyond the social networking and other technology platforms that have become increasingly familiar over the last fifteen years. We would also include the global financial system, energy system, production systems, global governance institutions, education, media, and national-level state bureaucracies as operating as platforms too (among many other systems). We therefore take the term 'platform' from its contemporary usage and place it into a political one, generalising the function of platforms to multiple different instantiations.

If platforms can describe all these different forms of vital infrastructure to the modern social world, what do they then have in common? At the most fundamental level, platforms are any system on which other entities depend, and in depending, are influenced by. Let us take the example of a platform such as Google. Google operates as a system – particularly its search and advertising technology elements – upon which many other entities – from websites to businesses to ordinary end users – depend. In so doing, this dependency gives the owner of the platform a particular mode of influence; it is this that can be termed platform power. For Google, this influence is insidious but omnipresent. 'Google search' is literally a synonym for internet-based enquiries, full stop; as such, the decisions embedded in the algorithms that power it will tend to help shape the everyday epistemology of the people who use it – to shape how knowledge is known and what knowledge is selected as being the most important or significant.[14] The elements included as 'defaults' within such important digital infrastructures of everyday life help shape our lives. 'Default' options, protocols, implicit and explicit rules: all of these constitute the ways in which platforms tend to influence human behaviour and world-views.

Platforms tend to work in two directions simultaneously. Most obviously, they influence the behaviour of those entities that depend in some way upon them. But they also work in the other direction: the more entities that depend on a platform, the more embedded and entrenched that platform will tend to become. To return to our example of Google, the more that Google search is used, the better it functions, and the more entrenched it will be as a result. For Facebook or any other social network, this would be the impressive social compulsion that develops after the user base hits a certain volume within a given population: it will become hard *not* to be a user. This double action can be termed *generative entrenchment*, wherein a system becomes more powerful the more it is depended upon, and shapes those entities that depend on it by becoming an important basis on which they depend.[15] These two directions occur together to reinforce one another. In other words it is generative, because it helps generate behaviour of those entities that are using it, while it is entrenched because that generative property fosters dependence and hence structural power. It is for this reason that within the domain of tech platforms, specific strategies have been developed to help push a given system towards the point of taking on the qualities of a platform[16] – the pathway to immense profitability and power.

We must clarify here that platforms *do not* correspond to the classical Marxist notion of base versus superstructure. This now very old idea puts in place a distinction between the domain of production (the economic 'base'), and the realms of culture, ideology, and religion (the 'superstructure'). Within this account, the (singular and unitary) base is seen as primary, the ultimate force driving the world, with the cultural superstructures being somewhat ephemeral elements with little causatory power of their own.[17] Such a simplistic binary is entirely out of keeping with the non-reductionist account of power that we have already set out. Thinkers of hegemony such as Ernesto Laclau and Chantal Mouffe were absolutely correct to criticize this kind of analysis of the world as reductive in nature.[18] Yet even for Gramsci, there was no straightforward acceptance of the base/superstructure argument. Indeed, a closer inspection of his *Prison Notebooks* demonstrates a more nuanced and non-linear relationship between the economic and the cultural.[19]

The concept that comes closest to hegemonic platforms for Gramsci is his idea of the historic bloc, which is a well-established hegemony, where hegemonic projects have worked over time to reorient the economy and other non-political domains into reflecting and reinforcing the political ones.[20] For Gramsci this was never a question of the economic dominating the political, but rather of there being a kind of reciprocal relationship where changes in one would help to create changes in the other, without either being necessarily dominant over the other.[21] While power relations from the economy will tend to produce power dynamics in the political sphere, politics can obviously affect the economic domain too. From policies relating to the labour market, to rules around private property, the economic sphere requires constant political maintenance.

We follow Gramsci here. There is no singular platform that determines, as in the base of classical Marxian legend, the configuration of political forces operating atop it. Tensions and dynamics within the economy do not direct the entirety of society as a kind of puppet show. Rather, we can observe multiple overlapping and interlocking platforms, each governing a different socially necessary function, with their own modes of influence. Such influence is never entirely deterministic, in the sense of mechanically constituting the behaviour of its users in an absolutely predictable sense. Instead, it is more like a series of different landscapes, each of which have specific contours that constitute the space of possibility for human action. In the words of design theorist Keller Easterling, platforms and infrastructures tend to function 'like an operating system, [making] certain things possible and other things impossible'.[22] It is always possible for individuals and groups to choose a pathway other than that of least resistance, but there will be costs (economic, energetic, psychological) associated with venturing too far. In this sense, platforms will tend to shape most behaviours and understandings roughly towards their intended (or evolved) ends, without being absolutely deterministic in scope.

Another useful point of reference here would be from the phenomenology of technology and the notion of 'affordances for action'.[23] Affordances are a way of thinking about how we perceive possibilities for action within an object or system. Designers often think about affordances when creating interfaces, to deliberately encode methods of use in the presentation of a designed object. However, the affordances for action are never entirely limited by design or intention, and often, more can be discovered over time. Think of a car – designed for use as a means of personal transportation, but equally amenable to use as a place to sleep, a mobile sound system, or even a murder weapon. Similarly, the affordances of platforms can never be precisely mapped out in advance, but rather emerge through use. What this means is that platform systems that emerge under a particular hegemonic power structure might have certain features encoded within them, whether through intentional design or through unintentional evolution. But the full range of affordances for action can never be entirely predicted or controlled for. This means that platforms have a Janus-faced nature – on the one hand operating as the great conditioners of human behaviour, but on the other hand acting as wellsprings of potential for resistance, transformation, and change.

Politics is often considered by journalists and political scientists as operating under some kind of set of 'rules'. For example, during high neoliberalism, Blairite and Clintonite centrists would often opine on a seemingly inviolable rule set of politics: the market was all that mattered, politicians should obey opinion polling, slick presentation was essential, finance capital was to be encouraged, and so on.[24] But if politics is a game, it is a recursive one. That means that the game is partly about the process of changing the rules under which it itself is played. It is a game in which all that constitute it, from the rules to the playing pieces to the board itself, are not solid and settled things. While for political scientists politics is akin to Chess, which has a set of rules with determinate strategies to be mastered, the radical, recursive instability of hegemonic politics more closely resembles the ancient Chinese and Japanese game of Go, where what is figure and what is ground is always ambiguous and under contention.

The recursive nature of politics means that periods where apparently firm 'rules' emerge are merely the artefact of hegemonic stability, including most obviously at the level of platforms. But even platforms, the most long-lasting elements of a political hegemony, can be altered. In altering them, the rules of the game can itself be changed, and beyond any playing of the game under any given set of rules, this constitutes the moment of most hegemonic potency. Take for example electoral systems. For years now the American Republican Party has become exceptionally adept at manipulating the various parameters of the US electoral system, from gerrymandering the borders of congressional districts to aggressively stacking courts with conservative justices, to imposing severe voter ID laws that make it harder for non-whites and the poor to actually vote.[25] All of these measures combine to slant the system towards them and against their opponents, even as the popular vote trends ever further against them. Though mainstream Democrats may decry such actions as unseemly, that only attests to the inability of liberals to conceive of politics at its fullest extent (e.g., as more than just debate, policy, and elections). Which is to say, hegemonic politics is always about rebuilding the ground on which it stands, the platforms on which it rests.

Why does the question of platforms matter? Because as the most structurally long-lasting modes of power, they tend to enable hegemony to operate at more expansive time scales and spatial scales than active political projects alone. If we think of the built environment, for example, buildings can last hundreds of years, and some roads in Europe continue to be in use in the same layout as were the roads of the old Roman Empire.[26] The structural legacies of prior political projects thereby get etched into the infrastructures of our world. While their effects cannot remain absolutely locked in to the specific direction of travel of a given hegemony under which they were created, certain tendencies will remain. This makes them an ideal method for ambitious political projects determined to have a lasting influence upon the world, building structural constraints that embed elements of their hegemonic juncture. The longest-lasting forms of hegemonic power are, in essence, platforms in nature. They continue to configure the tendencies of human behaviour for many generations to come.

Big Tech

As we have already discussed in some detail, perhaps the most notable example of platform power in the world around us today consists of 'big tech' – an entire sector of the economy devoted to information technology and its associated infrastructures. Here we include such social networking platforms as Facebook, Instagram, Twitter, Tencent, Weibo, and TikTok, as well as search and ad-tech platforms like Google, cloud-computing platforms such as Amazon Web Services, the makers of operating systems such as Microsoft, streaming content platforms like Spotify and Netflix, e-commerce platforms such as Alibaba, eBay and (again) Amazon, and 'lean market' platforms like Uber and Airbnb. Platforms constitute a new kind of organisational matrix to be exploited by the different forces contending for the political future of the planet in the wake of a rapidly eroding neoliberalism. However, in spite of this new role, we should consider the tech platforms to generally be characteristically neoliberal systems.

What do we mean when we describe technology platforms as neoliberal in character? As we saw in chapter 2, neoliberalism has been given many different competing definitions (as well as been routinely declared non-existent, at least by some anti-intellectual media commentators). At its core, though, we can consider it as a set of policies (privatisation, marketisation, outsourcing, deregulation), coupled with a world-view (that the market is the best information processor and the state exists only to enable it) and a set of actors who were crucial in its implementation (the Mont Pèlerin Society, neoliberal think-tanks, right-wing media operations, etc.).[27] Together, these constructed a hegemony, building and helping to influence the production of a number of key platforms. In turn, the traces of neoliberal policies and world-views will tend to be inscribed on the material infrastructures they leave behind. To say that big tech is essentially neoliberal in character means that it was shaped by neoliberalism, that it contributed to the sedimentation and embedding of neoliberalism, and that these effects continue into the post-neoliberal era. Let us examine some of these tendencies in more detail.

Take for example a typical social media platform such as Facebook, Twitter, Instagram or Weibo. Tech platforms tend in general to support a particular mode of engagement – that is to say, the essential business model rests upon the generation of content for free by users, in return for access to the platform. In turn, the platform monetises the attention of its users via the sale of advertising and uses the data generated by behaviour on platforms both to improve its own business and as a product to be bundled up and sold to advertisers and other interested parties.[28] This has led to the development of social platforms designed around disclosure, where competitive individualism and gamification or metricisation are pervasive. Disclosure of information, often glossed as a revolutionary openness (i.e., 'connecting the world'), is one of the core ideological convergences between neoliberalism and tech platform design. This radical openness has roots in the cultural constituents of Silicon Valley, particularly its right-libertarian elements which see openness (of certain kinds) as being inherently morally good. It is no coincidence that this kind of libertarian pseudo-openness also enables the basic business model of social media – free at the point of use, with data commodified – to work. While young users have partially learned to resist the presumption that everything should be shared (which is often literally embedded into the preferences of the social media app or site), older users are more oblivious or conditioned.

Accompanying this are typical user interface design conventions, such as omnipresent metrics: 'likes,' 'friends', 'engagement', 'shares'. Though such defaults might appear relatively objective and neutral, they are heavily influential on human behaviour. The direct rendering of otherwise tacit or unobservable social properties into hard numbers will tend to have two major effects. First, it enables comparison between users.[29] Second, it nurtures competitiveness and an identification of the metrics as an end in themselves, rather than as merely a measure of a more important process (e.g., sociality as such). This mirrors directly the use of metrics throughout advanced neoliberal management, particularly as deployed in areas which were traditionally non-market based, such as education and health. A commonly remarked upon problem with this expansion of targets is that practitioners and professionals will tend to simply game the system, aiming to maximise those things that are measured – while tacitly allowing everything not being measured to be ignored.[30] If you set a series of targets for health care, such as having doctors see all emergency patients within a certain amount of time, systems will tend to just meet that target to the letter and not in terms of its spirit (perhaps by seeing patients quickly and then triaging them to wait again for several hours before actual treatment is provided). What digital metrics tend to create is an environment in which social activities are gamed, and where 'engagement' with the apps is increased, which in turn maximises profits for the platform owners.

Among the many social habits and behaviour patterns that neoliberalism tends to teach is competitive individualism, which it shares most keenly with tech platforms. The proliferation of metrics, as well as radical openness and social panoptic access to the mass lives of others, aggressively supercharges an already ever-present sense of competition and individualism. Competition is a key social value of neoliberalism,[31] but it is also an important mechanism through which value in the marketplace is deemed to be generated. Individualism is one of the most important methods through which neoliberalism both valorises the market (for it is through consumption practices that individual identity can most easily be realised) and transforms the way we experience the world and think about politics. This is especially marked in the way we constitute the horizon of our interests. Collective interests are very different to those of merely ourselves or our immediate families, and it is atomised social relations that social media both recreate in digital form and expand within the fabric of our online interactions.

Digital platforms also tend to obfuscate the distinction between professionals and amateurs. This effect was much lauded in the early days of the internet, where the notion of citizen journalism was promoted as a method through which the powerful could be better held to account while at the same time ordinary people could participate in the media. The reality tends to be that competitive relations present in the workplace become incorporated into the everyday – as in the rise of micro-celebrities and influencers. Combined with this, tech platforms enable a blurring of work and leisure that further accelerates the expansion of work and market relations that are core to the neoliberal political project. This was never clearer than during the COVID-19 pandemic, where big tech kept many workers working from home, compressing the domestic and public spheres, as well as free time and work time, into a singular, constant time-space (what Italian Marxists once talked about as the 'social factory').[32]

The commodification of public digital space, and its expansion of work-based social relations, directly mirrors that occurring in the 'real world' of privately owned public spaces (or POPS) and large-scale private developments. Increasingly throughout the developed world, where public spaces such as parks, leisure facilities, and thoroughfares were once publicly owned, perhaps by municipal governments, they now tend to be controlled by private forces.[33] These POPS might appear to be just like the old public spaces, but they are controlled by corporations and private security, and have the right to remove anyone they choose. Similarly, the social worlds enclosed within social media platforms appear to be smoothly neutral, unobtrusive digital domains, but they are owned and controlled by private interests, and managed for profit above all else. This means that our digital spaces are largely controlled by technology corporations, for their own economic and political interests. Controls extend most obviously to the policing (or in their terms, 'moderation') of speech – political speech in particular. The politics of online speech have become highly contentious in the last five years, but what remains is the fact that increasingly our public spheres are conducted almost entirely within privately controlled domains. Transformations to the regulations that govern these domains, such as what content can be posted or not, are often opaque and can have significant influence on the modes of politics (and political organisation) that are possible through them. A good illustration of this is the dramatic effect of 'deplatforming' on the ability of certain alt-right figures to spread their political messages (e.g., commentators such as Milo Yiannopoulos and Alex Jones).[34] Though in that example we might be satisfied that the removal of such right-wing personages was justified and necessary to avoid harm, it effectively positions platform owners in increasingly influential roles as private censors.

Alongside the private control of our digital public spaces, there are other important modes of control embedded in the algorithms that organise the information with which we interact. Whether in terms of a Facebook News Feed or a Google search, our online universe is painstakingly arranged by complex networks of algorithms designed for specific purposes – usually to provide utility, but also (and more crucially) to engage the user so as to extract value. Decisions at the level of changes in algorithms can be massively influential. In 2018, Facebook changed the emphasis of its News Feed algorithm away from foregrounding news stories and towards privileging status updates from people users actually knew – a shift that worked to massively disadvantage political movements using the platform to share updates. Much of this is not intentional political activity by platform owners, but it can certainly have directly political effects. These effects are not limited to those intended by the designers of these systems. For instance, algorithmic systems have routinely been gamed by right-wing extremists to normalise search results that are outright racist.[35] In these respects, tech platforms serve as large-scale feedback-loop systems, which can be tuned through the algorithms that help to organise the information they contain. Feedback loops will tend to be non-linear in nature, often expanding out beyond the intended purposes in unpredictable ways. For example, while Facebook was revealed to have weighted the 'angry' response emoji significantly more strongly than any other response within its algorithmic timeline, largely for reasons of increasing engagement and hence profits, the non-linear result was a marked uptick in political polarisation and a general affective shift towards the furiously political, one in keeping with the emergence of American right-wing populism.

Moving beyond the realm of social media, platforms such as 'lean market' operations Uber, Postmates, Deliveroo and Airbnb have a particularly pernicious impact. While not operating in such subtle and influential fashions as Google or Facebook, they directly impact labour markets and have demonstrated themselves to be agents of increasing precarity within vulnerable workforces. These platforms have definite political effects, disrupting existing labour markets and disempowering workers through elimination of benefits and significantly increasing the rate of exploitation. This has led to the formation of new unions specifically designed to organise workers in these app-mediated digital workplaces, but the fight has been difficult.[36] In many cases these platforms embed the worst of neoliberal labour market reforms, and they mirror closely, but in digital-platform guise, the kinds of attacks on organised labour and established rights of the aggressive neoliberalism practiced by Margaret Thatcher and Ronald Reagan in the early 1980s.

Increasingly, platform regulations and platform algorithms are becoming the objects of political contention and debate, moving platforms out of their former position of false naturalisation and into the light of political conflict. This has led tech platforms to become considerably more vulnerable to political and economic regulation – for instance, in the US, the appointment of one of Amazon's fiercest critics to head the Federal Trade Commission, among other significant moves in recent years.[37] However, such controversial status has yet to threaten their position as central to social, economic, and political life.

Planetary Wall Street

Though theories of platforms first developed in and around computing-based industries, we do not believe they should be limited to that sphere alone. For instance, one absolutely necessary platform for the establishment and sedimentation of neoliberalism is the global financial system. Here we can observe many of the same dynamics we identified with big tech platforms like Google and Facebook. The global financial system has many complex functions within planetary-scale capitalism today, but one core operation is in directing capital from investors to businesses and projects that require it. Control of this infrastructure therefore confers an immense amount of power to govern the flows of investment and hence the basic direction of development within capitalism. The major institutions of finance capital also tend to use its power, both functional and economic, to manipulate legislators into deregulating finance and thereby allowing more profitable avenues for financial accumulation. In turn this leads to what has been termed financialisation – the insertion of finance-based mechanisms into more and more ostensibly non-financial elements of the economy.[38]

It was global finance, as well as an earlier era of technology firms, that aided in the expansion and embedding of neoliberalism in the early 1980s in Global North core nations like the US and UK. Particularly after the 'big bang' of deregulatory reforms in the late 1980s, financial flows were vital to neoliberalism's expansion to much of the rest of the world, as

corporations and governments came under ever more rigorous external management. Most important here has been the
expansion of debt, both at the level of individuals and nation-
states. Fiscal debt, the debt held by national governments,
effectively operates today as a kind of disciplinary mechanism. Pushed beyond a certain point, fiscal debt will lead to
financial repercussions, from massively more expensive borrowing through bond market price shifts or ratings-agency
revisions, to active measures like structural adjustment
requirements following access to European Union or International Monetary Fund money in a crisis situation. The
impact of this can be substantial, effectively forcing a hard
austerity politics on an otherwise-unwilling state (as was the
case following the EU fiscal debt crisis of 2009–11 for countries like Greece).[39] Even more seriously, structural adjustment
following state indebtedness is frequently used to force less
powerful states to employ disastrous hyper-neoliberal policies, such as the privatisation of their entire water services
sectors.[40] At the level of the state, then, finance has embedded
neoliberal policies, particularly in any kind of crisis situation.
While the period post-2016 and particularly since the COVID-
19 pandemic has seen looser public spending across much of
the world, the threat of structural adjustment and bond markets making borrowing unaffordable has not gone away.

On an individual and economic level too, financialisation
has served to embed neoliberal relations across society. Economically, financialisation means more and more economic
activities have a financialised component. Take cars for example. Most car manufacturers make more money from
leasing and car loan agreements than they do from actually
selling cars. Similarly, phone companies are really phone-
handset financing providers that happen to also run cellular
networks. This tends to have two effects, both characteristic
of platform logic. The first is that the increasing dependence
upon financial platforms across the broader economy aligns

with a strengthening of finance in general. It means more money flowing through financial circuits, which in turn means more potential financial activities being built off those financial flows, and increased financialisation. Secondly, though, it means that the activities of non-financial organisations become more and more suborned within financialised logics, which means they become more geared towards making money from debt.[41] This means a generalised expansion of debt levels throughout society as a whole.

For individuals and households, the period from the 1980s onwards was one characterised by a massive expansion in the availability of private credit, and personal borrowing increased substantially. In many respects this served to supplement what became fairly stagnant levels of wage growth in the developed world, enabling consumption when wages would not allow it. After all, debt enables control at the individual as well as at the national level. It binds individuals in various ways, both practically and psychologically. It creates practical issues in that it consumes their incomes and, as a result, influences them not to take certain kinds of risks. Debt also tends to create a certain psychological effect, pressurising individuals and imposing a bleak level of internalised discipline through mental health conditions such as depression and anxiety, a generalised weakening of mental space and a truncated horizon of political interests.[42]

This influence of finance reaches its apogee in the prevalence of a particular form of financialisation within the UK: the mortgage and the property market it underpins. If we were attempting to explain the political economy of the UK to an alien visitor, the first and most important thing to mention would be the influence of the property market on politics.[43] Though in recent years there has been much written about generational divides (between young progressives and older reactionaries), much of this can be explained simply by the relation an individual has to property ownership.[44] Those who own their own property tend to have a set of interests that more closely align with the right, and the converse is true of those who do not own their own homes. Those who acquired a mortgage on a property in the 1980s or '90s may well be sitting on an asset of considerable value now, which confers distinctive material interests. Governments pander to this key demographic – older people – who are also highly likely to vote. In turn, this has become a great constant, consistent from Thatcher all the way through to the pandemic environment that prevails as of this writing. Mortgages enabling property acquisition are the singular motor of increased personal wealth in the UK, and are effectively protected at all costs by successive administrations. This financial mechanism allows those in possession of property to accumulate wealth, backed by state policies, while those excluded are trapped in low-paid work and indebtedness. For some homeowners, it is the case that they will make more money from asset appreciation than from wage labour in any given year. In this fashion, homeownership and mortgages work to generate a particular class structure for British society at large, which is exploited by political forces to retain control.

Finance has obvious global effects too. One is the use of complex financial arrangements to avoid tax, whether by wealthy individuals or massive global corporations, often through use of 'offshore' facilities. This practice leads to the dramatic underfunding of states, with the largest corporations on Earth paying lower marginal tax rates than the average worker on the minimum wage, enhancing private power while leaving the public realm noticeably enfeebled.[45] Another pernicious impact is that of private equity, particularly when private equity firms treat otherwise-functional businesses as mere financial vehicles to be exploited for short-term profitability. Indeed, financialisation in general tends to promote a short-termism that radically limits the horizons in which individuals, households, governments, and corporations think about their actions in the world. The expansion of models of 'share-holder value' as the key metric for managers of corporations to be judged upon has meant that publicly traded companies will tend to focus largely on the short term in practice.[46] The inevitable result of this is a maximisation of profits in the short run, and hence of market capitalisation, share price, and dividends to shareholders. Through lobbying and other influence operations on governments and legislators, corporations will then tend to work to impose their short-term objectives on those organisations intended to preserve longer-term goals.

In the years since 2000, we can even identify considerable convergence between the platforms of finance and those of big tech, with the two becoming ever more closely intertwined. Big tech has relied for some time on the backing of venture capitalists for its start-up capital. Similarly, the world-views of senior staff working in finance and computing have many points of resemblance: they tend to express broad social liberalism, combined with a ruthless commitment to private power and liberated capitalism that is taxed as little as possible.[47] But increasingly, financialised logics and technological ones are merging or being intertwined. The emergence of 'fintech' – financial technology – such as blockchain and cryptocurrencies attests to the development of a new phase in the finance sector's use of and incorporation into digital technology. Financial operators, including large investment banks, increasingly identify fintech as a field of immensely profitable expansion, while tech giants like Facebook have sought to develop their own cryptocurrencies.

Neoliberalism Going Global

A characteristic development of advanced neoliberalism has been that it constructs a particular kind of global order, a set of supranational legal-regulatory regimes that worked to weaken democratic control over states. What this means in practice is akin to the kind of control achieved by global financial systems, the creation of systems of rewards and punishments at the global level that heavily incentivise certain behaviours and disincentivise others. Indeed, we can consider global financial systems and flows as one example of a global platform that creates a supranational order of control.

Let us examine the World Trade Organization (WTO), which through the regulation of global commerce, oversees binding commitments undertaken by states to not disrupt processes of trade liberalisation. Concealed behind technical and commercial vocabulary are distinctly political effects that prioritise markets and the free flow of goods over any other social objectives. When governments, perhaps under pressure from their electorates, want to break with neoliberal free market shibboleths on such issues as labour laws, hygiene standards, or limits on access to their markets for environmentally damaging goods, they often cannot do so without incurring massive fines from the WTO.[48] An illustrative example is food allergies labelling. This highly reasonable policy is considered by the WTO to be a 'technical barrier' to trade. In practice, wealthier nations and regional powers like the EU end up paying the fines in order to have a modicum of policy leeway, but poorer nations are obviously less able to do so.

Another example worth consideration here is intellectual property law. For decades, the WTO has sought to use its considerable powers to allow access to global markets to work as both a 'carrot' and 'stick' to convince non-Western nations to incorporate Western-style copyright and patent laws. Such regulations, while seemingly natural, are actually highly culturally specific; even in the West, they are relatively recent inventions, while other traditions for producing and owning culture often find them alien. Refusal to comply will tend to lead to fines or an inability to buy or sell key products, which might have significant economic or political effects. In so doing, global cultural policy is directed in favour of privatisation of access and rights.

Just as neoliberals rejected the state in theory but practically used it to extend market relations throughout society at the national level, so too did they put institutions to work at the global level. Large-scale legal institutions like the European Court of Justice, alongside financial and trade bodies such as the WTO, World Bank, and International Monetary Fund, were all used to help create barriers against the ability of democratic forces to obtain better protections from rampant market dynamics.[49] National-level states were called upon to enforce the expansion of market rule, and so too at the international level. As we have seen repeatedly within this chapter, platforms tend to seek to push political directionality into domains where they are hard to identify, challenge, or otherwise contend with. Global governance institutions present a neutral and technical front, but their rules tend to prevent basic democratic control and frequently lead states to act against their own best interests. This process of globalisation beyond the reaches of the state wasn't a secondary stage in the hegemonic path of neoliberalism. Rather, as historian Quinn Slobodian puts it, 'Neoliberalism as a body of thought . . . originated in an early twentieth century crisis about how to organize the whole earth.'[50] Indeed, neoliberalism depended upon globalism at both a philosophical and organisational level.

There are of course many more examples of global platforms we could examine. The globally distributed system of production that began to be established in earnest in the late 1970s, where supply chains are globally extensive and production processes disaggregated across numerous different companies, has become characteristic of globalised neolialism in manufacturing. This was not just a stark transformation of the economy, but partially a politically motivated attempt to rein in the power

of organised labour in the Global North, subcontracting much of
the raw material extraction, manufacturing, and assembly
to the developing world (particularly South-east Asia).[51] This
led to a destruction of highly unionised labour in countries
like the UK, US, and much of Europe. It also massively
expanded the economic might of China, with widespread geopolitical effects today. Like many processes, this is effectively
impossible to reverse, with most attempts to 'get jobs back' to
developed nations prevented by the raw economic advantages
of using the cheapest possible labour available. Though the
Trump era saw more barriers erected to certain forms of trade,
overall global manufacturing remains distributed.

A full treatment of the global energy system would also be
necessary to understand a large part of the history of the
world, certainly since the nineteenth century and even more
so since the emergence of oil as a crucial factor in enabling
expansive capitalist development.[52] While recent years are
seeing a sustained opposition to fossil fuel industrialists and
their domination of global energy infrastructures, they were
essentially victorious in pushing such opposition as forward
into the future as possible. This accomplishment has had significant political effects, and will have even more significant
environmental ones as we struggle to reduce carbon emissions
sufficiently to evade the very worst impacts of climate change.
Indeed, beyond the world of human-constructed infrastructures, we should consider platforms that are non-human in
nature, or at least which include us but precede us, such as the
various subsystems of the global environment. While not
human created, and hence not bearing any specific intention-
ality, the systems of the global biosphere, soil systems, water
systems, and weather systems support a particular mode of
human civilisation, or at least make it possible. The destabil-
isation of these systems is already creating immense problems
for human societies.[53] Therefore, any successful long-term
political project will of necessity include efforts to develop

solutions that adapt future paradigms of living to the new conditions which emerge, while mitigating carbon and other greenhouse gas emissions.

Surveillance, Serfs, and Post-capitalism

A claim that bears closer interrogation relates to whether platforms, and tech platforms in particular, are essentially a radically new form of power in the world, or whether they are more of an evolution of existing forms. Have platforms actually ended hegemony and replaced it with something else? Our answer has to be careful, as we certainly do not want to underestimate the novelty of the technology platforms, and the unique tendencies that they make possible. But much of the recent treatment of them has tended towards the hyperbolic and ahistorical. Platforms as such are certainly not new, and the influence of infrastructures on politics is long standing.

For legal scholar Shoshana Zuboff, 'surveillance capitalism' – the reliance of big tech on data as a source of revenue – constitutes a radical new evolution of capitalism itself.[54] It is certainly the case that tech platforms present a variety of novel features and have had a significant effect on global politics and world culture in the last decade, from the 'Arab Spring' revolutions to the emergence of neosocialism and neonationalist authoritarianism, from the collapse of editorial gatekeeping to innumerable innovative memetic cultural forms. Zuboff describes the new mode of power she thinks has emerged from tech platforms as 'instrumentarian': a comprehensive kind of behavioural modification through algorithmic technologies.[55] However, while, modern algorithms definitely allow for a more expansive range of behaviour modulating abilities, platforms have long manipulated human behaviour in diverse ways and through varied methods.

Ubiquitous data and its manipulation enable radically new ways of doing business, but the harms this has created seem like a continuation and expansion of existing ones, rather than being uniquely novel. For example, many have opined about the role of social media in manipulating political opinion in the years since 2016.[56] Yet the core issues remain ones that are resolutely traditional: a chronic lack of regulation, and too much money in politics. We agree that tech platforms enable disparities of economic resources to become more powerful than ever before in influencing politics, but this is a matter of quantitative and not qualitative change.

For a basically liberal thinker like Zuboff, it is the invasive surveillance side of the equation which is ultimately the source of harm to individuals and societies, rather than capitalism itself. Indeed, one of her central critiques is that behavioural prediction markets, grounded in extracted user data, are 'about us but not for us'[57] – implying that the issue is that this is a capitalism where we don't get to be consumers. This focus also tends to flatten several different modes of surveillance into one, which unhelpfully gathers together state surveillance of political dissidents and Facebook's tracking of user's consumer preferences. As Zuboff notes, one of the key issues she has with the activities of big tech is 'the degradation of the self-determining individual as the fulcrum of democratic life'.[58] We might well argue that the self-determining individual is largely a myth, found only in the pages of liberal political theory and never actually sighted in the wild. This liberal vision is common to much of the recent body of works criticising the negative political effects of big tech, framed, as they often are, either explicitly or implicitly around a prelapsarian past free of manipulative vice that has become corrupted by technology.[59] Yet, as we have argued, all platform infrastructures confer power upon those who own and control them, and are always influencing our behaviour in ways that are not directly amenable to democratic control.

Similarly, we remain unconvinced by arguments from more radical sources that big tech platforms have either replaced the capitalist system as such[60] or recreated a new kind of serfdom in digital form.[61] From our viewpoint in early 2022, capitalism seems to be operating much as it always has – its key constituent parts, such as private ownership of the means of production, extraction of surplus value, capital accumulation, wage labour, markets, and technological change are all present in today's economy of big tech. While the specific *mechanisms* of surplus-value extraction might have shifted, these do not affect the basic organisation of capitalism in itself. In terms of the latter argument, that the prevalence of big tech has shifted the basic power structures of global society towards ones more closely resembling medieval feudalism, we tend to see this assertion as obfuscating as much as enlightening. While the extraction of value in data gleaned from platform users' digital activities might bear some vague analogies to certain elements of serfdom, practically speaking these are very distinct. Such a viewpoint tends to ignore the manifold ways in which democratic control of platforms could be reasserted. Indeed, from increased regulation of content to anti-trust efforts to break apart digital monopolists, there are many ways in which democratic measures can enable control to be wrested back from platforms. The heightened rate of exploitation in which big tech engages is ultimately not a sign of a new political era so much as a testament to the (deliberate) weakness of late-era neoliberal governments at regulation.

What is distinctive, we would argue, about the rise of the big tech platforms is their ability to subsume many different pre-existing infrastructures – from media and advertising to finance and political organisation – within their singular logic. This is the distinctive property of ubiquitous computing and its control by private corporations. We can observe its impacts in the fact that for the last few years, the top ten companies in the world by market capitalisation are almost all tech firms. Indeed, they do now constitute something akin to the commanding heights of the global economy. We might consider this to be a new phase within capitalism, perhaps akin to the shift from Fordism to post-Fordism in the former industrial nations of the Global North.[62] However, it does not replace many of the basic operations of hegemony; rather, it refracts them, automates them, and proliferates them across the social world. In this sense, the basic hegemonic operations of antagonism, alliance, and passivity (or coercion, consent, and passive consent) are not so much replaced wholesale as reincarnated in a new guise.

At this stage it is worth considering what *could* break apart the basic political physics of hegemonic rule. After all, it is possible to imagine a world in which the automation of coercion was so generalised that the essential hegemonic equation of *coercion + consent* no longer requires the latter element. Perhaps a realm of pure automated force could break the basic logics of hegemony, enabling absolute coercion at the hands of sophisticated biosecurity algorithmic surveillance combined with militarised autonomous drone technologies. Though this kind of absolutely dystopian future is conceivable, and would surely break with hegemony as we know it, this would mark a very significant shift in global human political affairs.

Even the most tyrannical of totalitarian societies of the twentieth century required a degree of consensuality to assure their rule. For instance, in the politics of Nazi Germany, while coercion and violence were everywhere, studies of the era note persistent issues with efforts to retain the consent of the German population, and the specific ways in which Adolf Hitler's public image was manipulated and crafted to achieve it.[63] To take a more contemporary example, the authoritarian rule of China's Xi Jinping deploys many platform technologies to create an advanced system of control, with particular emphasis on surveillance and mass censorship combined with a programme of cultural domination, and even genocide. In perhaps the most sophisticated political deployment of digital technologies to suppress a population in the world today, the Chinese government also expends immense effort on attempts to retain at least the passive consent of majorities of the population at large.[64] As the above examples illustrate, outside of rather extreme dystopias of absolutely automated coercive violence, hegemony will continue to be the basic political logic enabling small groups to rule large, complex, societies.

Platforms as Class Infrastructures

How do platforms intersect with the theory of twenty-first-century hegemony we have put forward so far in this book? More specifically, how do they relate to coercion, consent, and material political interests? We have already written in some detail above about coercion and consent in the context of the role of technology platforms in changing (or not) the basic wiring of the economy and politics. But we still need to outline exactly how the interplay of coercion, consent, and the grey zone of passive consent work in terms of platforms in general. How do the mechanisms of influence, whether intentionally designed or unintentionally evolved, sit on this spectrum of political force?

We locate the vast majority of the effects of platforms – particularly those of big tech, finance, and global governance institutions – as being in the domain of passive consent. Though platforms sometimes operate in the worlds of active consent or active coercion, more often they occur as neutral-appearing backdrops to human activity, which situates them as agencies of passive consent. As we discussed earlier, platforms don't tend to absolutely force behaviour on their users, but rather shape it and modulate it along certain lines. They might do so through incentives, but often it is in an effort to construct a pathway of least resistance, where alternative approaches can be taken but where there will be costs for doing so. These costs can be literally monetary in nature, or less obvious energetic costs, or even psychological ones. This means that platforms work by configuring the pathway of least resistance: that which is followed by those of passive consent, who are not actively resisting the given system, but might not actively endorse it either. Here we could consider the example of all those who use Twitter but spend much of their time complaining of its pernicious influence on the quality and character of public discourse.[65] Critics such as these are fully aware of the negative effects of the platform but are unwilling to either break the habit of using it or incur the costs to their careers or social lives of disengaging from it. Though they complain, they are still passively consenting in their continued usage. From the standpoint of power, such complaints are essentially irrelevant, unless they result in groups actually taking action of some kind.

How do platforms embody particular class interests? Let us consider tech platforms and the class interests and political projects they represent. To do so means we must examine the conditions for their creation, which is ultimately the culture of Silicon Valley. The clustering of scientific expertise, technical nous, entrepreneurial flair and investment capital that would build Silicon Valley was already well under way by the late 1960s, and a distinctive culture was already emerging among those who were building it.[66] This culture had several sources. The influence of the counterculture upon it is well documented,[67] and a strand of American tech culture has always exhibited a commitment to utopian values that were at the same time egalitarian, libertarian, and collectivist, as well as a self-conscious identification with the politics of the counterculture and the New Left.[68] Meanwhile, a very specific internal culture had been associated with the computer-technology community since its early days at the MIT computer labs, characterised by a specific combination of libertarian individualism, radical empiricism, egalitarian belief in the value of free and open information, and commitment to the development of computing for its own sake – a complex of priorities and assumptions that journalist Steven Levy dubbed the 'hacker ethic'.[69] Obviously, this resonated in some ways with countercultural utopianism. Combined with these two cultural tendencies, we also find a right-libertarian politic that in many respects is easily integrated into the neoliberalism of the Austrian and Chicago schools. At its most extreme, such libertarianism might manifest itself in sympathy for the pseudophilosophy of Ayn Rand.[70] Paulina Borsook's landmark study of 'technolibertarianism', *Cyberselfish*, offers various anthropological explanations for the popularity of 'anarcho-capitalist' ideas in Silicon Valley, citing, for example, the tendency of coders to work alone for long periods, oblivious to the social and material relations that make that work possible.[71]

This is precisely the constituency identified by sociologists Luc Boltanski and Eve Chiapello as having to be recruited back into capitalist service following the cultural revolution of the 1960s. They explore the ways in which post-Fordist corporations and management theorists adopted an organisational culture extolling the virtues of networked collaboration, innovative creativity and decentralised decision-making, seemingly borrowing its rhetoric from the countercultural critique of bureaucratic capitalism in the 1960s.[72] Boltanski and Chiapello make a convincing case that a significant proportion of young graduates – heavily influenced by the romantic, bohemian critique of capitalism associated with the counterculture and the politics of 1968 – genuinely could not be persuaded to participate in the crucial business of managing capitalism, as long as its institutional culture retained the bureaucratic and conformist cast that typified the great corporations of the post-war era. Instead, they argue, capitalism had to adapt its practices to offer them more flexibility, more personal freedom, a sense of individuality and a degree of expressive agency: as employees, as potential managers and as consumers.

What we would add to this analysis is the observation that this is also the social constituency to which the tech industry has historically oriented most of its products and services, especially high-end innovations. Consider, for example, that Facebook's first user base was elite Harvard students and graduates, and that the first suites of smartphone apps were based on the functionality of devices like the Palm Pilot and the Filofax, typically only used by high-earning professionals working in information-rich, highly networked environments. Boltanski and Chiapello already showed in the late 1990s that the ideal member of this social constituency was the 'networker': someone capable of various types of collaborative and communicative work on many scales, but ruthless in monitoring the efficiency and productivity of every relationship in which they engaged.[73] Most of these key technologies have developed with the almost explicit aim of enabling (or even obliging) the user to become the ideal networker. As such, they offer this key constituency significant compensations for their participation in a social system led by the tech industry and the finance sector, by offering them fantastic enhancements in their communicative and productive possibilities. At the same time, they work to recruit this layer of workers/consumers into the culture that the tech and finance coalition produces (and desires to produce), actively working to bring the behaviour, and hence the subjectivity, of those workers/consumers in line with the norms of that culture. The products of big tech tend to exemplify the values and interests of their creators, in turn building habits and promoting world-views that closely resemble their own.

In this way, the values of the elites involved in directing investment, design, and marketing of big tech products and services become embodied in the materiality of those systems, in all the different features that we analysed earlier in this chapter. It is important to note here that platforms do not therefore have a necessary character – it was not inevitable that big tech would take on its present shape. Indeed, alternative visions of both capitalist and socialist social computing were trialled and could have been realised under the correct broader socio-political conditions.[74] But given the particular set of elite interests at work among big tech's founders and leading managers, they will tend to incorporate systems that represent and enhance those interests in the technologies they build, both as intentional design choice and as unintentional cultural mimesis. Platforms thus act both to embed themselves (through generative entrenchment) and to realise the interests of their owners, managers, and elite workers. In so doing, they act in some respects like educational systems – as manufacturing bases for human subjectivity, helping shape and sculpt the political horizons of their users.

The Strange, Long Death of Neoliberalism

What, then, can we say about our present moment, this time of the ending of neoliberalism and the emergence of hegemonic crisis across the world? The long, slow, doom of neoliberalism is a process which is uneven and spasmodic; it is a state of decay more than a sudden, ruptural ending. In the terms we have developed in this chapter, this is the emergence of a hegemonic crisis, but one in which many, if not all, of the key platforms of neoliberalism remain more or less intact. We can consider the present crisis as beginning with the 2008–9 financial and fiscal debt crises, then laying somewhat dormant until the ruptures of 2016 with Brexit, the election of Donald

Trump, and the emergence of serious neosocialism throughout much of the Global North, before reaching a culmination
with 2020–21 and the COVID-19 pandemic. The two book-
ends of this emergence of the crisis are marked by massive
state spending on a scale never seen outside of wartime.
Particularly from 2016 onward, there have been increasingly
numerous claims that neoliberalism is either over, or in the
process of ending. But what is the nature of this ending?

There has been a collapse in the authority of neoliberalism
at the level of media narrative, political discourse, and popular consent (though it is important to note that neoliberalism
never saw broad positive support but merely had passive
acceptance).[75] Increasingly, media discourse has moved
beyond the terms established by peak neoliberalism, along
with politicians and other key leaders who no longer call
upon its frameworks to justify and legitimate policy and
ideology. This collapse is not matched by the state of play in
the domain of platforms – whether within finance, energy,
logistics or technology. Here we find that most of the characteristic infrastructures of neoliberalism remain basically
unbroken. Further, the legacy platforms that neoliberalism
leaves behind in its wake shape its very collapse, and indeed
its contention and replacement. It is as if we contend the suc-
cession to neoliberalism within its own hollowed-out body, a
hegemonic battle among its gleaming bones and rotting
organs.

Never was this more apparent than in the COVID-19 pandemic, where within the UK and Europe at least, massive state
responses, often held up as demonstrating the absolute end of
neoliberalism, were executed through absolutely neoliberal
means. In the UK, this meant large-scale state spending on
outsourced initiatives, with the state's largesse filtered through
the private sector. This led to many embarrassing scandals as
the government relied upon companies established by political
cronies.[76] Moreover, it was the infrastructures of big tech itself

that enabled much of the policy approaches used in 2020–21, and that enabled much of the economy and society to continue even under conditions of lockdown. Without the ability to move most information-based labour online, it is doubtful that Western states would have embraced lockdown with as much alacrity as they did. Equally, big tech offered a variety of new strategies to surveil populations and monitor the prevalence of the disease.[77] This crisis portends the end of neoliberalism, but it is a strange end – one that leaves most of its long-lasting infrastructures in place.

While public opinion, common sense, and even political discourse can shift relatively swiftly, it is much more difficult to transform immense, complex and expensive platform infrastructures. Infrastructures remain, both internal to states and across them, that will work to help maintain neoliberal social relations, even in the retreat of the active projects that sustain it. This strange, long death of neoliberalism inflects our present moment strategically, because any attempt to supplant it obligates some engagement with the fact that much of the material infrastructure it developed and helped to shape remains enormously socially and politically powerful. If we are in a hegemonic crisis (and we are), then it is a crisis that will partly be conditioned by these legacy platforms.

The hegemonic crisis of neoliberalism is by this juncture actually more like a set of nested crises: a political crisis of consent and legitimation for neoliberalism itself, combined with a global health crisis in the shape of the pandemic, nested within a geopolitical crisis (the emergence of multipolarity and particularly China as a competitor global hegemon) and set against a broader backdrop of the global environmental crisis of anthropogenic climate change. These crises are interlinked in various interesting ways, and they form the backdrop for all politics today. The common senses of the past decades have been smashed apart, and new political forces have sprung up to contend for power in their wake. The dynamics of hegemonic crisis tend to push existing systems into instability, and the battle for a new hegemony consists of two closely related aspects: first, to amass significant power through alliances, resources, and institutional positions; and second, to do so in service of a political project which is able to stabilise enough elements of the political system (and all the subsystems that support it) to deliver on enough of the interests of the population, particularly those elements directly aligned with the leading forces. Such a stabilisation relies not just on raw power or popularity, but also on an ability to find a particular mixture of policies necessary to work with the conditions of the crisis and enable a degree of stability.

This means that the politics of hegemonic crisis are always about more than just politics, and that they require the refinement of policies to allow for experimentation and the development of some kind of 'solution' to the crisis itself – a new point of relative stability. This is what neoliberalism was able to at least somewhat successfully do in the 1980s, outcompeting the new social movements and the left within the capitalist world. Today, this means neosocialism, illiberal authoritarian nationalism, and remnant political centrism are all competing to find fixes for the concatenated crises we face. In the next chapter we will begin to think about how the left in particular can position itself to win this crisis.

PART III:

THE FUTURE WAR
OF POSITION

6

STRANGE TIMES

Since 2008, the neoliberal world has been subject to an interlocking and mutually intensifying set of nested crises.[1] Though
for a time it seemed as if some of these could be defused (such
as the great financial crisis), by now it is clear that we are
watching a slow-motion demolition, with a series of explosive
charges chaining off from one another to bring the great
edifice down. The most serious and significant of these is the
ecological crisis, which is why any strategic programme to
address any of them must tackle this one head on. Increasingly,
this shapes all other sets of social relations and interactions,
and in particular it shapes the increasingly defensive posture
taken by sections of capital that depend on fossil fuel extraction, and of other social groups allied with them.

The specific crisis to which we have given most attention in
these pages is the catastrophic loss of legitimacy suffered by the
technocratic political class since the 2008 financial crisis, and
the general difficulty of maintaining even minimally passive
consent for neoliberalism while pre-2008 consumption levels
remain unattainable for many workers. At the same time, the
long-term consequences of neoliberalism itself have been an
entirely predictable set of dislocations of labour markets, of
urban and rural environments and of social networks on multiple scales, all of which have given rise to an exponential increase
in loneliness, mental illness and various symptoms of social dys-
function.[2] Like all great systems, hegemonic neoliberalism sewed
the seeds of its own destruction, whose fruits it must now reap.

What clearly is *not* in crisis is the power of platform capitalism, or the guiding hand of financial capital. Unsurprisingly,

as retail outlets closed the world over during the COVID-19 pandemic, profits for Amazon soared, and its everyday usage has become normalised for even larger proportions of entire populations.[3] This isn't just a question of historically unprecedented levels of capital accumulation, or of ever-growing market share by one particularly successful online retailer. Amazon's global ordering, warehousing, retail and delivery systems are in many cases becoming the very infrastructure of everyday commerce. While labour theorists rightly point to the strategic potential of workers directly engaged in Amazon's logistical operations,[4] to date Amazon has had little trouble resisting large-scale efforts towards the unionisation of its workforce.[5] At the same time, the ubiquitous use of video-conferencing applications to facilitate all aspects of institutional and social life during the pandemic has marked a new watershed in the normalisation of platform sociality, while hugely benefitting the shareholders of the relevant corporations.[6] The price of Bitcoin, meanwhile, though subject to the same levels of extreme volatility that have characterised its entire history to date, has continued to defy all predictions of an irreversible long-term collapse. Perhaps by the time this book is published, this will finally have occurred; but even if it does, the point has been made. The tech sector now retains and asserts the right to impinge upon even the historically most sacred monopoly of the banks: the ability to create money. We can be confident that the administration of Joe Biden will continue to gesture towards the regulation of cryptocurrency, given the enduring ties between Biden and the established credit industry. However, it is doubtful such measures will have much impact. Indeed, the convergence of Wall Street and big tech will likely continue into the post-neoliberal era.

Post-neoliberalism

There are no market-centric solutions to a pandemic. Nor can such an approach arrest the long-term decline of neoliberal legitimacy, as has been clear since the beginning of the COVID-19 crisis. After all, neoliberal norms have been deeply embedded within key institutions at every scale over a period of decades, and the technocratic political class remains utterly committed to them, despite its ever-waning authority. This set of conditions gives rise to endless confusion over the question of whether neoliberalism is 'over'. Our answer is that given the entrenchment of neoliberalism in a range of sectors and institutions, it will be decades before it is entirely 'over'. Still, it is also clearly in retreat, especially at the level of broad ideological legitimacy.

It should be obvious why, in 2022, we can observe that neoliberal norms do not enjoy the legitimacy that they once did. The US president is, at the time of writing, trying to get a bill through Congress that would actively enhance the power of organised labour in the United States.[7] The UK government has engaged in unprecedented levels of peacetime borrowing and spending to keep the economic show on the road, while hundreds of thousands of workers have been furloughed. The vast bulk of that expenditure has been funnelled directly into the balances of private corporations with personal links to government ministers,[8] rather than into the creation of publicly owned and democratically accountable infrastructure. Even figures such as French president Emmanuel Macron have now declared some kind of decisive break with neoliberal orthodoxy to be necessary and unavoidable.[9]

On the political right, at least in the Atlantic Anglosphere, the emergent form of politics is a kind of clientelist authoritarian nationalism. Governments like those of Donald Trump and Boris Johnson have appealed more or less explicitly to specific sections of the electorate, promising special treatment for them and pain for their perceived enemies, with almost no real attempt made to cohere these promises into an overarching ideological narrative. Johnson, for example, has promised direct investment in former industrial regions that have switched their electoral allegiance from Labour to the Conservatives, while pointedly failing to promise the same to those who haven't.[10] Arguably this is just a less extreme form of precisely the political logic informing the projects of figures such as Vladimir Putin in Russia, Narendra Modi in India, Jair Bolsonaro in Brazil, Viktor Orbán in Hungary, and Andrzej Duda in Poland. In all cases some appeal is made to a notion of national identity and national sovereignty, but the consistency and coherency of these appeals is debatable. What is clear is that this is a different form of capitalist authoritarianism to that which typified the New Right in the 1970s and '80s, even while there are points of overlap and family resemblance. While reactionary in character, it does not usually seek to combine economic liberalisation with Victorian social values (as did Margaret Thatcher and Ronald Reagan). Instead, it is much more focussed on the border, cultural exclusivity, outright racism (of a much more flagrant type), and quasi-autarkic economic rhetoric. We might consider it either 'neoliberalism in one country', or, perhaps better, an illiberal, reactionary Keynesian software running on the hardware of the post-neoliberal state.

In this context, the legatees of the Third Way have tried desperately to hold back the tide of historical change, seeking to restore the reputation of the neoliberal political class at least as competent managers of contemporary capitalism. At the time of writing, this has played out very differently in the US and the UK. In the former, the Democratic establishment under Biden, having defeated the challenge from the left posed by Bernie Sanders, has made significant concessions to progressive constituencies and demands, putting forward the most ambitious reform programme since the 1960s. Indeed, it is the first since that time that might, if enacted, genuinely empower workers at the expense of employers (however slightly).[11] Given that at the time of writing, there seems little to no prospect of this measure passing under the current administration, this might be considered an irrelevance; but to have come as close as they have, and to have exposed the thinness of the political base upon which objections to reforms now rests, must itself count as a significant political advance, and has at least conferred new levels of public legitimacy on left-wing demands. In the UK, by contrast, the Labour leadership that replaced Jeremy Corbyn's has engaged in an entirely counterproductive assault on his legacy and reputation, flagrantly disregarding the unifying and left-wing platform on which Keir Starmer was elected leader. Starmer and his allies have been engaged in a project to re-establish full bureaucratic control of the Labour Party's institutions and elected offices, deliberately alienating and demoralising the left-wing majority of its members, without any apparent regard for Labour's reputation with the wider electorate. The consequences have been predictably disastrous for the party's poll ratings and electoral performance, despite the extraordinary sycophancy that most of the media class has demonstrated towards Starmer for the past year and a half. The simplest conclusion to draw is that, in England and Wales at least, the residual neoliberal political class would rather cling to its remaining institutional privileges than allow the organised left to make an effective political challenge to Johnson. But what is most striking, from a wider historical perspective, is how unpopular this seems to be making them with the wider public. This is further evidence that the loss of hegemonic legitimacy suffered by the professional political class between 2008 and 2015 cannot be recovered without a significant reversal of the neoliberal direction of travel, such as Biden has already clearly signalled in the US. In Scotland, of course, no government which does not at least claim commitment to such a reversal is capable of commanding any legitimacy.

Perhaps more importantly, the re-emergence of collective resistance on the part of some of the most oppressed subaltern groups has also marked a significant break with a long period of technocratic neoliberal hegemony. The Black Lives Matter (BLM) movement was not born in 2020, but it achieved a new level of public visibility in the summer of that year, in the US and around the world, with obvious cultural effects. By the following year, even England's national football team felt moved to make gestures of explicit allegiance to this movement, to the disgust of conservative commentators.[12] The conjunctural significance of BLM cannot be overstated. On both sides of the Atlantic, nothing indexed the hegemony of neoliberalism more than the abeyance of black radicalism after 1992, and the widespread acquiescence to mass incarceration of young black men. Throughout this period, much of black commercial popular culture was hegemonised by somewhat neoliberal themes of competitive acquisitiveness and anomic individualism.[13] This era of political quietism went alongside the rise of meritocratic multiculturalism, ultimately culminating in the spectacle of the Obama presidency: a black president who did very little for black people, but everything for his Wall Street backers; the ultimate destination of the Third Way. As such, the re-emergence of universalist, collectivist, militant, black-led anti-racism is a development of extraordinary significance,[14] and one which portends the scale of the crisis facing neoliberalism at this time.

On a global scale, the pandemic period of 2020–2 will also be remembered as marking a new phase in the emergence of China as a world power with a distinctive approach to the resolution of a range of social problems. The pandemic began there, but it was also, apparently, brought under control in China long before it was in Europe, the Americas or Australia.[15] This isn't the least bit surprising. China's system of state-directed developmental capitalism had the institutional capacity to cope with an emergency on this scale in ways that Western states – hollowed out by decades of outsourcing, underfunding and democratic decline – struggled to imitate. This is not to make any judgement on the desirability or ethicality of China's one-party authoritarianism; it is merely to observe that if the Chinese Communist Party, along with the platform capitalists of Silicon Valley and the planetary financial engineers of Wall Street, was one of the true winners of the twentieth century, then its position as such has only been confirmed by the pandemic. It has been during this time that Xi has sought significant extension of his powers. At home this has meant a massive crackdown on the power of China's own tech oligarchs, such as Jack Ma of Alibaba, as well as the intensification of a cultural conservatism (against such classic moral-panic targets as video games and 'effeminate' men) combined with a continuation of the genocide of the Uyghur people in its westernmost areas. Abroad, this has involved an explosion of aggressive 'wolf warrior' diplomacy,[16] a full subsumption of Hong Kong under the laws of the mainland, and bellicose rhetoric directed at such familiar objects of ire as Taiwan.

Most recently in February 2022 we have also seen another immense geopolitical rupture, with the Russian invasion of Ukraine. This large-scale military action combined with threats to NATO countries of nuclear war has already led to a significant response in the form of the EU states and America arming Ukraine, as well as an extensive economic and financial sanctions programme. Unlike China, Russia has made little effort to project a cultural or technical hegemony beyond its fostering of dependence on their gas reserves. But the very emergence of Russia into outright conflict attests to a more general weakening of not just the hegemony of the political class, but also the Atlanticist world order that accompanied the end of the Cold War in the early 1990s.

Whether geopolitical dislocations of this nature will have any effect upon political culture and expectations in the West is an open question. Certainly, popular demands and the force of circumstances have already pushed the Biden administration towards a dirigiste programme of government-led recovery that has no real precedent since the 1960s. The combination of massive geopolitical risk, inflation and cost of living crises, energy crises, a global hegemonic crisis of the political elites, and the remaining effects of the pandemic create a uniquely febrile global conjuncture.

The Weakness of the Left

Despite the long-term abatement of neoliberal hegemony, the organised left remains weak and far from power in most of the world. Neither the Corbyn nor the Sanders movements were able to achieve their ultimate objectives of winning elections and forming governments, while the organisational gains of each were limited and remain somewhat tenuous. A full analysis of either of these situations would take a book in itself,[17] but we can make some general remarks about the limits that each encountered. On the one hand, each faced determined opposition from those sections of the professional political class that are most entrenched in the institutions of the Democratic and Labour Parties respectively: opposition that was able to thwart their ultimate aims, if not to launch a distinctive alternative project. On the other hand, neither was able to extend its coalition to include key sections of the electorate that have been successfully hegemonised by that centrist political class since the 1990s. Arguably, in both cases, a key problem was the relative weakness of the left among constituencies with particular investments in the limited forms of cosmopolitanism that technocratic neoliberalism had normalised: middle-class Remain voters in the UK,[18] and older

Southern black voters in the US,[19] still loyal to the Obama administration and its legatee Joe Biden.

However, the overall consequences of these defeats have been quite different in the two countries. In the UK, defeat for the radical left came at an actual general election, which featured a dramatic loss of support both from cosmopolitan liberals and from working-class Leave voters. While many myths and misunderstandings have been circulated about the UK's 2019 election result, it is true neither that the election witnessed a dramatic transfer of support from Labour to Conservative among working-class voters, nor that the Conservatives even won more votes than Labour among working-age citizens. What *did* happen is that the twenty-year accumulation of support for the Tories among the ever-growing population of property-owning retirees in post-industrial constituencies finally passed a tipping point, allowing the Conservatives to win a landslide within the UK's absurd, winner-takes-all electoral system.[20] Having subsequently lost control of the Labour leadership, and having thrown away the chance to institute significant democratic reforms to the party while Corbyn was in charge, the left finds itself on the defensive and in retreat.

In the US, by contrast, Biden's victory in the Democratic presidential primary saw Sanders and elements of his campaign incorporated into the Democratic campaign for the White House, producing precisely the kind of broad-based social coalition that Labour had been unable to sustain, while the influence of the Sanders movement on Biden's governing programme has been striking. This is partly because of Sanders's far-greater success, compared to Corbyn, in popularising his agenda with the general public (especially the young) between 2015 and 2019;[21] it is also partly because centrist control of the Democratic Party machine was never ultimately threatened by the rising left, outside of specific localities, and so felt no need to engage in a revanchist counter-attack once the immediate threat of a Sanders presidential candidacy had passed. Whatever the local circumstances may have been, the partial success of the Sanders campaign in shifting the balance of American political forces is significant. At the time of writing, any judgements as to its significance must be cautious and provisional: Republicans and neoliberal Democrats in the legislature could yet derail Biden's entire programme, and indeed as of February 2022 the Senate appears to be doing exactly this. Nonetheless, moving from the position in which the organised left found itself in 2016 (i.e., complete political irrelevance), to the point of having a serving president actively seeking to pass pro-union legislation, looks like the most significant phase of political success for the American left since the mid 1970s. This demonstrates that while the left remains in a politically and socially weak position, by any historic standard, its position of weakness is not fixed or irreversible.

If this seems like a rather trite observation it is one that cannot be stated enough times and that many on the left forget too easily. The key problem for progressive and counter--hegemonic forces is always that of how to make meaningful political gains from a starting position of relative weakness. The Corbyn project's defeat was partly due to a configuration of opposing forces that was simply more powerful, and thus less surmountable, than its equivalent obstacles in the US; the right-wing domination of the media, in particular, is even more complete in the UK. But significant gains could have been made had Corbyn and his key advisors not behaved consistently as if the position that they were working from was one of far-greater strength than it was. In retrospect, Corbyn's rejection of all offers of co-operation from other opposition parties in April 2017 looks like a catastrophic error: there was never any way that the UK electoral system was going to deliver Labour a working parliamentary majority, so such offhand rejection of co-operation with other parties was nonsensical and counterproductive. At the same time, the single greatest failure of Corbynism – the absence of any significant reform to Labour's internal democratic procedures – should also be understood as a consequence of the failure to read the balance of forces and to appreciate the scope of those ranged against the left.

This claim may sound counter-intuitive. After all, the typical explanation given for Corbyn's failure to implement his programme is that he and his closest allies were frightened of provoking a split within the Parliamentary Labour Party were they to press home such reforms. Doesn't this demonstrate that they were too conscious of their weakness, rather than oblivious to it? On the contrary, it revealed a more fundamental misunderstanding of the situation: the mistaken belief that there was some way to convert the right-wing of the Labour Party from enemies into allies of Corbynism, or perhaps a commitment to the idea of the 'Labour Party' over and above its specific political contents. Their avoidance of a fight with the right only gave the latter more time to regroup and attack. Believing, mistakenly, that they might be only a few months away from government, and assuming that the Labour Party already constituted a broadly anti-neoliberal coalition, Corbyn and his allies failed to build such a coalition beyond the Labour Party, while avoiding a 'divisive' but winnable conflict with their most immediate and implacable enemies within it.

Of course, the gains of Corbynism cannot be simply dismissed. Despite the depressing political situation at the time of writing, the organised left in much of the UK is larger, more visible to itself and others, more intellectually dynamic and socially diverse, and demographically younger than at any time since the collapse of the late 1980s. In both the US and the UK, the progressive movement has made the most significant advances where it has consisted of a complex ecology of complementary forces and projects, rather than a singular organisation seeking to abrogate all political and ideological functions to itself. In the UK, the best example has probably been the emergence and growth of a mutually amplifying ecology of left media and political education projects, to include Novara Media, *Tribune* magazine, *New Socialist*, the journalism of Owen Jones, The World Transformed festival and its national network of local events, as well as longer-established outlets such as *Red Pepper* magazine. In the US, a significant upswing in labour militancy in some sectors has played a key role in shifting the balance of forces,[22] while the diverse range of organisations and media projects that have emerged from, or been boosted by and allied with, the Sanders movement – from the Sunrise Movement and the Democratic Socialists of America to *Jacobin* magazine and a host of popular podcasts – have enabled pressure to be brought to bear across a range of sites, from mainstream electoral politics to the cultural fringe. In both cases a striking feature has been the way that previously highly segregated strands of left-wing politics and activism have converged around a relatively coherent programme, combining the pursuit of significant social reforms via electoral politics with a commitment to community organising, consciousness raising, and trade union organising.[23]

Emergent Dynamics

The key points of social and political antagonism that have emerged in these contexts have been familiar for much of the past century or so. The fundamental inequalities produced by capitalism continue to be a key source of grievance, while the net beneficiaries of capital accumulation (including millions of retirees who do not formally belong to the ruling class, but whose incomes are dependent upon stock market prices and housing asset values) push back against most efforts to

mitigate them permanently. The long struggle against the legacies of colonialism carries on, intersecting with class struggles
in increasingly visible ways as it becomes ever more apparent
that the gains of the civil rights era have accrued largely to a
small black professional class.[24] The limits of meritocratic
liberal feminism are also becoming clearer all the time, as
women outside the professional classes struggle to derive
many benefits from the opportunities that it has theoretically
extended to them. Simultaneously, anti-feminism, hostility to
anti-racism and general social conservatism – the key impe-
tuses of reactionary politics since the 1960s – have become
powerful poles of attraction for various groups.

Above all looms the threat of climate disaster. Indeed, if
any issue has the potential finally to shake the middle-class
beneficiaries of cosmopolitan neoliberalism out of their com-
placency, then this is it. But by the same token, reactionary
forces – most of all those allied to carbon-intensive industry,
landownership and property development – will probably
seek to mobilise these resentments against any threat to their
wealth and power. We can expect determined efforts by them
and their allies to convince poor workers that any serious
attempts to reduce or eliminate the causes of climate change
are against their immediate interests; and, more importantly,
to engineer political opportunity structures so as to make
this, at least in the short-to-medium term, effectively true.
One reason for a renewed interest in industrial policy among
sections of the reactionary right[25] is surely the desire to
re-align the short-term economic interests of low-paid workers with those of carbon capital and property developers.

At the global scale this crisis continues through increasingly
volatile geopolitics, where new lines of conflict are emerging,
from the rise of China and Putin's new incursions into Eastern
Europe, to broader increasing national authoritarianism.
Simultaneously, much of the world faces significant pressures
from demographic shifts; in particular, the developed world

and China are afflicted by rapidly ageing populations. All the while, the technologies of big tech serve to undermine the traditional media logics that enabled information to be easily corralled towards serving the interests of traditional professional elites. In combination, the loss of authority of hegemonic neoliberalism, the expansion of geopolitical tensions, the rising demographic crisis and climate crisis will constitute the context in which the future battles for global hegemony will be fought.

Pessimism and Optimism

There is no more familiar quotation from Antonio Gramsci, at least in the English-speaking world, than his cherished slogan 'pessimism of the intellect, optimism of the will', which in fact he borrowed from the French writer Romain Rolland.[26] The reason the phrase is so often cited, in many languages, is that it clearly expresses an intellectual and affective disposition which, indeed, every radical must cultivate at times. However, we would suggest that its importance goes beyond a useful piece of advice on managing one's own emotional state, a register in which the phrase has almost become an unfortunate cliché. Arguably, this formula expresses something crucial about the strategic orientation required to prosecute a progressive political project with any success; or perhaps it would be better to say that it describes the affective disposition that is always necessary in order to be able to *strategise*, individually or collectively. 'Pessimism of the intellect' implies an entirely realistic and honest assessment of the state of the balance of forces in any given historical situation, and a determination to avoid the error of overestimating the strength of one's own side. We have already given the experience of Corbynism as one example of such an error in practice. We could also point to the generations of revolutionaries throughout the past century who have made the strategic mistake of conducting themselves as if a full-scale social and political revolution were much more likely in the near future than it clearly was: perhaps the far-left paramilitary radicalism of the early 1970s (the Weather Underground, the Red Army Faction, the Red Brigades, etc.) would be the most perfect example. But this phenomenon still manifests itself today in the tendency of many leftists to analyse contemporary historical situations using tools and terms of reference derived solely from the key moments of immediately pre-revolutionary European history (Russia in early 1917, Germany in 1918–19, etc.). In a country where no more than 25 percent of the population adheres to anything like a socialist ideology, and where trade union militancy has not approached revolutionary levels within living memory, nothing is more absurd than the spectacle of socialists declaring with solemn sincerity that they will never compromise with liberals. This is precisely the behaviour of those who lack the pessimism of reason, proceeding as it does from a refusal to face the reality of the balance of forces.

Yet, at the same time, such simplistic sectarianism also proceeds from an absence of optimism of the will. The only reason to refuse to co-operate with potential political allies, however short term the potential alliance, is that there is no chance whatsoever of altering the political trajectory of those allies, even minutely, in the direction of one's own objectives. If there is any such possibility, then there is no reason not to try. The refusal to do so – a decision to cling instead to a position of self-consciously ineffectual political purity – is a manifestation of precisely that fetishistic attachment to weakness that the German philosopher Friedrich Nietzsche famously called 'ressentiment'. Ressentiment (literally: resentment) is the disposition of those who allow themselves to behave as if their current position of weakness were unalterable or unimprovable in any way.

This is what 'pessimism of the intellect, optimism of the will' really involves: a full and rigorous acceptance that the current balance of forces puts us in a relatively weak position, and a refusal to behave as if that position of weakness were irreversible. We might describe this as an attitude of radical realism: radical because it looks always to the nearest available 'root system' to intervene in, the nearest set of social relations and institutions that has a clear determining effect on other sets thereof; radically realistic because it never seeks to make such interventions all at once, but generally identifies a multi-stage strategy (with room for the emergence of new strategies along the way). Unlike certain strands of eschatological Marxism, hegemonic politics doesn't seek a messianic, total redemption of the world in a single gesture. Instead, it looks to the machinic nature of power, the fact that systems can be engaged with through the parts which constitute them.

Why is this distinct from mere reformism, which ultimately seeks only to mitigate the social effects of capitalism? Because its objective is always to use a given stage of hegemonic power as the ground from which to conduct the next level of a hegemonic project: to use reforms to make more reforms possible, and to keep moving the balance of forces in favour of progressive classes and social groups. To effect hegemony from below is not simply a means to ameliorate the worst excesses of capitalism, but rather is a matter of constructing a counter-power in stages, with no final stopping point. Such a process of assembling power piece by piece is necessarily one which is highly context specific – the exact pieces, the order of accumulation, the forces that need to be allied with, the resources to be drawn upon, and so on, will be highly specific to a given place and time. Next we turn to the strategies we will need for the crises we face.

7

STRATEGIES FOR FUTURE WARS

As we have shown, hegemony is always a matter of smaller groups assembling the resources necessary to rule or lead larger groups. This holds true both for ongoing relations of hegemony and for all projects of counter-hegemony. It is more challenging to counter existing hegemonic relations than it is to maintain them, because the process of their maintenance tends to produce layers of embedded power and influence, crystallising and institutionalising the very power relations which produce them. As such, any counter-hegemonic strategy must seek to assemble the largest set of forces that it possibly can. As the examples in the preceding chapters have illustrated, hegemony is a matter of creating as large as possible an aggregation of interests – a social bloc, in other words – and orienting them towards appropriate horizons of realisability. At a political level, this means the creation of coalitions – be they within, between or across institutions such as political parties, trade unions, community organisations, media projects, and particular sectors of the economy. At the same time, as Ernesto Laclau and Chantal Mouffe have reminded us many times,[1] hegemonic politics cannot function without an antagonistic dimension: a 'dichotomic frontier' that must be drawn between the coalition – however broad – and its political antagonists. Friends require enemies, at a political level. Neither of these dimensions can be ignored: there can be no successful politics that fails either to define enemies, or to win as many friends as it plausibly can.

Of course, as we have stressed in our discussions of passive consent, on any given terrain many political agents will be neither actively friendly nor hostile to any given political project; in turn, in many situations the maintenance of certain constituencies in that position of passivity will be a crucial component of hegemonic strategy. For example, efforts to persuade Conservative-inclined voters simply not to bother voting against the Labour Party was a key function of New Labour strategy in the UK from 1995 to 2010, while the demobilisation of working-class, progressive and black Democrats, demoralised by the politics of Hillary Clinton, was a necessary precondition for Donald Trump's victory in 2016.

The necessity of political coalition building is nowhere more starkly illustrated than in the UK, where the Conservative Party and its supporters enjoy such a dominant position within both electoral politics and key media institutions that the party has been in government for 80 of the past 120 years (discounting the periods of national government during the two world wars, in which they also participated). It is now very clear that the period during which the UK had an effective two-party system – 1945–79 – was exceptional, and entirely coterminous with the history of British Fordism. And yet, even under Corbyn, Labour has continued to behave as if it were fighting an electoral battle with the Tories on equal terms.

The Green New Deal

What, under present circumstances, might count as an appropriate horizon of realisability? And what might be the constituent elements of a counter-hegemonic coalition that could be oriented in its direction? Ultimately, any attempt to answer such questions can only amount to a 'best guess'; but this by no means absolves us of the responsibility to devote as much attention to them as we possibly can, and to make the very best assessments that we are able to. With these provisos in mind, we would argue that the general set of proposed reforms and political ambitions that are named by various commentators the 'Green New Deal'² constitutes an ambitious but achievable horizon on which to focus. Indeed, given the stakes of the climate emergency, there seems little point in aiming at any less ambitious target. The Green New Deal would amount to a package of reforms enacted at a national or regional supranational level, leading to the wholesale decarbonisation of the productive economy as well as a significant redistribution of resources and work so as to reduce social inequality and maximise the social capacity for useful and creative labour. There is no question that its implementation would meet with fierce resistance from a coalition of forces opposed in part to any significant measures to reduce carbon emissions, and, more significantly, to any large-scale shift in power from capital to labour or from corporations to citizens.

The question, then, is: what kind of counter-coalition might the left be capable of assembling, and on what terms, against such opposition? Who are the constituencies that the left might mobilise? Perhaps more importantly – if we are to remain at a level of abstraction that makes these observations useful in different national local contexts – what are the factors that determine how well specific constituencies might or might not be mobilised?

Unsurprisingly, given our arguments so far, the first issue is that of common interests: the basis upon which any coalition of social forces must be formed. One of the great virtues of the Green New Deal programme is that it seeks to articulate the long-term interest of the vast majority of humans in drastically reducing carbon emissions with a range of other interests, realisable at different temporal scales and beginning with the most mundane and short-term interests of workers in finding stable, predictable and remunerative employment. To a certain extent this means that the classic conflict of interest between capital and labour is likely to inform patterns of sympathy and antagonism to the project. On the other hand, there will be sectors of capital that have more to gain than to lose – at least in the medium term – from the implementation of a Green New Deal. As such, it will be politically crucial to try to identify those fractions of capital and to drive hard wedges between them and those sections of their class who have more to lose than to gain. Obviously this means the fossil fuel sector will be isolated completely, whereas sectors exclusively devoted to the development and deployment of renewable energy will be entirely incorporated; however, careful analysis will be required to determine, for example, which sections of the tech sector can be brought into a pro–Green New Deal social bloc, and which cannot.

Within the subaltern social classes (i.e., all except the capitalist class proper, and the most elite sections of the professional political class), most groups will have some obvious interest in at least certain aspects of the Green New Deal's programme. But the extent, obviousness and intensity with which this interest will be immediately apparent will vary hugely between social and demographic groups and economic sectors. Issues to consider here will include, of course, the relative extent to which various groups are dependent upon wages, and would thereby benefit from the programme's implementation of conditions for effective full employment (thereby enormously improving the position of workers in the labour market). But they will also include, for example, the extent of different groups' dependence on public services, as well as their level of access to forms of asset wealth that may render them independent of wages or services. At the same time, differences of race, gender and sexuality may well come into play, depending on the extent to which any specific iteration of the Green New Deal sets out deliberately to redress imbalances of power along those axes.

Political Consciousness Raising

While these calculations of 'objective' material interest are useful, they only give a very rough idea as to which constituencies are most likely to be articulable into a broad assemblage/bloc oriented towards a Green New Deal (or any other progressive objective). In any case, a key factor determining the likelihood of such an outcome is the relative degree of *political consciousness* typical of the social groups in question. 'Political consciousness' here is a loose but useful term, referring to two main sets of variables (which are often closely related). On the one hand, it refers to the issue of how the group's members tend to conceptualise their interests at the present time: Towards which horizon of realisability are they oriented? In other words, in good old-fashioned Marxist jargon, what is their level of class consciousness? This itself will be an effect of the strength of various ideological and political tendencies within the group, the historical legacy of others, the level of influence enjoyed by various media outlets, and so on. For example, groups of workers following very similar occupations might be inclined towards defensive nationalism, cautious reformism or even revolutionary socialism depending on these factors: consider the varying political allegiances of European industrial and post-industrial communities during the past few decades.[3] On the other hand, 'political consciousness' may be taken to refer to the more general issue of levels of education and access to information; we might call this simply 'political education'. Whether there is any real distinction between class consciousness and political education is a moot point; but for the sake of argument, we might assume that it is possible, for example, for people living in communities with strong radical traditions to maintain a generally radical, utopian, socialistic and even internationalist outlook without being particularly well informed about the minutiae of current affairs (or, for that matter, revolutionary theory).

By the same token, highly educated and well-informed citizens do not necessarily develop any form of class consciousness, beyond that of corporate loyalty to the professional and managerial elite. However, all of the evidence of recent years is that levels of education and information *do* have a bearing upon how easy it is for political forces, of whatever character, simply to reach and make contact with various social groups. While this phenomenon has become strikingly visible in the age of massive online media platforms, it isn't new: after all, it was always easier to spread new ideas among the dense, information-rich populations of cities than in the countryside. To be clear, we are not saying that, for example, workers without university degrees are tendentially more conservative than those with them. We are merely offering a material explanation for the growing correlation between, for instance, support for the Democrats or the Labour Party and possession of a university degree (which is an undeniable empirical fact).[4] We can see here that while levels of class consciousness and levels of political education are clearly closely related, they can also be conceptualised as discrete, observable features that each contribute to the degree to which specific social groups might or might not be easy for radical and progressive projects to connect with, ally with, recruit and mobilise.

Variable Reachability

This issue of what we might call the *variable reachability* of different social constituencies is one that is too often ignored by attempts to formulate viable left strategies. How many well-meaning political projects have foundered on the laudable, but entirely unrealistic, assumption that it is the most highly exploited and oppressed groups who should always be the easiest to mobilise? Indeed, every far-left group that has ever failed to win mass support among the residents of a municipal housing project (e.g., a council estate) or in a low-wage workplace has encountered this phenomenon. Every commentator who has ever complained about the pre-dominance of 'middle class' students and young graduates at protests, or on left-wing canvassing drives, has been effectively observing the same phenomenon. To be very clear, we are making no comment on the relative *importance* of reaching and mobilising either of these respective constituencies. The intuition that it is the most oppressed groups in society whose interests most clearly express themselves in demands for radical change is one that is entirely consistent with our perspective here. The task of radicalising and organising poor workers is crucial and indispensable for any left project, and will continue to be so as long as the general feature of the capitalism mode of production obtain. But the history of 'the left' since before the term was coined (at least as far back as the English Revolution)[5] makes very clear that there are times when intermediate and highly educated layers are much easier to reach, while others are unlikely be to radicalised and mobilised outside of a more general process of radicalisation. Under present circumstances, as a general rule, workers with high levels of education and/or who are 'extremely online' are easier to reach than those whose information sources – the tabloid press, right-wing YouTube, and so on – are largely impermeable to left channels.

Taking account of these key factors – objective interests, political consciousness and reachability – helps to explain why, for example, poor workers might often be very difficult to bring into an effective coalition, where they have low levels of consciousness and are very hard to reach; whereas, for example, highly educated managers whose children attend state schools might well be easier to mobilise. This doesn't mean that the task of poor workers can be abandoned, but only that it must at times be understood as operating at a different temporality to comparable tasks that might be achievable in the short term. In other words, the work of consciousness raising is always crucial, but current levels of consciousness must be considered when assessing the likelihood of mobilising particular constituencies at particular speeds.

We can illustrate these ideas with reference to a particular British social group that has clearly *not* been mobilised effectively in recent years, but which would seem to be an obvious candidate for such mobilisation: schoolteachers in the UK. Notoriously politically acquiescent, they are especially so when compared to their counterparts in other countries.[6] For various reasons, they have never been seen as a priority target for left propaganda. However, as perpetual victims of neoliberal rationalisation and discipline, with a high level of education and a direct interest in the defence, extension and democratisation of public provision, they ought to be seen as a key constituency towards which such propaganda should be directed. The fact that they have not been viewed as such, but have usually been overlooked in favour of social groups who are more clearly marginalised (but far harder to reach), is indicative of the lack of strategic thinking on the British left.

Modes of Organisation

So far in this chapter we have made numerous remarks about what 'the left' should do. But who exactly should undertake these tasks, and through what means? What types of collective actor, incarnated by what types of institution, do we need in the twenty-first century? Broadly speaking, most debates on this issue revolve around the question of how far the institutional and organisational forms typifying 'the left' at the high-water mark of its historical success in the mid-twentieth century (unions, mass parties, revolutionary parties) should be replicated today, and how far we need organisational forms that seem more appropriate to an age of extreme social complexity, global networked communications, and a general reluctance to defer to all forms of received authority.[7] Various commentators have identified this division between the politics of '1917' and that of '1968'.[8] Indeed, political philosopher Rodrigo Nunes has recently made a persuasive case that much of the global left is still caught in a melancholic relationship with one or both of these moments,[9] unable to accept the implications of their passing or the limitations of their animating visions. Of course, '1917' and '1968' are really just convenient shorthands here for 'centralised, professionalised, top-down', and 'radical egalitarian, devolved, distributed'; thus we need not worry ourselves here about their strict historical accuracy.

The fact is, as Nunes elucidates so well, that arguments over political organisation have been going on since at least the time of the debates between Marxists and anarchists in the 1870s,[10] and all of the subsequent history has made one thing quite clear: there is simply no one form or principle of organisation that is appropriate to radical and progressive politics in every context. Centralised, professionalised political parties, open democratic assemblies, self-organised networks, disciplined bureaucracies, local affinity groups: all may have roles to play in specific contexts, and only a complex ecology of such institutions and practices is likely to be able to sustain an effective counter-hegemonic movement.

We might illustrate these principles by comparing the specific cases of the movements that coalesced around, and partially survived, the campaigns to elect Bernie Sanders and Jeremy Corbyn respectively. In both cases, the reconstruction of a politically functional organised left required the emergence or revivification of a range of organisations fulfilling a number of strategic functions in relation to the major parties: organising for the nomination of progressive candidates; campaigning for progressive polices both internally and externally; and facilitating political education and information flow between activists, candidates, policy makers and the intellectuals. In the UK, a great deal of this work had to be undertaken by a singular organisation – Momentum – that was only formally established in 2016, with a smaller sister organisation, The World Transformed, responsible for supporting political education efforts. While there was some overlap between the range of roles undertaken by Momentum / TWT and those carried out in the US by the newly invigorated Democratic Socialists of America, the distribution of roles within that country's ecology of organisations – including DSA, Justice Democrats and Sunrise Movement (both formed in the wake of Sanders's 2016 presidential bid) – arguably made for a more dynamic and flexible approach that also enabled more sustained gains in a variety of local and institutional contexts. These differences were almost certainly exacerbated by the fact that the range and scope of pro-Corbyn media was much smaller than those of progressive media in the US, while the British outlets with the largest audiences were far newer and less established than their American counterparts. In the British context, despite the advantage of having control of the party leadership for a few years, the new movement was arguably starting from a considerably lower base, owing to the far-weaker state of left media in England and Wales.

Airy talk of an 'organisational ecology' may sound vague; however, an inability to conceptualise the question of organisation in these terms appears all too often as a debilitating obstacle to effective political strategy. As one of us has argued elsewhere,[11] there is likely no singular organisational form that will work as a political panacea. A key example here is the question of the role of the political party. Since the nineteenth century, both utopian anarchists and conservative pessimists have asserted that the party form inevitably leads to the concentration of power in the hands of increasingly self-perpetuating and defensive party elites.[12] At the same time, others have defended the party form as the only effective vehicle for militant political organisation in complex industrial and post-industrial societies.[13] While European politics has seen a proliferation of small new left-wing parties enter national legislatures since the 1970s (enabled by the widespread use of proportional representation for legislative elections), in the US and the UK the key question facing the left is normally that of whether to organise as a faction inside the principle of the party of 'the left', to attempt to exert pressure thereon solely by external means, or to try (almost always fruitlessly) to institute an electoral alternative. Debates on this issue are often characterised by a chronic confusion between issues of identity and strategy: between those who see the mass party of the centre left as a terrain on which to struggle with factional rivals, and those who see it primarily as a potential point of identification. The latter group generally feel that membership in the party must be conditional upon a close alignment at any one time between its perceived politico-ethical identity – or that of its leadership – and that of the individual member, while the former see this as a situation to be struggled for rather than a condition for membership as such.

The problem with such debates is that they distract from the key strategic issue, which is to identify the organisational functions which must be carried out and then to determine the best organisational instrument with which to execute them. Within a successful organisational ecology, a range of functions will have to be executed, but there is no need to make predetermined assumptions about whether they must all be carried out by a singular institution, or whether a range of different organisations and collective bodies can undertake these tasks. In general, we think it important to assume that it will be highly unlikely that any one organisation will be able to execute them all. Gramsci proposed that the modern communist party be understood as a 'modern prince' – a reference to Niccolò Machiavelli's hypothetical potentate, which stressed the imagined unity and comprehensiveness of the mass party as a collective actor.[14] That may well have been appropriate to the highly centralised socio-technical context of emergent Fordism, but it was already clear to the radicals of the 1960s and '70s that the more fluid and complex world of post-Fordism would require different approaches; our own era of platform capitalism, in turn, has once again presented us with an unfamiliar terrain of struggle. The point here is that no singular institutional prescription can be regarded as definitive, while tasks must be allocated unsentimentally to the bodies most capable of carrying them out. In the case of the Anglo-American mass parties, for example, they should be used as vehicles for the election of ideologically progressive legislators where such an objective is potentially realisable, and as potential platforms for the dissemination of socialist propaganda; however they should probably not be expected to fulfil any other roles except contingently and under very unusual circumstances. In our view, one error of recent years was for leftist movements to go 'all in' on a purely electoralist strategy. Indeed, the disappointments of the Corbyn project cast a particularly harsh light on such naivety.

None of this is to say that if current circumstances change, it may not become more productive to found new parties or merely to agitate outside of any party. At the same time, of course, trade unionism, community organising and many forms of 'direct action' will often be of greater importance to movement building than any type of electoral or party-based tactics. The point here is simply to avoid any unnecessary limitations on the understanding of what forms of political organisation and intervention may be required – or even simply useful – for the building of progressive political forces.

Persuasion, Education, Narration

In the Anglophone literature on hegemony, the most common understandings of the concept link it directly with ideas of consent and political persuasion. We have tried to correct this bias by stressing the extent to which hegemony always has material, institutional and technological components. Nevertheless, as we have made clear, this doesn't mean that the classic understanding of hegemonic/counter-hegemonic struggle as a battle over 'common sense' is any way mistaken. While any social bloc or political force must be assembled on the basis of common interests, the role of *political narration* is crucial in giving direction to any such formation and of convincing potential members of the bloc that its interests align with theirs. By 'political narration' we mean the process of describing current, recent and historic events in terms which make sense from the perspective of the bloc and its project, and which make the coming-together of that bloc and the pursuit of that project seem logical, desirable and (ideally) inevitable. For example, the classic study of hegemonic crisis in British politics and culture – Stuart Hall et al.'s *Policing the Crisis* – is essentially a study of how the New Right sought to build a narrative of social crisis in terms that facilitated the organisation of class fractions into a bloc committed to neo-liberal economics and authoritarian social policy. The relative success and failure of Sandersism and Corbynism lay partly in their relative capacities to narrate recent history in terms that made it seem possible and desirable for a broad coalition of social forces to mount a decisive challenge to neoliberalism. Corbyn in particular was simply unable to do this; instead, he fell back repeatedly on a moral condemnation of 'austerity' and its social consequences, rather than lodge any kind of political critique of neoliberalism as such.[15] Because of this limitation, he was never able to convince large numbers of working-class voters – who had suffered more from decades of post-industrial neoliberalism than from recent contractions of public spending – that he was speaking in their interests.

The battle for common sense is not only a question of high-level propaganda and counter-propaganda, but also of sustained political education and consciousness raising. The English left in particular, hampered by the chronic anti-intellectualism of English culture,[16] has been notoriously bad at prioritizing political education for its supporters and activists. The collapse of the Corbyn project in the wake of the 2019 election defeat is surely the most obvious consequence of this weakness. Indeed, throughout Corbyn's time in office, no serious effort was made by the party or its leadership to extend and deepen educational provision for party members and supporters: even Momentum undertook none of this work between 2015 and 2020. The task was left to the tiny, woefully underfunded network of activists working through TWT, whose audience was inevitably self-selecting and already highly educated, despite the extremely effective and creative work undertaken by the organisation. The naivety that led a large proportion of Corbyn's supporters to vote for Keir Starmer as his replacement, and the demoralisation that led so many of them simply to leave the party soon after his victory, were all symptomatic of the very low level of education and political consciousness that they had been enabled to attain as party members.

From a socialist perspective, the work of political education partly involves simply equipping partisans with enough historical, factual and institutional knowledge to be effective political actors and proselytisers. However, properly understood, it must also involve consciousness raising as such. By 'consciousness raising' we mean precisely the process by which subjects are enabled to conceptualise their interests within the highest-possible horizon of realisability, and to understand their political agency in terms not limited by those of hegemonic legacy liberalism. If nothing else, this generally means inculcating in political activists and partisans enough awareness of the nature of historical change to equip them emotionally and intellectually for long-term struggle – including repeated experiences of defeat. This generally requires that they should experience, at least occasionally, an empowering sense of solidarity with others committed to the same project, without this necessarily reifying into a fixed, exclusionary sense of identity. What is at stake here is not shared identities as such, but a shared experience of collective becoming and of collectively actualisable potential.

In practice this means that propaganda and political agitation must go on, like all other forms of organisation, at multiples scales and in multiple forms. What is required is both formal education and narration, and the promotion of cultural forms capable of cultivating empowered and empowering affects, experiences of 'collective joy'[17] and shared experiences of possibility. What all of this activity must have in common to be politically effective is an orienting sense of partisanship, however vague: the sense that many kinds of social activity – from localised mutual aid to various manifestations of the expressive arts to economics and policy making – are all 'on the same side' as the broad socialist project.[18]

Putting Platforms to Use

Under the circumstances that we have been describing, the intelligent deployment of new communications technologies is a crucial aspect of any future political strategy, whatever its orientation. The centrality of social media to contemporary public life is self-evident, although it can be argued that they largely serve to magnify the existing strengths and weaknesses of both left and right: the left is able to use social and platform media to disseminate creative and engaging propaganda at almost zero cost; in response, the right is able to use its financial resources to completely saturate key audience segments with its own messaging, however detached from lived experience. In the most extreme manifestations of the same logic, leftist campaigners in both the UK and the US have learned how to use platform technologies and mobile communications to facilitate mass face-to-face campaigning in key localities, and even to sustain community organising, while the fringe operators of the 'alt right' have become adept at disseminating the wildest fantasies to keep their followers entertained, distracted, and almost entirely unable to act in their own most immediate interests.

For the left, the lessons of the past decade are extremely mixed. At the moments of greatest hope – such as the aftermath of the 2017 UK general election – it has seemed as if the 1990s dream of a form of mass participatory democracy facilitated by internet technologies was at last being realised.[19] On the other hand, at the moments of greatest despair, vast social media platforms – exclusively controlled by unaccountable and impossibly wealthy corporations – have demonstrated a genuinely terrifying capacity to effectively rewire the very perceptual apparatus and material consciousness of huge populations of hapless individual subjects.[20]

As such, a clear medium-range objective of any twenty-first-century socialism must be the wresting of major platforms from monopoly corporate control.[21] To be effective, it would require major international, intragovernmental co-ordination and a high level of participation by platform users across the globe. It is perfectly possible to imagine that within the foreseeable future, some kind of viral campaign could lead to a mass global boycott of major platforms, forcing them to transition to some form of user-owned status. However, such a direct confrontation between international socialist forces and the platform capitalists of Silicon Valley is unlikely to happen anytime soon – or at least, no sooner than the implementation of Green New Deal programmes will be required for the very preservation of human civilisation.

The Progressive Fractions of Capital

Under these circumstances, to simply identify Silicon Valley as the leading fraction of capital, and therefore the principal enemy of progressive forces, is not a tenable strategy. In 'Americanism and Fordism', Gramsci himself posited the need to identify 'progressive' tendencies at the leading edge of capitalism, and the need to recognise how, for example, Ford and his colleagues advanced the forces of production.[22] From an eco-socialist perspective, the most urgent political task is to continue, and exacerbate, the ongoing isolation of those fractions of capital still directly dependent upon massive carbon emissions. This will inevitably involve making alliances with other fractions of capital, in particular those sections of the tech sector most invested in renewable energy production and least aligned with the conservatism of carbon capital or the neoliberalism of the finance sector. Ultimately, the aim should be to constitute a new progressive bloc that would inevitably have to include sections of the capitalist class, while excluding the most reactionary.

This does not involve any retreat from the task of organising labour in all sections of the economy, including the tech and platform-enabled sectors. Just as we saw during the mid-twentieth century, the constitution of a progressive assemblage/bloc is only possible when sections of the working class are able to enter into it from positions of relative and increasing strength. Industrial manufacturers were persuaded to make major concessions to labour not because they were progressive, but because the gains that they were offered for making them outweighed the risks posed by a refusal to compromise with the increasingly militant and well-organised working class. As such, classical and innovative forms of labour organisation remain a clear priority for any project oriented towards the constitution of a new progressive bloc. It is crucial to grasp the whole argument here: while we do not believe that some final confrontation between labour and capital is imaginable within the timescale required to prevent climatic and civilisational breakdown, and while we believe that pragmatic strategic objectives must orient all of the political activity of progressive forces, this does not constitute a withdrawal from class struggle or the effort to build class consciousness.

We make these observations at a necessarily high level of generality, and they raise as many questions as they answer. Which sections of the tech sector might have the potential to be incorporated into a progressive assemblage/bloc? What is our approach to the financial sector going to be? The reigning hegemonic bloc still consists of the alliance between tech and finance, so it would be tempting to imagine simply disaggregating this bloc into its two key components as a progressive strategic objective, perhaps understanding technologies such as cryptocurrency as a potential means by which to use the tech sector to undermine the power of finance. But this would be too simplistic: key sections of the tech sector are obviously regressive in their political orientations, social effects and implications, and could not form part of any imagined progressive bloc. Does this apply, as certain persuasive studies would suggest, to all of the current major social media platforms?[23] What about finance? Given that key sections of finance capital seem to be in the process of at least accepting the need for radical action on the environment, will it be necessary to accept some of those sections as elements of any such bloc? Can any such outcome really be countenanced, given that a direct attack on and reduction of the power of finance must be an immediate objective of even the most modest reform programme under present circumstances?[24] None of these questions are easy to answer, and any serious attempt to do so would require a book in its own right – or several. However, there is room enough here to briefly point to their salience, and to the urgency of some attention being given to them.

Speaking to Interests

The historic task of the left is always to weaken the power of capital and its agents, while building forms of democratic counter-power. At times, this necessitates alliances with sections of capital, in order to disaggregate existing hegemonic blocs; still, the abstract logic of class struggle remains the same. While we accept and affirm the post-Marxist claim that the common interests of those who must co-operate to weaken the power of capital and enhance that of the *demos* cannot be conceptualised purely in class terms, we also reject any claim that they can be effectively conceptualised in terms other than those defined by common interests. In practice, this means that there are two related types of discourse that are inimical to the success of any political project seeking to transcend the limits of liberalism and conservatism: moralism, and liberal identarianism.

Firstly, and most simply, all forms of moralism should be avoided. This has been a theme of radical commentary since Marx's day, but one only has to compare the fates of Corbyn and Sanders to see how salient it remains. We hope here that we have offered a clear theoretical account of *why* moralistic discourse is so fatal to attempts to build popular progressive movements. By its very nature, in its appeal to norms in themselves, moral discourse does not appeal to interests. It can be argued that certain kinds of moral discourse, such as the 'capability approach' of thinkers like Martha Nussbaum and Amartya Sen,[25] does appeal to an idea of shared interests. But it often does so only with reference to interests conceptualised at a very high level of realisability, with no attention to the necessary steps to be followed from the present until the moment of realisation; and where it avoids such pitfalls, it clearly does not take on the character of moralism, however ethical it may be.

This is all very abstract, but in practice, the principle for which we are advocating could not be simpler: if you want to persuade people to follow you, tell them what's in it for them. Don't confuse the issue with arguments over right and wrong.

The other key pitfall to avoid is liberal identarianism.[26] This is to say: politics or discourse that treats the achievement, defence, expression or recognition of a personal identity as an end in itself. This is absolutely *not* synonymous with the 'identity politics' first named in the 1970s by the pioneers of black feminist and queer politics of the Combahee River Collective.[27] From the perspective of the great collective liberation movements of that period, social identities such as 'black' or 'gay' were ways of identifying common sets of interests, common horizons of aspiration and realisability. They were not reified modes of being, or positions from which individualised claims could be made on the state, community or other institutions. They were not essential existential facts to be expressed and guarded against all possible incursion or pollution. On the contrary, they were vectors of collective becoming through which sets of interests could be expressed and then aligned with others for the fuller realisation of wider interests within ever-expanding horizons of realisability. Put in other words by the philosopher Judith Butler: 'Identity ought not to be the foundation for politics. Alliance, coalition and solidarity are the key terms for an expanding left.'[28]

We recommend this approach not merely because it aligns with our theoretical preconceptions, but because the history of the past half century has made clear that both short- and long-term political objectives – for example, of feminism and the women's movement – have been best served when they have been understood by their participants as projects for the expression and realisation of common interests rather than for the expression of a definable identity.[29]

None of this is to say that moral sentiments, altruism and the dignity of heroic self-sacrifice should have no place in the culture of the left. It is instead to argue for a politics – even an ethic – of solidarity, properly conceived.[30] The experience of solidarity is not an experience of shared identity, even if it is true that shared and expansive identities can facilitate the cultivation of solidarity;[31] it is rather a shared consciousness of the mutuality of interest, and of the enhanced capacity for the realisation of interests that derives from collective action. As such, it is something experienced primarily at the psycho-corporeal level of affect, rather than at the level of cognition or decision.

One feature of a politics of interests will necessarily be an attention to questions of affect, insofar as affective experience is always related to the expressibility and realisability of interests. Here, perhaps, we can identify an approach to the question of political motivation and political rationality which avoids the pitfalls of both individualised 'rational choice' theory (assuming that all optical actors make wholly logical and self-interested calculations), and 'irrationalist' theories of political psychology, from values theory to psychoanalysis. Our contention is that there is a certain rationality to political behaviour, but that that rationality will be expressed in collective behaviours more often than in private choices, and more often at the level of 'mood', 'vibe' and senses of possibility than at the level of verbal discourse, identity, or definite policy preferences. The basic claim underlying this approach is that political behaviour is always motivated by the expression and attempted realisation of interests, but that it is constrained by the various factors which limit the consciousness, expression and realisation of them.

For Gramsci, the great theorist of hegemonic power, 'every relationship of "hegemony" is necessarily an educational one'.[32] So too for us today: to win a new hegemony ultimately means to expand the consciousness, expression and realisability of the interests of the left.

8

THE PROMISE OF NEOSOCIALISM

Ultimately, the purpose of all of our claims and observations in this book is to contribute to the furtherance of a progressive, egalitarian, democratic politics capable of confronting the enormous challenges of a collapsing neoliberalism, destabilising geopolitics, and impending climate catastrophe. Such a project cannot be advanced without significantly increasing the power of workers, citizens and the institutions through which they are able to exercise collective power, vis-à-vis corporations, capitalists and the institutions that serve their interests. In other words, it must have a socialist dimension, even if it recognises that the full substitution of absolutely non-capitalist forms of social relations for the existing ones to realistically be a distant prospect.

At the same time, to have any hope of success, it must have a populist dimension, identifying key popular demands, narrating recent events and proposing programmatic solutions that align various progressive demands with each other – expressing sets of interests as demands that have not yet been publicly expressed as such. In the UK, at the time of writing, it is very obvious that such a politics would put forward a programme for the post-pandemic reconstruction of British society while clearly identifying the entire period of neoliberal hegemony (including the New Labour government) as one that has left the country less able to face this challenge than it should have been. As Ernesto Laclau and Chantal Mouffe have always insisted, such a politics must have an antagonistic dimension, identifying the social groups – above all, in this case, financial and property speculators – who have benefitted from a programme of neoliberal financialisation and whose interests must be curtailed if everyone else's are to be even partially realised. But it must also have a positive vision for reconstruction; and indeed, this is the core discursive function of the Green New Deal as a package of programmatic demands.

At the same time, a twenty-first-century socialism must have a fundamentally democratic character. It is important to understand that, although the language and priorities may differ, little of what we have written here would seem controversial to many of our enemies. In many places the political right has already abandoned neoliberal rhetoric and some features of neoliberal policy, in the attempt to construct a new assemblage/bloc that includes the most reactionary sections of tech and finance, as well as the property and energy industries. In both the US and the UK, at least, the growing number of homeowning retirees – legatees of both the post-war social settlement and the neoliberal property boom – are increasingly central to this bloc, at least in electoral terms; meanwhile, large numbers of workers of all types are excluded from it, except for those retained within it by virtue of their alignment with revanchist white supremacism or patriarchal reaction. Arguably since the days of the premiership of Silvio Berlusconi in Italy, we've been seeing the emergence of a kind of neofascism (or at the very least a reactionary neo-nationalism) predicated on control of media platforms and reaction against Third Way cosmopolitanism.

In the US the spectacle of Donald Trump's presidency provoked a degree of rapprochement between the new socialist left and the inheritors of technocratic liberal neoliberalism, although bitter fractional rivalries (and continuous disappointments for the left) persist. In the UK, by contrast, the defenders of Third Way common sense seem resolute in their preference for indefinite Conservative rule over any threat of government by the left. This raises an alarming prospect to which the socialist left should be sensitive: the re-emergence of a centrist bloc, still subservient to tech and finance, that presents itself as the only legitimate alternative to neofascism. This is, of course, precisely what has occurred in France under Emmanuel Macron. Such a bloc would almost certainly try to deploy the authoritarian technocratic ideology that already defines the shared common sense of much of the Silicon Valley elite,[1] promising technological (and technical) solutions to the climate crisis in return for the further erosion of any residual elements of meaningful popular sovereignty.

The assertion of popular sovereignty cannot imply the mere defence of existing liberal democratic institutions. Without a strong critique and persuasive analysis of their self-evident failures, it will not be possible to convince any significant sections of the public that the left has any viable remedies for them. Again, this was one of the great failures of Corbynism: while it was able to offer a strong economic critique of austerity and of the post-Fordist financialisation of the economy, it was never able to offer a political critique of the decay of representative democracy and the wider socio-political costs of neoliberalism. The political right, by contrast, was able to offer Brexit as a diagnosis of – and imagined solution to – the palpable decline of democratic efficacy since the 1970s.[2]

At the time of writing, the political prospects for the left in Britain look bleak; across the Atlantic there is rather more cause for hope, but little for tremendous enthusiasm. In other parts of Europe things are going little better, except, arguably, in Portugal and Spain, where coalitions of the left and centre left have managed to form governments with some success in recent years. If there is cause for hope, however, it lies in the objective deployment of the kinds of analytical methods that we have used and developed throughout the course of this book. From our perspective, platform capitalism poses major challenges for progressive politics. Nevertheless, it probably offers more opportunities than did post-Fordism, which rendered effective collective organisation across so many fronts virtually impossible. Moreover, the number and range of social constituencies with a direct objective interest in advancing the cause of socialism is growing, not shrinking. Ultimately there is no guarantee of success, no avoiding the fact that at any moment in history, the odds are always stacked against the forces of progress and human emancipation. But by attending to the issues we have focussed on here, we at least have a chance of avoiding some of the worst mistakes of the recent past.

GLOSSARY OF KEY TERMS

Active consent – active alliance, conscious agreement, or broad allegiance with a hegemonic project

Alliance – the process by which one group begins to develop common cause with others

Articulation – the practice of building alliances of class fractions through finding common cause in shared interests; the emergence into clarity of a hegemonic project

Assemblage – any set of social elements, and the relations between them, that is more than the sum of its parts

Assemblage/bloc – see 'social bloc'; a term we use occasionally merely to emphasise that every bloc is also an assemblage (although there are many other kinds of assemblage that are not blocs)

Chain of equivalence – a set of demands, symbols, or interests from more than one group that haven't been articulated into relation with each other; a basic form of alliance

Class fraction – a social group organised around a common interest, smaller than a Marxist or sociological class, with a specific subset of interests, often coalescing around shared culture and/or presence within a specific productive sphere (e.g., technology workers, financial workers)

Coercion – the application of force, or the threat of force, for political effect; how hegemonic groups tend to deal with those who cannot be rendered either passive or consenting

Common sense – a system of social norms and cognitive frameworks that shape the perception of interests

Conjuncture – a political moment within a given space and time, or the set of forces contending within that moment and place; often used in the sense of 'conjunctural analysis', meaning an examination of the interplay of a set of forces in a given political moment

Consciousness raising – the effort to expand political horizons and material interests

Good sense – a common sense, or a portion thereof, aligned with the best available interests of a given group

Hegemonic bloc – a set of actors and class fractions with aligned interests operating within a given hegemonic project; also a particular form of assemblage

Hegemonic crisis – the collapse of a hegemonic regime at a given scale (locally, nationally, regionally, or globally)

Hegemonic leadership – the ability to set a direction of travel for a group, set of groups, society, nation, or organisation

Hegemonic project – the collective practice of building, contending, or defending a system of hegemony; both more and less than 'winning power'

Hegemonic regime – a systemic hegemony that can be exported, generalised, and imposed on other states or regions, towards a global predominance

Hegemony – a system of power where a small group leads a larger one, typically seen in complex societies

Material interest – the basic unit of political motivation, which links the structural positioning of individuals to their agency in the world; often complex and inconsistent

Passive consent – a form of consent lacking either assent/belief or opposition/contention; the most minimal form of consent (through inaction) necessary to leave hegemonic power unperturbed

Platform – an infrastructure for some element of social life; any system which is widely relied upon by a group of actors

Political horizon – the personal or collective scale on which interests are considered

Settlement – a particular kind of systemic hegemony, expressed as a time period, with its own relatively stable set of ruling common senses (e.g., the 'post-war settlement' of 1945–75)

Social bloc – a coalition of distinct class fractions aligned around a common interest or interests

Structure of feeling – the semi-articulated sense of being within a particular conjuncture, often through culture

Subaltern – any non-hegemonic group or class; those who are led and not leading; also those excluded from a system of rule

Systemic hegemony – any long-lasting system of power where multiple domains, from the ostensibly political to the cultural, economic and infrastructural, have been harmonised and serve to mutually reinforce one another over time; more or less what Gramsci calls a 'historic bloc'

NOTES

Introduction

1. Antonio Gramsci, *Selections from the Prison Notebooks*, ed. Quintin Hoare and Geoffrey Nowell Smith (London: Lawrence & Wishart, 1971), 276.
2. In this we distinguish our account from the mass of political science and popular journalistic political commentary. The former largely obsesses about the minutiae of conventional electoral politics and psephologically surveys. The latter stenographically conveys gossip about elected representatives as if it were astute analysis.
3. Perry Anderson, *The H-Word: The Peripeteia of Hegemony* (London: Verso, 2017).

1 Who Won the Twentieth Century?

1. Anthony Barnett, *The Lure of Greatness: England's Brexit and America's Trump* (London: Unbound, 2017).
2. Alex Nunns, *The Candidate: Jeremy Corbyn's Improbable Path to Power* (New York: OR Books, 2016).
3. Bob Rigg, 'Bernie Sanders Has Morphed into a Serious Contender', *openDemocracy*, 2015, opendemocracy.net.
4. David Runciman, 'Nobody Knows Anything: Why Is Politics So Surprising?', *Political Quarterly*, 11 December 2017, political-quarterly.org.uk.

5. David Harvey, *A Brief History of Neoliberalism* (Oxford: Oxford University Press, 2007); Jeremy Gilbert, *Neoliberal Culture* (London: Lawrence & Wishart, 2016); Alana Lentin and Gavan Titley, *The Crises of Multiculturalism: Racism in a Neoliberal Age* (London: Zed Books, 2011); William Davies, *The Limits of Neoliberalism: Authority, Sovereignty and the Logic of Competition*, rev. ed., Theory, Culture and Society (London: SAGE, 2017).

6. Jeremy Gilbert, 'The Second Wave: The Specificity of New Labour Neo-liberalism', *Soundings* 26, no. 26 (1 March 2004): 25–45.

7. Jeremy Gilbert, *Anticapitalism and Culture: Radical Theory and Popular Politics* (Oxford: Berg, 2008).

8. Richard Seymour, *Corbyn: The Strange Rebirth of Radical Politics*, 2nd ed. (London: Verso, 2017).

9. Martin Kettle and Lucy Hodges, *Uprising!: The Police, the People, and the Riots in Britain's Cities* (London: Pan Books, 1982).

10. Seumas Milne, *The Enemy Within: The Secret War against the Miners* (London: Verso, 2004).

11. George McKay, *Senseless Acts of Beauty: Cultures of Resistance since the Sixties* (London: Verso, 1996), 11–74.

12. Melinda Cooper, *Family Values: Between Neoliberalism and the New Social Conservatism* (New York: Zone Books, 2017).

13. Stuart Hall et al., *Policing the Crisis: Mugging, the State and Law and Order* (London: Macmillan, 1978).

14. Andrew Gamble, *The Free Economy and the Strong State: The Politics of Thatcherism* (Durham, NC: Duke University Press, 1988).

15. Alan Finlayson, *Making Sense of New Labour* (London: Lawrence & Wishart, 2014); Gilbert, 'The Second Wave'.

16. Anthony Giddens, *The Global Third Way Debate* (Cambridge, UK: Polity Press; Malden, MA: Blackwell Publishers, 2001); Paul Smith, *Millennial Dreams: Contemporary Culture and Capital in the North*, Haymarket Series (London: Verso, 1997).

17. Andrew Pierce, 'Horror as Cameron Brandishes the B Word', *Times* (London), 5 October 2005, thetimes.co.uk.

18. However, some commentators would later claim exactly such a transition, from neoliberalism to authoritarian populism. See, for example, Gideon Rachman, 'The Trump Era Could Last 30 Years', *Financial Times*, 4 February 2019, ft.com. As we will argue later, there is good reason to think that this is not a smooth transition of global orders and that we have actually entered a period of hegemonic crisis.

19. 'General Election: Trump vs. Sanders', Real Clear Politics, 2016 polling data, realclearpolitics.com.

20. Mark Blyth, *Great Transformations: Economic Ideas and Institutional Change in the Twentieth Century* (New York: Cambridge University Press, 2002).

21. Colin Crouch, *Post-Democracy* (Cambridge, UK: Polity Press, 2004); Colin Crouch, *The Strange Non-death of Neoliberalism* (Cambridge, UK: Polity Press, 2013).

22. Tony Judt, *Ill Fares the Land* (New York: Penguin, 2010).

23. See, for example, 'British Social Attitudes 37', NatCen Social Research, natcen.ac.uk.

24. Ron Formisano, *American Oligarchy: The Permanent Political Class* (Champaign: University of Illinois Press, 2017).

25. Costas Lapavitsas, *Profiting without Producing: How Finance Exploits Us All* (London: Verso, 2013).

26. Martin Kettle, '2015 General Election: It's the Economy, Stupid! (Well, Maybe Not . . .)', *Guardian*, 14 January 2014, theguardian. com.

27. Timothy Bewes and Jeremy Gilbert, *Cultural Capitalism: Politics after New Labour* (London: Lawrence & Wishart, 2000).

28. Costas Lapavitsas and Stathis Kouvelakis, 'Syriza's Repressive Turn', Verso blog, 8 October 2018, versobooks.com.

29. Olivier Tonneau, 'Macron's Tragedy Is That He Still Believes in a Discredited Economic System', *Guardian*, 8 May 2017, theguardian.com.

30. Jonathan Hopkins, 'Technocrats Have Taken Over Governments in Southern Europe. This Is a Challenge to Democracy.' *EUROPP* (blog), 24 April 2012, blogs.lse.ac.uk.

31. Fritz W. Scharpf, 'Monetary Union, Fiscal Crisis and the Disabling of Democratic Accountability', in *Politics in the Age of Austerity* (Cambridge, UK: Polity Press, 2013).

32. 'Higher Education: Success as a Knowledge Economy', white paper, UK government official website, 16 May 2016, gov.uk.

33. 'Statement from the New Prime Minister Theresa May', UK government official website, 13 July 2016, gov.uk; 'Britain, the Great Meritocracy: Prime Minister's Speech', UK government official website, 9 September 2016, gov.uk; Jo Littler, *Against Meritocracy: Culture, Power and Myths of Mobility* (London: Routledge, 2017); 'Prime Minister Visits Families in North East to Mark One Year to EU Exit', UK government official website, 29 March 2018, gov.uk.

34. Justin Schlosberg, *Should He Stay or Should He Go? Television and Online News Coverage of the Labour Party in Crisis*, Media Reform Coalition, 2016, mediareform.org.uk.

35. Mike Phipps, *For the Many . . . : Preparing Labour for Power* (New York: OR Books, 2017).

36. 'Ed Miliband Admits Pledge to Freeze Energy Prices Could Lead to Higher Bills before Next Election', *Telegraph*, 25 September 2013, telegraph.co.uk.

37. Roger Simon, *Gramsci's Political Thought: An Introduction* (London: Lawrence & Wishart, 2015).

38. Michel Foucault, *The History of Sexuality*, 1st Vintage Books ed. (New York: Vintage Books, 1988), 94.

39. Harvey, *Brief History of Neoliberalism*.

40. Perry Anderson, 'Renewals', *New Left Review* 1, no. 1 (2000): 1–20.

41. Giovanni Arrighi, *Adam Smith in Beijing: Lineages of the Twenty-First Century* (London: Verso, 2007).

42. Tariq Ali, *Pirates of the Caribbean: Axis of Hope* (London: Verso, 2008).

43. Gabriel A. Almond, R. Scott Appleby and Emmanuel Sivan, *Strong Religion: The Rise of Fundamentalisms around the World* (Chicago: University of Chicago Press, 2003).

44. Todd Gitlin, *The Twilight of Common Dreams: Why America Is Wracked by Culture Wars*, 1st ed. (New York: Metropolitan Books, 1995).

45. Vijay Prashad, *The Poorer Nations: A Possible History of the Global South* (London: Verso Books, 2014).

46. Kristin Ross, *May '68 and Its Afterlives* (Chicago: University of Chicago Press, 2002); Robert Gildea, James Mark and Anette Warring, eds., *Europe's 1968: Voices of Revolt*, 1st ed. (Oxford: Oxford University Press, 2013); Todd Gitlin, *The Sixties: Years of Hope, Days of Rage* (New York: Random House, 2013).

47. Giovanni Arrighi, Terrence Hopkins and Immanuel Wallerstein, *Antisystemic Movements* (London: Verso, 1989).

48. Gitlin, *The Sixties*.

49. Eric J. Hobsbawm, *Age of Extremes: The Short Twentieth Century, 1914–1991* (London: Michael Joseph, 1994).

50. Ibid.; Donald Sassoon, *One Hundred Years of Socialism: The West European Left in the Twentieth Century* (London: I.B. Tauris, 2013).

51. Charles W. Eagles, *The Civil Rights Movement in America* (Jackson: University Press of Mississippi, 2012); Charles McKelvey, *The African-American Movement: From Pan-Africanism to the Rainbow Coalition* (New York: General Hall, 1994); Charles V. Hamilton and Kwame Ture, *Black Power: Politics of Liberation in America* (New York: Knopf Doubleday, 2011); Jeffrey Ogbonna Green Ogbar, *Black Power: Radical Politics and African American Identity*, rev. ed. (Baltimore: Johns Hopkins University Press, 2019).

52. Ogbar, *Black Power*.

53. Ward Churchill and Jim Vander Wall, *Agents of Repression: The FBI's Secret Wars against the Black Panther Party and the American Indian Movement* (Boston: South End Press, 1988).

54. Ibid.

55. Jeremy Gilbert, *Common Ground: Democracy and Collectivity in an Age of Individualism* (London: Pluto Press, 2014), 11.

56. Sheila Rowbotham, *Woman's Consciousness, Man's World* (London: Penguin, 1973).

57. Murray Bookchin, *Post-scarcity Anarchism* (Berkeley, CA: Ramparts Press, 1971).

58. Gerry Kennedy, 'Growing up in a Commune', *Guardian*, 27 April 2005, theguardian.com.

59. Daniel Chauvey, *Autogestion* (Paris: Éditions du Seuil, 1970); John Medhurst, *That Option No Longer Exists: Britain 1974–76* (Arlesford: Zero Books, 2014).

60. Carl Freedman, *The Age of Nixon: A Study in Cultural Power* (London: Zero Books, 2012); Jefferson Cowie, *Stayin' Alive: The 1970s and the Last Days of the Working Class* (New York: New Press, 2012); Penny Lewis, *Hardhats, Hippies, and Hawks: The Vietnam Antiwar Movement as Myth and Memory* (Ithaca, NY: ILR Press, 2013).

61. Hall, *Policing the Crisis*, 218–326.

62. Bruce J. Schulman and Julian E. Zelizer, eds., *Rightward Bound: Making America Conservative in the 1970s* (Cambridge, MA: Harvard University Press, 2008).

63. Raymond Williams, *Marxism and Literature* (London: Oxford University Press, 1977); William E. Connolly, *Capitalism and Christianity, American Style* (Durham: Duke University Press, 2008).

64. See Hall, *Policing the Crisis*.

65. Kate Nash, *Contemporary Political Sociology: Globalization, Politics, and Power*, 2nd ed. (Chichester, UK: Wiley-Blackwell, 2010).

66. Angela McRobbie, *The Aftermath of Feminism* (London: SAGE, 2008); Nancy Fraser, *Fortunes of Feminism: From State-Managed Capitalism to Neoliberal Crisis* (London: Verso, 2013).

67. Michelle Alexander, *The New Jim Crow: Mass Incarceration in the Age of Colorblindness*, rev. ed. (New York: New Press, 2012).

68. Ross, *May '68*.

69. Aubrey Walter, *Come Together: The Years of Gay Liberation, 1970–73* (London: Gay Men's Press, 1980); Hamilton and Ture, *Black Power*.

70. Steven Levy, *Hackers: Heroes of the Computer Revolution – 25th Anniversary Edition* (New York: O'Reilly Media, 2010).

71. Fred Turner, *From Counterculture to Cyberculture: Stewart Brand, the Whole Earth Network, and the Rise of Digital Utopianism* (Chicago: University of Chicago Press, 2010).

72. Ibid.; Paulina Borsook, *Cyberselfish: A Critical Romp through the Terribly Libertarian Culture of High Tech*, 1st ed. (New York: PublicAffairs, 2000); Richard Barbrook and Andy Cameron, 'The Californian Ideology', *Science as Culture* 6, no. 1 (January 1996): 44–72.

73. Jim McGuigan, *Neoliberal Culture* (London: Springer, 2016); Patricia Ventura, *Neoliberal Culture: Living with American Neoliberalism* (New York: Routledge, 2016); Gilbert, *Common Ground*.

74. Nick Srnicek, *Platform Capitalism* (Cambridge, UK: Polity Press, 2017).

75. Karl Marx et al., *Capital: A Critique of Political Economy*, vol. 3, *The Process of Capitalist Production as a Whole* (London: Penguin, 1991), 334–43.

76. Martin Kenney, ed., *Understanding Silicon Valley: The Anatomy of an Entrepreneurial Region* (Stanford, CA: Stanford University Press, 2000), 15–67.

77. Levy, *Hackers*, 151–278.

78. Juan Pablo Pardo-Guerra, 'Creating Flows of Interpersonal Bits: The Automation of the London Stock Exchange, c. 1955–90', *Economy and Society* 39, no. 1 (February 2010): 84–109.

79. Francis Fukuyama, *The End of History and the Last Man* (New York: Free Press / Maxwell Macmillan International, 1992), 39–51.

80. Martin Jacques, *When China Rules the World: The End of the Western World and the Birth of a New Global Order* (New York: Penguin, 2009).

81. See Stephen Silver, 'Apple Taken to Task for Actions of Chinese Suppliers in "Complicit" Documentary', *AppleInsider*, 24 May 2018, appleinsider.com.

82. Mike Featherstone, John Urry and Nigel Thrift, *Special Issue on Automobilities* (London: SAGE, 2004); Campbell Jones et al., *Against Automobility* (Malden, MA: Blackwell, 2006).

83. Connolly, *Capitalism and Christianity, American Style*; Ashley Dawson, *Imperial Ecologies* (London: Lawrence & Wishart, 2010).

84. Timothy Mitchell, *Carbon Democracy: Political Power in the Age of Oil* (London: Verso, 2013).

85. See Williams, *Marxism and Literature*.

86. Mike Davis, *Planet of Slums* (London: Verso, 2007).

87. Srnicek, *Platform Capitalism*.

88. Shoshana Zuboff, *The Age of Surveillance Capitalism: The Fight for a Human Future at the New Frontier of Power* (London: Profile Books, 2019).

89. Paul Gilroy, *The Black Atlantic: Modernity and Double Consciousness* (London: Verso, 1993).

90. Those that did emerge were either often more weakly formally innovative (for example the mid-00s London dubstep sound, quickly elided into the mush of American EDM) or globally locally sourced but more abstruse sounds (Chicago's footwork and Durban's *gqom*, for example), lacking in an ability to reconfigure the mainstream of global music.

91. Jonathan Sterne, *MP3: The Meaning of a Format* (Durham, NC: Duke University Press, 2012).

92. Jeremy Gilbert, 'Capitalism, Creativity and the Crisis in the Music Industry', *openDemocracy*, 14 September 2012, opendemocracy.net.

93. Glen Peoples, 'Recording Industry 2015: More Music Consumption and Less Money, That's Digital Deflation', *Billboard*, 7 January 2016, billboard.com.

94. Adam Rasmi, 'Streaming Has Helped the Music Industry Recover—to Half Its Peak Size', *Quartz*, 3 April 2019, qz.com.

95. Simon Reynolds, *Retromania: Pop Culture's Addiction to Its Own Past* (London: Faber & Faber, 2011).

96. Roger Eatwell, *Fascism: A History* (New York: Penguin, 1996); Leon Trotsky, *Fascism: What It Is, How to Fight It* (New York: Pathfinder, 1984).

97. Vanessa R. Schwartz, *Spectacular Realities: Early Mass Culture in Fin-de-Siècle Paris* (Berkeley: University of California Press, 1998).

98. Mica Nava, *Visceral Cosmopolitanism: Gender, Culture and the Normalisation of Difference* (Oxford: Berg, 2007).

99. Lapavitsas, *Profiting without Producing*.

100. 'Final Consumption Expenditure (Current US$), Data', World Bank, https://data.worldbank.org/indicator/NE.CON.TOTL.CD.

101. Paul Addison, *The Road to 1945: British Politics and the Second World War*, rev. ed. (London: Random House, 2011).

102. Alan Finlayson, *Making Sense of New Labour* (London: Lawrence & Wishart, 2003).

103. Manuel Castells, *The Rise of the Network Society* (Oxford: Blackwell, 2011), 415–16.

104. George Steinmetz and Erik Olin Wright, 'The Fall and Rise of the Petty Bourgeoisie: Changing Patterns of Self-Employment in the Postwar United States', *American Journal of Sociology* 94, no. 5 (March 1989): 973–1018.

105. Stuart Hall and Martin Jacques, *New Times: The Changing Face of Politics in the 1990s* (London: Verso, 1989).

106. Eatwell, *Fascism*.

107. Ross McKibbin, *Classes and Cultures: England 1918–1951* (Oxford: Oxford University Press, 1998).

108. Pierre Bourdieu, *Distinction: A Social Critique of the Judgement of Taste* (Cambridge, MA: Harvard University Press, 1984); Luc Boltanski and Eve Chiapello, *The New Spirit of Capitalism*, trans. Gregory Elliot, rev. ed. (London: Verso, 2018).

109. Jeremy Gilbert, *Twenty-First Century Socialism* (Cambridge, UK: Polity Press, 2020).

110. Nicos Poulantzas, 'On Social Classes', *New Left Review* I/78 (March/April 1973).

111. Antonio Gramsci, *Selections from the Prison Notebooks*, trans. Quintin Hoare and Geoffrey Nowell Smith (London: Lawrence & Wishart, 1971), 96.

112. Simon, *Gramsci's Political Thought*.

113. Ian Clark, *Hegemony in International Society* (Oxford: Oxford University Press, 2011).

114. Gramsci, *Prison Notebooks*, 12.

2 Actually Existing Neoliberalism

1. Jeremy Gilbert, 'What Kind of Thing Is "Neoliberalism"?', *New Formations* 80, no. 80 (November 12, 2013): 7–22.

2. See Philip Mirowski, *Road from Mont Pelerin – the Making of the Neoliberal Thought Collective* (Cambridge, MA: Harvard University Press); William Davies, *The Limits of Neoliberalism: Authority, Sovereignty and the Logic of Competition*, rev. ed., Theory, Culture and Society (Los Angeles: SAGE, 2017).

3. David Harvey, *A Brief History of Neoliberalism* (Oxford: Oxford University Press, 2007).

4. Steve Cohn, *Competing Economic Paradigms in China: The Co-evolution of Economic Events, Economic Theory and Economics Education, 1976–2016*, Routledge Contemporary China Series 171 (London: Routledge, 2017); Julian B. Gewirtz, *Unlikely Partners: Chinese Reformers, Western Economists, and the Making of Global China* (Cambridge, MA: Harvard University Press, 2017).

5. Gewirtz, *Unlikely Partners*; Christopher Connery, 'Ronald Coase in Beijing', *New Left Review* 115 (January–February 2019).

6. Anthony Barnett, *This Time: Our Constitutional Revolution* (London: Vintage, 1997); Harvey, *Brief History of Neoliberalism*; Davies, *Limits of Neoliberalism*.

7. Jeremy Gilbert, 'The Second Wave: The Specificity of New Labour Neo-liberalism', *Soundings* 26, no. 26 (1 March 2004): 25–45.

8. Farhad Manjoo, 'Silicon Valley's Politics: Liberal, with One Big Exception', *New York Times*, 6 September 2017, nytimes.com.

9. Anthony Giddens, *The Global Third Way Debate* (Cambridge, UK: Polity Press, 2001).

10. Charles Moore, *Margaret Thatcher: The Authorized Biography* (New York: Alfred A. Knopf, 2013).

11. Pierre Dardot and Christian Laval, *The New Way of the World: On Neoliberal Society* (London: Verso, 2013).

12. Paulina Borsook, *Cyberselfish: A Critical Romp through the Terribly Libertarian Culture of High Tech*, 1st ed. (New York: PublicAffairs, 2000). We could add to these claims the further observation that a distinctive strain of postmodern, antinomian libertarianism persisted at the borders between hacker culture and the counterculture since at least the 1950s (evinced by phenomena such as the strange pseudo-religion of 'Discordianism', popularised by the novelist Robert Anton Wilson), eventually influencing the libertarian culture of Silicon Valley significantly. See Erik Davis, *High Weirdness: Drugs, Esoterica, and Visionary Experience in the Seventies* (Cambridge, MA: MIT Press, 2019).

13. Harvey, *Brief History of Neoliberalism*, 158.

14. Raymond Williams, *The Long Revolution* (London: Chatto & Windus, 1961).

15. Tony Judt, *Ill Fares the Land* (New York: Penguin, 2010).

16. Richard G. Wilkinson and Kate Pickett, *The Spirit Level: Why Greater Equality Makes Societies Stronger* (New York: Bloomsbury, 2010).

17. Indeed, we can consider these 'levels' to be analytical functional domains, rather than absolute structural or topological ones which exclude the other. They are an artefact of our tools of analysis, rather than actual geographies of power in the real world.

18. Georg Lukács, *History and Class Consciousness* (London: Merlin Press, 1975).

19. Ernesto Laclau, *Politics and Ideology in Marxist Theory: Capitalism, Fascism, Populism* (London: New Left Books, 1977);

Tony Bennett, 'Theories of the Media and Society', in *Culture, Society and the Media*, ed. Michael Gurevitch (London: Routledge, 1988), 26–51; Barry Hindess and Paul Q. Hirst, *Mode of Production and Social Formation: An Auto-Critique of Pre-capitalist Modes of Production* (London: Palgrave Macmillan UK, 1977).

20. Nicholas Abercrombie, Stephen Hill and Bryan S. Turner, *The Dominant Ideology Thesis* (London: G. Allen & Unwin, 1980).

21. See Sean Creaven, *Marxism and Realism: A Materialistic Application of Realism in the Social Sciences*, Routledge Studies in Critical Realism (London: Routledge, 2000); Jonathan Joseph, *Hegemony: A Realist Analysis* (London: Taylor & Francis, 2002).

22. Sutton Trust, *The State of Social Mobility in the UK*, 2017, suttontrust.com; 'Neoliberalism: Oversold? – Finance and Development, June 2016', International Monetary Fund, imf.org.

23. Karl Marx, *Capital* (London: Lawrence & Wishart, 2003).

24. Michael D. Shear and Michael Barbaro, 'In Video Clip, Romney Calls 47% "Dependent" and Feeling Entitled', *The Caucus* (blog), September 17, 2012, thecaucus.blogs.nytimes.com.

25. In this sense we examine ideology as fundamentally in the domain of an ontological intervention, rather than an epistemological one, whose effects are not in the domain of the true or false, so much as in the realm of function, process and causality.

26. Louis Althusser, *On the Reproduction of Capitalism: Ideology and Ideological State Apparatuses* (London: Verso, 2014), 261–5.

27. Pat Thompson, 'Bringing Bourdieu to "Widening Participation" Policies in Higher Education: A UK Case Analysis', in *Routledge International Handbook of the Sociology of Education*, ed. Michael W. Apple, Stephen J. Ball and Luís Armando Gandin, Routledge International Handbooks (London: Routledge, 2010), 318–28; Althusser, *On the Reproduction of Capitalism*.

28. Abercrombie, Hill and Turner, *The Dominant Ideology Thesis*.

29. Shamus Rahman Khan, *Privilege: The Making of an Adolescent Elite at St. Paul's School*, Princeton Studies in Cultural Sociology

(Princeton, NJ: Princeton University Press, 2011); Jo Littler, *Against Meritocracy: Culture, Power and Myths of Mobility* (London: Routledge, 2017).

30. Aeron Davis, *Reckless Opportunists: Elites at the End of the Establishment* (Manchester: Manchester University Press, 2018).

31. Davies, *Limits of Neoliberalism*; Jeremy Gilbert, *Common Ground: Democracy and Collectivity in an Age of Individualism* (London: Pluto Press, 2014).

32. Dieter Plehwe, 'Neoliberal Think Tanks and the Crisis', in *Liberalism and the Welfare State: Economists and Arguments for the Welfare State*, ed. Roger Backhouse (New York: Oxford University Press, 2017), 192–211; Philip Mirowski, *Never Let a Serious Crisis Go to Waste: How Neoliberalism Survived the Financial Meltdown* (London: Verso, 2013).

33. Mark Blyth, *Austerity: The History of a Dangerous Idea* (Oxford: Oxford University Press, 2015).

34. Margaret Thatcher, 'Let Our Children Grow Tall', speech to the Institute of Socioeconomic Studies Foundation, 15 September 1975, available at margaretthatcher.org; see Plehwe, 'Neoliberal Think Tanks.

35. Margaret Thatcher, interview for *Director* magazine, 4 July 1983, available at margaretthatcher.org.

36. Alan Travis, 'Thatcher Was to Call Labour and Miners "Enemy within" in Abandoned Speech', *Guardian*, 2 October 2014, theguardian.com.

37. Margaret Thatcher, 'No Such Thing as Society', interview for *Woman's Own*, 23 September 1987, available at margaretthatcher.org.

38. Moore, *Margaret Thatcher*.

39. 'Tony Blair's Conference Speech 2005', *Guardian*, 27 September 2005, theguardian.com.

40. Margaret Thatcher, 'Speech to Overseas Bankers', 7 February 1978, available at margaretthatcher.org; John Gray, *Hayek on Liberty*, 3rd ed. (London: Routledge, 1998), 151.

41. 'Tony Blair's Speech in Full', *BBC News*, 28 September 1999, news.bbc.co.uk.

42. Dardot and Laval, *New Way of the World*.

43. Margaret Thatcher, 'Press Conference for American Correspondents in London', 25 June 1980, available at margaretthatcher. org; Claire Berlinski, *'There Is No Alternative': Why Margaret Thatcher Matters* (New York: Basic Books, 2008).

44. Leonard Downie Jr, '364 British Economists Assail Thatcher's Policies', *Washington Post*, 31 March 1981, washingtonpost. com.

45. The term 'subaltern' is at the heart of an entire subfield of Gramscian-inspired work.

46. Antonio Gramsci, *Selections from the Prison Notebooks*, trans. Quintin Hoare and Geoffrey Nowell Smith (London: Lawrence & Wishart, 1971), 343.

47. Peter D. Thomas, *The Gramscian Moment: Philosophy, Hegemony and Marxism*, Historical Materialism 24 (Leiden: Brill, 2009), 16.

48. 'Full Text: Brown's Mansion House Speech', *Guardian*, 17 June 2004, theguardian.com.

49. J.L. Austin, *How to Do Things with Words: The William James Lectures 1955* (Oxford: Clarendon Press, 1962).

50. Ibid., 147.

51. Judith Butler, *Gender Trouble: Feminism and the Subversion of Identity* (New York: Routledge, 1999); Judith Butler, *Bodies That Matter: On the Discursive Limits of 'Sex'* (New York: Routledge, 2011).

52. Paul S. Agutter and Denys N. Wheatley, *Thinking about Life: The History and Philosophy of Biology and Other Sciences* (Dordrecht: Springer, 2010).

53. Jacques Derrida, 'Signature Event Context', in *Margins of Philosophy*, trans. Alan Bass (Chicago: University of Chicago Press, 1982), 309–30.

54. Stuart Hall and Alan O'Shea, 'Common-Sense Neoliberalism', *Soundings* 55, no. 55 (December 13, 2013): 9–25.

55. Lester K. Spence, *Stare in the Darkness: The Limits of Hip-Hop and Black Politics* (Minneapolis: University of Minnesota Press, 2011).

56. Christine Geraghty, *Women and Soap Opera: A Study of Prime Time Soaps* (Cambridge, UK: Polity Press, 1991); Christine Geraghty and David Lusted, eds., *The Television Studies Book* (New York: St. Martin's Press, 1998); Robert C. Allen and Annette Hill, *The Television Studies Reader* (London: Routledge, 2010).

57. Laurie Ouellette and James Hay, *Better Living through Reality TV: Television and Post-Welfare Citizenship* (Malden, MA: Blackwell, 2008).

58. Chris Tryhorn, 'Big Brother Cleared of Neglect', *Guardian*, 18 September 2006, theguardian.com. Although the producers of the show were cleared, their intentions in the casting decisions that they had made are very clear from the details of the case.

59. David Lee, 'Networks, Cultural Capital and Creative Labour in the British Independent Television Industry', *Media, Culture and Society* 33, no. 4 (10 May 2011): 549–65.

60. Mark Fisher, *Capitalist Realism: Is There No Alternative?* (Winchester, UK: Zero Books, 2010).

61. Will Brooker and Deborah Jermyn, eds., *The Audience Studies Reader* (London: Routledge, 2003); Laurie Ouellette, ed., *The Media Studies Reader* (London: Routledge, 2013).

62. Ouellette and Hay, *Better Living*.

63. Alan Finlayson, *Making Sense of New Labour* (London: Lawrence & Wishart, 2003); Helen Dickinson, 'From New Public Management to New Public Governance: The Implications for a "New Public Service" ', in *The Three Sector Solution*, ed. John Butcher and David Gilchrist (Canberra: Australian National University Press, 2016); Chris Lorenz, 'If You're So Smart, Why Are You under Surveillance? Universities, Neoliberalism, and New Public Management', *Critical Inquiry* 38, no. 3 (1 March 2012): 599–629.

64. Alan Finlayson, 'Financialisation, Financial Literacy and Asset-Based Welfare', *British Journal of Politics and International*

Relations 11, no. 3 (August 2009): 400–21; Costas Lapavitsas, *Profiting without Producing: How Finance Exploits Us All* (London: Verso, 2013).

65. Colin Leys, *Market-Driven Politics: Neoliberal Democracy and the Public Interest* (London: Verso, 2003).

66. Allan Barton, 'Public Choice Theory and Economic Rationalism: The Basis of New Public Management', in *Research in Public Policy Analysis and Management* 11, part B (2001), chap. 29, 571–88.

67. Colin Crouch, *The Strange Non-Death of Neo-Liberalism* (Cambridge, UK: Polity Press, 2013).

68. Steven Pressman, 'What Is Wrong with Public Choice', *Journal of Post Keynesian Economics* 27, no. 1 (1 October 2004): 3–18.

69. Nancy MacLean, *Democracy in Chains: The Deep History of the Radical Right's Stealth Plan for America* (New York: Viking, 2017).

70. Rachel Ormston and John Curtice, eds., *British Social Attitudes: The 32nd Report* (London: NatCen Social Research, 2015), 74-101, available at bsa.natcen.ac.uk.

71. Ibid., 102–21.

72. See Frédéric Lordon and Gabriel Ash, *Willing Slaves of Capital: Spinoza and Marx on Desire* (London: Verso, 2014), chap. 1.

73. Christina Beatty and Steve Fothergill, 'Jobs, Welfare and Austerity: How the Destruction of Industrial Britain Casts a Shadow over the Present-Day Public Finances', project report, Centre for Regional, Economic and Social Research, Sheffield Hallam University, 2016, shura.shu.ac.uk.

74. Richard Sennett, *The Corrosion of Character: The Personal Consequences of Work in the New Capitalism* (London: W.W. Norton & Company, 2011); Guy Standing, *The Precariat: The New Dangerous Class*, rev. ed. (London: Bloomsbury Academic, 2016).

75. Stuart Hall et al., *Policing the Crisis: Mugging, the State and Law and Order* (London: Macmillan, 1978).

76. 'Perceptions Are Not Reality', *Ipsos MORI*, 9 July 2013, ipsos. com; 'Perceptions of How Tax Is Spent Differ Widely from

Reality', *YouGov*, 9 November 2014, yougov.co.uk; 'Perceptions and Reality: Public Attitudes to Immigration,' *Ipsos MORI*, 2 January 2014, ipsos.com.

77. Gramsci, *Prison Notebooks*, 328.

78. Ernesto Laclau and Chantal Mouffe, *Hegemony and Socialist Strategy* (London: Verso, 1985); Lawrence Grossberg, 'On Post-modernism and Articulation', *Journal of Communication Inquiry* 10, no. 2 (24 July 2016): 45–60. NB this is only a *tendency* of Laclau and Mouffe's thought and some of its interpretations; it is also possible to read their theories of 'antagonism' as precisely stressing the importance of recognising points of non-commensurability between different sets of demands.

79. Laclau and Mouffe, *Hegemony and Socialist Strategy*, 146.

80. This is absolutely not the Lacanian 'real' that thinkers such as Slavoj Žižek posit as the 'unpresentable kernel' of all discourse. It is simply material social reality that can be very easily apprehended and represented by almost anybody.

81. Gabriel de Tarde, *L'opinion et La Foule* (Paris: F. Alcan, 1901).

82. Fisher, *Capitalist Realism*.

83. Jane McAlevey, *No Shortcuts: Organizing for Power in the New Gilded Age* (New York: Oxford University Press, 2016); Gary Daniels and John McIlroy, eds., *Trade Unions in a Neoliberal World: British Trade Unions under New Labour*, Routledge Research in Employment Relations 20 (London: Routledge, 2009); Stuart Hall, 'The Neo-liberal Revolution', *Cultural Studies* 25, no. 6 (17 October 2011): 705–28; Harvey, *Brief History of Neoliberalism*.

84. 'Ipsos MORI Research Reveals Widespread Pessimism Regarding the Future of Young People', Intergenerational Foundation, 23 July 2014, if.org.uk; Juliette Jowit, 'What Is Depression and Why Is It Rising?', *Guardian*, 4 June 2018, theguardian.com; 'Depression', World Health Organization, who.int/mental_health/management/depression/en.

85. Maurizio Lazzarato, *Experimental Politics: Work, Welfare, and Creativity in the Neoliberal Age*, Technologies of Lived Abstraction (Cambridge, MA: MIT Press, 2016).

86. Lizabeth Cohen, *Making a New Deal: Industrial Workers in Chicago, 1919–1939*, 2nd ed. (Cambridge: Cambridge University Press, 2008).

87. Eric J. Hobsbawm, *Age of Extremes: The Short Twentieth Century, 1914–1991* (London: Michael Joseph, 1994), chap. 10.

88. Arthur Marwick, *The Sixties: Cultural Revolution in Britain, France, Italy, and the United States, c.1958–c.1974* (London: A&C Black, 2011).

89. 'The Crisis of Democracy', Trilateral Commission, http://trilateral.org/file/8.

90. Standing, *Precariat*; Lazzarato, *Experimental Politics*.

91. Abercrombie, Hill and Turner, *The Dominant Ideology Thesis*.

92. However, we do not endorse the polemical conclusions of this book, to the effect that there is no dominant ideology under 'late capitalism' and that ideology plays no significant role in securing the compliance of subaltern groups to elite rule; we think that the entire history of neoliberal hegemony since the time of the book's publication (1980) has comprehensively undermined these claims. The volume nevertheless remains a classic, crucial contribution to the debate, and a necessary corrective against any simplistic or mechanistic understanding of ideology.

93. Ngai-Ling Sum and Bob Jessop, *Towards a Cultural Political Economy: Putting Culture in Its Place in Political Economy* (Cheltenham, UK: Edward Elgar, 2013). 261–392.

94. Daniels and McIlroy, *Trade Unions in a Neoliberal World*.

95. Sennett, *Corrosion of Character*; Richard Sennett, *The Culture of the New Capitalism* (London: Yale University Press, 2007).

96. Michel Foucault and Jean Khalfa, *History of Madness* (New York: Routledge, 2006); Michel Foucault, *The Birth of the Clinic: An Archaeology of Medical Perception* (New York: Vintage, 1994); Michel Foucault, *Discipline and Punish: The Birth of the Prison* (New York: Vintage, 1979).

97. Michel Foucault, *The History of Sexuality* (New York: Vintage, 1980).

98. Peter L. Berger and Thomas Luckmann, *The Social Construction of Reality: A Treatise in the Sociology of Knowledge* (New

York: Anchor Books, 1990); Barry Lee, ed., *Philosophy of Language: The Key Thinkers*, Continuum Key Thinkers (London: Continuum, 2011).

99. Michel Foucault, Arnold I. Davidson and Graham Burchell, *The Birth of Biopolitics: Lectures at the Collège de France, 1978–1979* (Mannheim: Springer, 2008).

100. Davies, *Limits of Neoliberalism*.

101. Lazzarato, *Experimental Politics*.

102. Mark Olssen, John A. Codd and Anne-Marie O'Neill, *Education Policy: Globalization, Citizenship and Democracy* (London: SAGE, 2004); Melissa Benn, *School Wars: The Battle for Britain's Education* (London: Verso, 2012).

103. Harvey, *Brief History of Neoliberalism*; Davies, *Limits of Neoliberalism*.

104. Johanna Oksala, 'Feminism and Neoliberal Governmentality', *Foucault Studies* 16 (22 August 2013): 32.

105. Davies, *Limits of Neoliberalism*; Mirowski, *Road from Mont Pelerin*.

106. Harvey, *Brief History of Neoliberalism*.

107. Alan Milchman and Alan Rosenberg, 'Marxism and Governmentality Studies: Toward a Critical Encounter', *Rethinking Marxism* 14, no. 1 (March 2002): 132–42; Frank Pearce and Steve Tombs, 'Foucault, Governmentality, Marxism', *Social and Legal Studies* 7, no. 4 (17 August 2016): 567–75.

108. Alison Hearn, 'Meat, Mask, Burden', *Journal of Consumer Culture* 8, no. 2 (July 2008): 197–217; Richard Seymour, *The Twittering Machine* (London: Indigo Press, 2019).

109. Michel Foucault, *Security, Territory, Population: Lectures at the Collège de France, 1977–78* (Basingstoke: Palgrave Macmillan, 2007).

110. Lazzarato, *Experimental Politics*.

111. Gilles Deleuze, 'Postscript on the Societies of Control', *October* 59 (1992): 3–7.

112. Manuel DeLanda, *Intensive Science and Virtual Philosophy* (London: Bloomsbury, 2013).

113. Harvey, *Brief History of Neoliberalism.*

114. Martin Kettle and Lucy Hodges, *Uprising!: The Police, the People, and the Riots in Britain's Cities* (London: Pan Books, 1982); George McKay, *Senseless Acts of Beauty: Cultures of Resistance since the Sixties* (London: Verso, 1996).

115. Andy Beckett, *Promised You a Miracle: UK80–82* (London: Penguin, 2016).

116. Anthony Barnett, *Iron Britannia* (London: Allison & Busby, 1982); Beckett, *Promised You a Miracle.*

117. Tariq Ali, *Pirates of the Caribbean: Axis of Hope* (London: Verso, 2008.

118. Perry Anderson and Suleiman Ali Mourad, *The Mosaic of Islam: A Conversation with Perry Anderson* (London: Verso, 2016).

119. Étienne Balibar and G. M. Goshgarian, *Violence and Civility: On the Limits of Political Philosophy*, Wellek Library Lectures (New York: Columbia University Press, 2015).

120. Gramsci, *Prison Notebooks*, 169–71.

121. Crawford Brough Macpherson, *The Political Theory of Possessive Individualism: Hobbes to Locke* (Oxford: Oxford University Press, 1988).

122. Michel Foucault, *Society Must Be Defended: Lectures at the Collège de France, 1975–76* (York: Picador, 2003), 12–64.

123. Lawrence Freedman, *Strategy: A History* (Oxford: Oxford University Press, 2013).

124. Gramsci, *Prison Notebooks*, 238–40.

125. Ibid., 170, 394, 405.

3 Persuasion and Passivity

1. Allyson Pollock, *NHS Plc: The Privatisation of Our Health Care* (London: Verso, 2005).

2. Ibid.

3. Dexter Whitfield, *Public Services or Corporate Welfare: Rethinking the Nation State in the Global Economy* (London:

Pluto Press, 2001); Dexter Whitfield, 'New Labour's Attack on Public Services: Modernisation by Marketisation?: How the Commissioning, Choice, Competition and Contestability Agenda Threatens Public Services and the Welfare State: Lessons for Europe', *Socialist Renewal*, 5th ser., no. 3 (2006); Alan Finlayson, *Making Sense of New Labour* (London: Lawrence & Wishart, 2003); Colin Leys, *Market-Driven Politics: Neoliberal Democracy and the Public Interest* (London: Verso, 2003).

4. Mike Gerrard, *A Stifled Voice* (London: Pen Press, 2006).

5. Ibid.

6. Roger Simon, *Gramsci's Political Thought: An Introduction* (London: Lawrence & Wishart, 2015), 24.

7. Antonio Gramsci, *Selections from the Prison Notebooks*, trans. Quintin Hoare and Geoffrey Nowell Smith (London: Lawrence & Wishart, 1971), 107.

8. The history of engagements between the two bodies of thought can be traced back at least to Voloshinov's critical essay *Freudianism*, first published in the 1920s: Valentin N. Voloshinov and Neal H. Bruss, *Freudianism: A Critical Sketch* (Bloomington: Indiana University Press, 1987). It can then be traced through the work of thinkers ranging from Adorno, Fromm, Marcuse, Barthes, Lacan and Althusser to more recent thinkers such as Žižek. There is no space here to defend our claim that few of these attempts to reconcile the two bodies of thought have ever been very successful; we can merely elucidate that in our view, while all have introduced powerful insights, they have almost all done so at the expense of one or other of the key radical aspects of historical materialist thought: its materialism, its historicism, or its anti-individualism.

9. The French term *agencement* might more normally be translated as 'arrangement' or 'construction', but 'assemblage' is the better translation in this context.

10. Gilles Deleuze and Félix Guattari, *A Thousand Plateaus: Capitalism and Schizophrenia* (Minneapolis: University of Minnesota Press, 1987); Manuel DeLanda, *New Philosophy of Society:*

Assemblage Theory and Social Complexity (New York: Continuum, 2006).

11. See Lawrence Grossberg, *We Gotta Get out of This Place: Popular Conservatism and Postmodern Culture* (New York: Routledge, 1992); Jeremy Gilbert, *Anticapitalism and Culture: Radical Theory and Popular Politics* (Oxford: Berg, 2008); Panagiotis Sotiris, 'Lignes de fuite, minorités et machines de guerre: Repenser la politique deleuzienne', *Revue Periode*, 2014, revueperiode.net; Alex Williams, *Political Hegemony and Social Complexity: Mechanisms of Power after Gramsci* (Basingstoke: Palgrave Macmillan, 2019).

12. Anne Showstack Sassoon, *Gramsci's Politics*, 2nd ed., Contemporary Politics (London: Hutchinson, 1987), 119–26; Christine Buci-Glucksmann, *Gramsci and the State* (London: Lawrence & Wishart, 1980), 260–80.

13. Robert Brenner, *The Economics of Global Turbulence: The Advanced Capitalist Economies from Long Boom to Long Downturn, 1945–2005* (London: Verso, 2006), 77–8.

14. 'Full Transcript: Donald Trump's Jobs Plan Speech', *Politico*, 28 June 2016, politico.com; Anthony Barnett, *The Lure of Greatness: England's Brexit and America's Trump* (London: Unbound, 2017).

15. Annie Kelly, 'The Alt-Right: Reactionary Rehabilitation for White Masculinity', *Soundings* 66, no. 66 (15 August 2017): 68–78.

16. Laurie Ouellette, 'The Trump Show', *Television and New Media* 17, no. 7 (August 2016): 647–50.

17. William E. Connolly, *Capitalism and Christianity, American Style* (Durham, NC: Duke University Press, 2008).

18. Bari Weiss and Damon Winter, 'Opinion, Meet the Renegades of the Intellectual Dark Web', *New York Times*, 8 May 2018, nytimes.com.

19. Manuel DeLanda, *Intensive Science and Virtual Philosophy* (London: Bloomsbury, 2013).

20. Jeremy Gilbert, 'This Conjuncture: For Stuart Hall', *New Formations* 96, nos. 96–97 (1 March 2019): 5–37.

21. Grossberg, *We Gotta Get out of This Place*; Lawrence Grossberg, *Bringing It All Back Home: Essays on Cultural Studies* (Durham, NC: Duke University Press, 1997); Lawrence Grossberg, *Caught in the Crossfire: Kids, Politics, and America's Future* (Boulder: Paradigm Publishers, 2005); Lawrence Grossberg, *Cultural Studies in the Future Tense* (Durham, NC: Duke University Press, 2010).

22. Ernesto Laclau and Chantal Mouffe, *Hegemony and Socialist Strategy* (London: Verso, 1985), 9.

23. Louis Althusser, *For Marx*, rev. ed., Radical Thinkers (London: Verso, 2005), 178.

24. Stuart Hall, 'Signification, Representation, Ideology: Althusser and the Post-structuralist Debates', *Critical Studies in Mass Communication* 2, no. 2 (18 May 2009): 91–114; Jennifer Daryl Slack, 'The Theory and Method of Articulation in Cultural Studies', in *Stuart Hall: Critical Dialogues in Cultural Studies*, ed. David Morley and Kuan-Hsing Chen, Comedia (London: Routledge, 1996).

25. Ronald Reagan, 'A Time for Choosing', speech, 27 October 1964, Ronald Reagan Presidential Library, National Archives and Records Administration.

26. Deleuze and Guattari, *A Thousand Plateaus*, 232–309.

27. Ibid.; Gilles Deleuze, *Difference and Repetition* (London: Athlone Press, 1994).

28. John Sides, Michael Tesler and Lynn Vavreck, 'How Trump Lost and Won', *Journal of Democracy* 28, no. 2 (2017): 34–44.

29. Zack Beauchamp, 'A New Study Reveals the Real Reason Obama Voters Switched to Trump', *Vox*, 16 October 2018, vox.com.

30. Joe Kennedy, *Authentocrats: Culture, Politics and the New Seriousness* (London: Repeater, 2018).

31. Jon Cruddas, 'Labour Can't Afford to Lose Its Working-Class Heartlands by Backing Remain', *Guardian*, 26 June 2019, theguardian.com.

32. 'British Social Attitudes 37', NatCen Social Research, natcen.ac.uk.

33. Michel Aglietta, *A Theory of Capitalist Regulation* (London: Verso, 2016).

34. Ibid.; Robert Boyer and Yves Saillard, eds., *Regulation Theory: The State of the Art* (London: Routledge, 2002).

35. Ash Amin, ed., *Post-Fordism: A Reader*, Studies in Urban and Social Change (Oxford: Blackwell, 1994).

36. David Harvey, *The Condition of Postmodernity* (London: Wiley, 1989).

37. Stephen A. Marglin, ed., *The Golden Age of Capitalism: Reinterpreting the Postwar Experience*, UNU-WIDER Studies in Development Economics (Oxford: Clarendon Press, 2007).

38. Ibid.

39. Gramsci, *Prison Notebooks*, 277–320.

40. Ibid., 304–6.

41. Susan Kingsley Kent, *Gender and Power in Britain, 1640–1990* (London: Routledge, 1999), 287–334.

42. Gramsci, *Prison Notebooks*, 286.

43. John H. Hamer, 'Money and the Moral Order in Late Nineteenth and Early Twentieth-Century American Capitalism', *Anthropological Quarterly* 71, no. 3 (July 1998): 138.

44. We could note here, for example, the shifting importance in the funding and administration of the fine arts from the activities of individual wealth financiers to the programs administered by central governments, such as the Federal Arts Project (1935–43) and the UK Arts Council (founded 1946). We could also note the passing of the great age of financier philanthropy.

45. George H. Nash, 'The Conservative Intellectual Movement in America: Then and Now', *National Review*, 26 April 2016, nationalreview.com.

46. Steven Fielding, Peter Thompson and Nick Tiratsoo, *England Arise! The Labour Party and Popular Politics in 1940s Britain* (Manchester: Manchester University Press, 1995).

47. Marglin, *Golden Age of Capitalism*.

48. Ben Pimlott, Dennis Kavanagh and Peter Morris, 'Is the "Postwar

Consensus" a Myth?', *Contemporary Record* 2, no. 6 (June 1989): 12–15.

49. Deleuze and Guattari, *A Thousand Plateaus*, 406.

50. Gilbert Simondon, *L'individuation psychique et collective: À la lumière des notions de forme, information, potentiel et métastabilité*, L'Invention Philosophique (Paris: Aubier, 1989), 25–8.

51. Ibid., 551–6.

52. Selina Todd, *The People: The Rise and Fall of the Working Class, 1910–2010* (London: John Murray, 2014).

53. Donald Sassoon, *One Hundred Years of Socialism: The West European Left in the Twentieth Century* (London: I.B. Tauris, 2013); Eric J. Hobsbawm, *Age of Extremes: The Short Twentieth Century, 1914–1991* (London: Michael Joseph, 1994).

54. Andrea Cossu, 'Commemoration and Processes of Appropriation: The Italian Communist Party and the Italian Resistance (1943–48)', *Memory Studies* 4, no. 4 (18 October 2011): 393.

55. William Blum, *Killing Hope: U.S. Military and CIA Interventions since World War II* (Monroe, ME: Common Courage Press, 1995), 27–32.

56. Connor Woodman, *Spycops in Context: A Brief History of Political Policing in Britain*, Centre for Crime and Justice Studies, 2018, 14, crimeandjustice.org.uk.

57. Anthony Carew, 'The Politics of Productivity and the Politics of Anti-Communism: American and European Labour in the Cold War', *Intelligence and National Security* 18, no. 2 (June 2003): 73–91.

58. Fielding, Thompson and Tiratsoo, *England Arise!*

59. Gramsci, *Prison Notebooks*, 175–85.

60. Peter H. Lindert, 'Three Centuries of Inequality in Britain and America', in *Handbook of Income Distribution*, vol. 1 (Amsterdam: Elsevier, 2000), chap. 3, 167–216.

61. Marglin, *Golden Age of Capitalism*.

62. Larry Ceplair, *Anti-Communism in Twentieth-Century America: A Critical History* (Santa Barbara, CA: Praeger, 2011).

63. Marglin, *Golden Age of Capitalism*.

64. David Butler and Gareth Butler, *Twentieth-Century British Political Facts, 1900–2000*, 8th ed. (New York: St. Martin's Press, 2000), 141–59.

65. Jim Tomlinson, *Democratic Socialism and Economic Policy: The Attlee Years, 1945–1951* (Cambridge: Cambridge University Press, 2002), 290–5.

66. Fielding, Thompson and Tiratsoo, *England Arise!*

67. Paul Addison, *The Road to 1945: British Politics and the Second World War*, rev. ed. (London: Random House, 2011).

68. Noreen Branson, *History of the Communist Party of Great Britain*, vol. 4 (London: Lawrence & Wishart, 1997).

69. Addison, *Road to 1945*.

70. Sassoon, *One Hundred Years*.

71. Hobsbawm, *Age of Extremes*, 109–41.

72. Ross McKibbin, *Classes and Cultures: England 1918–1951* (Oxford: Oxford University Press, 1998).

73. Ibid.

74. Sassoon, *One Hundred Years*, 15–16.

75. Addison, *Road to 1945*.

76. Ibid.; McKibbin, *Classes and Cultures*; Ross McKibbin, *Parties and People: England 1914–1951* (Oxford: Oxford University Press, 2011); Todd, *The People*.

77. Rudolf Klein, *The Politics of the National Health Service*, Politics Today (London: Longman, 1983), 18–20.

78. Hywel Francis and David Smith, *The Fed: History of the South Wales Miners in the Twentieth Century* (London: Lawrence & Wishart, 1980), 52–69.

79. Ibid., 354.

80. Gramsci, *Prison Notebooks*, 302.

81. It is important to note here that Foucault would not have accepted the formulation according to which Fordist sexual culture was simply 'repressive'; rather, he would have seen it as actively facilitating a very particular set of behaviours and ways of thinking and talking about sexuality. See Foucault, Michel Foucault, *The History of Sexuality* (New York: Vintage, 1980).

82. Shelagh Delaney, *A Taste of Honey: A Play* (New York: Grove Press, 1959); Simone de Beauvoir, *The Second Sex* (New York: Knopf, 1953); Lynne Reid Banks, *The L-Shaped Room* (London: Chatto & Windus, 1960); Doris Lessing, *The Golden Notebook* (London: M. Joseph, 1962).

83. Jeffrey Weeks, *Sex, Politics and Society: The Regulation of Sexuality since 1800*, 4th ed., Themes in British Social History (London: Routledge, 2018), 307–8.

84. Barnor Hesse, ed., *Un/Settled Multiculturalisms: Diasporas, Entanglements, 'Transruptions'* (London: Zed Books, 2000), 6.

85. Tony Sewell, *Keep on Moving: The Windrush Legacy: The Black Experience in Britain from 1948* (London: Voice Enterprises, 1998); Paul Gilroy, *There Ain't No Black in the Union Jack: The Cultural Politics of Race and Nation* (Chicago: University of Chicago Press, 1991).

86. Philip Mirowski, *Road from Mont Pelerin – the Making of the Neoliberal Thought Collective* (Cambridge, MA: Harvard University Press).

87. Stuart Hall et al., *Policing the Crisis: Mugging, the State and Law and Order* (London: Macmillan, 1978); Jeremy Gilbert, 'After '68: Narratives of the New Capitalism', *New Formations* 65, no. 65 (1 November 2008): 34–53.

88. John Medhurst, *That Option No Longer Exists: Britain 1974–76* (Arlesford: Zero Books, 2014).

89. 'British Social Attitudes 37'.

90. Brenner, *Economics of Global Turbulence*.

91. Todd Gitlin, *The Sixties: Years of Hope, Days of Rage* (New York: Random House, 2013).

92. Robert Gildea, James Mark and Anette Warring, eds., *Europe's 1968: Voices of Revolt*, 1st ed. (Oxford: Oxford University Press, 2013); Immanuel Wallerstein, '1968, Revolution in the World-System', *Theory and Society* 18, no. 4 (July 1989): 431–49.

93. Brenner, *Economics of Global Turbulence*.

94. Hall, *Policing the Crisis*, 1–138.

95. Edmund Frow and Ruth Frow, *Engineering Struggles: Episodes in the Story of the Shop Stewards' Movement* (Manchester: Manchester Free Press, 1982); John Barker, *Bending the Bars* (Hastings: ChristieBooks, 2006); Penny Lewis, *Hardhats, Hippies, and Hawks: The Vietnam Antiwar Movement as Myth and Memory* (Ithaca, NY: ILR Press, 2013).

96. E.P. Thompson, *The Making of the English Working Class* (London: Victor Gollancz, 1965).

97. McKibbin, *Parties and People.*

98. Sassoon, *One Hundred Years.*

99. McKibbin, *Parties and People.*

100. Kevin Williams, *Read All About It!: A History of the British Newspaper* (Routledge, 2009).

101. Kenneth R. Minogue and Michael D. Biddiss, eds., *Thatcherism: Personality and Politics* (New York: St. Martin's Press, 1987).

102. John Ehrman, *The Eighties: America in the Age of Reagan* (New Haven: Yale University Press, 2005).

103. Andy Beckett, *Promised You a Miracle: UK80–82* (London: Penguin, 2016).

104. Sheila Rowbotham, *Edward Carpenter: A Life of Liberty and Love* (London: Verso, 2009).

105. Colin Campbell, *The Romantic Ethic and the Spirit of Modern Consumerism* (New York: Springer, 2018); Luc Boltanski and Eve Chiapello, *The New Spirit of Capitalism*, trans. Gregory Elliot, rev. ed. (London: Verso, 2018).

106. Campbell, *Romantic Ethic.*

107. Hall, *Policing the Crisis.*

108. Beckett, *Promised You a Miracle.*

109. Hall, *Policing the Crisis*; Stuart Hall, *The Hard Road to Renewal: Thatcherism and the Crisis of the Left* (London: Verso, 1990); Andrew Gamble, *The Free Economy and the Strong State: The Politics of Thatcherism* (Durham, NC: Duke University Press, 1988).

110. Hall, *Policing the Crisis.*

111. Andrew Hartman, *A War for the Soul of America: A History of the Culture Wars* (Chicago: University of Chicago Press, 2015), 200–21; Bruce J. Schulman and Julian E. Zelizer, eds., *Rightward Bound: Making America Conservative in the 1970s* (Cambridge, MA: Harvard University Press, 2008), 153–67; James Curran, Julian Petley and Ivor Gaber, *Culture Wars: The Media and the British Left* (Edinburgh: Edinburgh University Press, 2005), 5–25.

112. Jefferson Cowie, *Stayin' Alive: The 1970s and the Last Days of the Working Class* (New York: New Press, 2012).

113. Philip A. Thomas, 'The Nuclear Family, Ideology and AIDS in the Thatcher Years', *Feminist Legal Studies* 1, no. 1 (March 1993): 23–44; Brody Levesque, 'Why Ronald Reagan's Legacy Should Be Vilified, Not Sanctified', *LGBTQ Nation*, 6 February 2011, lgbtqnation.com.

114. Judith Clifton, Francisco Comín and Daniel Díaz Fuentes, *Privatisation in the European Union: Public Enterprises and Integration* (Dordrecht: Kluwer Academic Publishers, 2003), 91; Yeheskel Hasenfeld and Jane A. Rafferty, 'The Determinants of Public Attitudes toward the Welfare State', *Social Forces* 67, no. 4 (June 1989): 1027; David Marsh, 'Public Opinion, Trade Unions and Mrs Thatcher', *British Journal of Industrial Relations* 28, no. 1 (March 1990): 57–65.

115. Adam Przeworski, 'Constraints and Choices', *Comparative Political Studies* 42, no. 1 (7 November 2008): 4–30.

116. 'Ronald Reagan From the People's Perspective: A Gallup Poll Review', *Gallup*, 7 June 2004, news.gallup.com; W. Carl Biven, *Jimmy Carter's Economy: Policy in an Age of Limits*, Luther Hartwell Hodges Series on Business, Society and the State (Chapel Hill: University of North Carolina Press, 2002).

117. Robert D. Putnam, *Bowling Alone: The Collapse and Revival of American Community* (London: Simon & Schuster, 2001), 84–98; Richard Sennett, *The Corrosion of Character: The Personal Consequences of Work in the New Capitalism* (New York: Norton, 1998).

118. Mike Featherstone, *Consumer Culture and Postmodernism*, Theory, Culture and Society (London: SAGE, 1991); Naomi Klein, *No Logo: Taking Aim at the Brand Bullies* (New York: Picador, 2000).

119. Mica Nava, *Changing Cultures: Feminism, Youth and Consumerism*, Theory, Culture and Society (London: SAGE, 1992).

120. Ulrich Beck and Elisabeth Beck-Gernsheim, *Individualization: Institutionalized Individualism and Its Social and Political Consequences*, Theory, Culture and Society (London: SAGE, 2002); Zygmunt Bauman, *Liquid Modernity* (Cambridge, UK: Polity Press, 2013).

121. Nava, *Changing Cultures*.

122. Sean Nixon, *Hard Looks: Masculinities, Spectatorship and Contemporary Consumption* (New York: St. Martin's Press, 1996).

123. H. Tunstall et al., 'Geographical Scale, the "Feel-Good Factor" and Voting at the 1997 General Election in England and Wales', *Transactions of the Institute of British Geographers* 25, no. 1 (April 2000): 51–64; Sarah Butt, 'How Voters Evaluate Economic Competence: A Comparison between Parties in and out of Power', *Political Studies* 54, no. 4 (24 June 2016): 743–66.

124. Butt, 'Economic Competence'.

125. Jane Green and Chris Prosser, 'Learning the Right Lessons from Labour's 2015 Defeat', British Election Study, 2015, british-electionstudy.com.

126. Julie D'Acci, *Defining Women: Television and the Case of Cagney and Lacey* (Chapel Hill: University of North Carolina Press, 1994).

127. Zygmunt Bauman, *Community: Seeking Safety in an Insecure World* (Cambridge, UK: Polity Press, 2013); Sennett, *Corrosion of Character*.

128. Imelda Whelehan, *Overloaded: Popular Culture and the Future of Feminism* (London: Women's Press, 2000).

129. Anna Marie Smith, *New Right Discourse on Race and Sexuality: Britain, 1968–1990*, Cultural Margins 1 (Cambridge, UK: Cambridge University Press, 1994).

130. Steven Vertovec and Robin Cohen, eds., *Conceiving Cosmopolitanism: Theory, Context and Practice* (New York: Oxford University Press, 2002).

131. Fernand Braudel, *Civilization and Capitalism, 15th–18th Century* (Berkeley: University of California Press, 1992).

132. Richard Barbrook and Andy Cameron, 'The Californian Ideology', *Science as Culture* 6, no. 1 (January 1996): 44–72.

133. Jeremy Gilbert, 'The Second Wave: The Specificity of New Labour Neo-Liberalism', *Soundings* 26, no. 26 (1 March 2004): 25–45.

134. Mirowski, *Road from Mont Pelerin*.

135. Harvey, *Brief History of Neoliberalism*.

136. Colin Leys, *End of Parliamentary Socialism: From New Left to New Labour* (London: Verso, 2019).

137. Geoff Mulgan, *Life after Politics: New Thinking for the Twenty-First Century* (London: Fontana Press, 1997).

138. Pierre Dardot and Christian Laval, *The New Way of the World: On Neoliberal Society* (London: Verso, 2013).

139. Ibid.; Finlayson, *Making Sense of New Labour*.

140. Niall Ferguson, *The Ascent of Money: A Financial History of the World* (New York: Penguin, 2008); Dardot and Laval, *New Way of the World*, 5.

141. Finlayson, *Making Sense of New Labour*.

142. 'Prawn Cocktail Offensive', *Wikipedia*, 7 August 2019, wikipedia.org; David Coates, 'Capitalist Models and Social Democracy: The Case of New Labour', *British Journal of Politics and International Relations* 3, no. 3 (24 June 2016): 284–307; Anthony Giddens, 'The Rise and Fall of New Labour', *New Perspectives Quarterly* 27, no. 3 (20 July 2010): 32–7.

143. Aled Rhys Davies, *The City of London and Social Democracy: The Political Economy of Finance in Britain, 1959–1979*, Oxford Historical Monographs (Oxford: Oxford University Press, 2017).

144. Tracey Jensen, 'Welfare Commonsense, Poverty Porn and Doxosophy', *Sociological Research Online* 19, no. 3 (4 November 2014):

1–7; Kim Allen et al., 'Welfare Queens, Thrifty Housewives, and Do-It-All Mums', *Feminist Media Studies* 15, no. 6 (30 July 2015): 907–25; Shawn A. Cassiman, 'Resisting the Neo-liberal Poverty Discourse: On Constructing Deadbeat Dads and Welfare Queens', *Sociology Compass* 2, no. 5 (September 2008): 1690–1700.

145. Maurizio Lazzarato and Joshua D. Jordan, *The Making of the Indebted Man: An Essay on the Neoliberal Condition*, Semiotext(e) Intervention Series 13 (Los Angeles: Semiotext(e), 2012).

146. Pat Walker, *Between Labour and Capital* (Hassocks: Harvester Press, 1979).

147. John Clarke and Janet Newman, *The Managerial State: Power, Politics and Ideology in the Remaking of Social Welfare* (London: SAGE, 1997); Timothy Bewes and Jeremy Gilbert, *Cultural Capitalism: Politics after New Labour* (London: Lawrence & Wishart, 2000).

148. Anthony Barnett, *This Time: Our Constitutional Revolution* (London: Vintage, 1997).

149. Liz Emerson, 'University Vice-Chancellor Pay: Still a Scandal', Intergenerational Foundation, 19 February 2019, if.org.uk.

150. Sara Ahmed, *On Being Included: Racism and Diversity in Institutional Life* (Durham, NC: Duke University Press, 2012).

151. Angela McRobbie, *The Aftermath of Feminism* (London: SAGE, 2008); Catherine Rottenberg, *The Rise of Neoliberal Feminism*, Heretical Thought (New York: Oxford University Press, 2018); Nancy Fraser, *Fortunes of Feminism: From State-Managed Capitalism to Neoliberal Crisis* (London: Verso, 2013).

152. Giddens, 'Rise and Fall of New Labour'.

153. Gilbert, 'The Second Wave'; Jo Littler, *Against Meritocracy: Culture, Power and Myths of Mobility* (London: Routledge, 2017).

154. Littler, *Against Meritocracy*, 33.

155. Melissa Benn, *School Wars: The Battle for Britain's Education* (London: Verso, 2012).

156. Richard G. Wilkinson and Kate Pickett, *The Spirit Level: Why Greater Equality Makes Societies Stronger* (New York: Bloomsbury, 2010).

157. Jeffrey Weeks, *The World We Have Won: The Remaking of Erotic and Intimate Life* (London: Routledge, 2007).

158. Mark Blyth, *Austerity: The History of a Dangerous Idea* (Oxford: Oxford University Press, 2015).

159. Sarah Lyall, 'Cameron Warns Britons of Austerity', *New York Times*, 7 June 2010, nytimes.com.

160. Rebecca Bramall, Jeremy Gilbert and James Meadway, 'What Is Austerity?', *New Formations* 87, no. 87 (24 March 2016): 119–40.

161. Blyth, *Austerity*; Helen Thompson, 'Austerity as Ideology: The Bait and Switch of the Banking Crisis', *Comparative European Politics* 11, no. 6 (9 September 2013): 729–36.

162. Nick Srnicek, *Platform Capitalism* (Cambridge, UK: Polity Press, 2017).

163. Robin Murray, Jeremy Gilbert and Andrew Goffey, 'Post-Post-Fordism in the Era of Platforms', *New Formations* 84, no. 84 (20 October 2015): 184–208.

164. Zygmunt Bauman, *Modernity and the Holocaust* (Ithaca, NY: Cornell University Press, 2000).

165. Stuart Hall and Martin Jacques, *New Times: The Changing Face of Politics in the 1990s* (London: Verso, 1989).

166. Paolo Gerbaudo, *The Digital Party: Political Organisation and Online Democracy* (London: Pluto Press, 2018).

167. Keir Milburn, *Generation Left*, Radical Futures (Cambridge, UK: Polity Press, 2019).

168. Roger McNamee, *Zucked: Waking up to the Facebook Catastrophe* (New York: Penguin, 2019).

169. Ferguson, *Ascent of Money*, 41–52.

170. Jeremy Gilbert, 'Disaffected Consent: That Post-Democratic Feeling', *Soundings: A Journal of Politics and Culture* 60, no. 1 (29 August 2015): 29–41.

4 The Nature of Interests

1. Richard Swedberg, 'Can There Be a Sociological Concept of Interest?', *Theory and Society* 34, no. 4 (August 2005): 359–90.

2. Oliver Marchart, *Post-Foundational Political Thought: Political Difference in Nancy, Lefort, Bafiou and Laclau*, Taking on the Political (Edinburgh: Edinburgh University Press, 2008); Ernesto Laclau and Chantal Mouffe, *Hegemony and Socialist Strategy* (London: Verso, 1985).

3. André Gorz, *Farewell to the Working Class: An Essay on Post-industrial Socialism*, Pluto Classics (London: Pluto Press, 1997); Michel Maffesoli, *The Time of the Tribes: The Decline of Individualism in Mass Society*, Theory, Culture and Society (London: SAGE, 1996); Kate Nash, *Contemporary Political Sociology: Globalization, Politics, and Power*, 2nd ed. (Chichester, UK: Wiley-Blackwell, 2010); Barry Hindess and Paul Q. Hirst, *Mode of Production and Social Formation: An Auto-Critique of Pre-capitalist Modes of Production* (London: Palgrave Macmillan UK, 1977).

4. Louis Althusser, *On the Reproduction of Capitalism: Ideology and Ideological State Apparatuses* (London: Verso, 2014); Nicos Poulantzas, *State, Power, Socialism*, Radical Thinkers (London: Verso, 2014).

5. Louis Althusser, *For Marx* (London: Verso, 2010).

6. Hindess and Hirst, *Mode of Production*; Laclau and Mouffe, *Hegemony and Socialist Strategy*.

7. Gail Lewis, 'The Incompatible Menage a Trois: Marxism, Feminism, and Racism', in *Women and Revolution: A Discussion of the Unhappy Marriage of Marxism and Feminism*, ed. Lydia Sargent (Montréal: Black Rose Books, 1981), 93.

8. E.P. Thompson, *The Making of the English Working Class* (London: Victor Gollancz, 1965); E.P. Thompson, *The Poverty of Theory, or An Orrery of Errors* (London: Merlin Press, 1995), 140–55.

9. Laclau and Mouffe, *Hegemony and Socialist Strategy*, 121.

10. Ernesto Laclau, *On Populist Reason* (London: Verso, 2007).

11. Steven Kettell and Peter Kerr, 'The Brexit Religion and the Holy Grail of the NHS', *Social Policy and Society*, 22 January 2021, 1–14.

12. Laclau, *On Populist Reason*.

13. 'England's New Rentier Alliance', Political Economy Research Centre, https://www.perc.org.uk/project_posts/englands-rentier -alliance.

14. Henri Bergson, W. Scott Palmer and Nancy Margaret Paul, *Matter and Memory* (Mansfield Centre, CT: Martino Publishing, 2011).

15. Gilles Deleuze, *Bergsonism* (New York: Zone Books, 1988); Keith Ansell-Pearson, 'The Reality of the Virtual: Bergson and Deleuze', *Modern Language Notes* 120, no. 5 (2005): 1112–27.

16. Manuel DeLanda, *Intensive Science and Virtual Philosophy*, Transversals (London: Continuum, 2011).

17. Gilles Deleuze, *Difference and Repetition* (London: Athlone Press, 1994), 209–12.

18. Ngai-Ling Sum and Bob Jessop, *Towards a Cultural Political Economy: Putting Culture in Its Place in Political Economy* (Cheltenham: Edward Elgar Publishing, 2015).

19. It's important to note that our use of Deleuzian terminology here is deliberately casual: it serves an important analytical purpose for us, but we also make no claim to strict fidelity to Deleuze's specific concepts. In particular, Deleuze's emphatic differentiation between the 'virtual' and the 'possible' certainly warrants detailed exploration, particularly with regard to our usage of these terms as almost synonymous. But there is no room to explore this issue further here.

20. Maria Sobolewska and Robert Anthony Ford, *Brexitland: Identity, Diversity and the Reshaping of British Politics* (Cambridge, UK: Cambridge University Press, 2020), 230–49.

21. To use a term proposed by Emily Hicks in 1981, such interests are *nonsynchronous*: Emily Hicks, 'Cultural Marxism: Nonsynchrony

and Feminist Practice', in Sargent, *Women and Revolution*, 219–38.

22. Jodi Dean, *The Communist Horizon* (London: Verso Books, 2012).

23. Jeremy Gilbert, 'This Conjuncture: For Stuart Hall', *New Formations* 96, nos. 96–97 (1 March 2019): 5–37.

24. Laclau and Mouffe, *Hegemony and Socialist Strategy*; Ernesto Laclau, *New Reflections on the Revolution of Our Time: Ernesto Laclau*, Phronesis (London: Verso, 1990).

25. Nicholas Abercrombie, Stephen Hill and Bryan S. Turner, *The Dominant Ideology Thesis* (London: G. Allen & Unwin, 1980).

26. Althusser, *On the Reproduction of Capitalism*.

27. Laclau, *On Populist Reason*, 110–17.

28. Althusser, *On the Reproduction of Capitalism*.

29. Michel Foucault and Paul Rabinow, *The Foucault Reader*, 1st ed. (New York: Pantheon Books, 1984), 60.

30. Gilles Deleuze and Félix Guattari, *A Thousand Plateaus: Capitalism and Schizophrenia* (Minneapolis: University of Minnesota Press, 1987), 25, 196.

31. Sobolewska and Ford, *Brexitland*.

32. Ibid., 59–71.

33. Ibid., 46.

34. Anthony Giddens, *The Global Third Way Debate* (Cambridge, UK: Polity Press, 2001).

35. Luc Boltanski and Eve Chiapello, *The New Spirit of Capitalism*, trans. Gregory Elliot, rev. ed. (London: Verso, 2018).

36. James Curran, Ivor Gaber and Julian Petley, *Culture Wars: The Media and the British Left*, Communication and Society (London: Routledge, 2019).

37. David Featherstone, *Solidarity: Hidden Histories and Geographies of Internationalism* (London: Zed Books, 2012); Frits L. van Holthoon and Marcel van der Linden, eds., *Internationalism in the Labour Movement, 1830–1940*, Contributions to the History of Labour and Society 1 (Leiden: Brill, 1988).

38. 'Tory Landslide, Progressives Split', Datapraxis, https://www. dataprax.is/tory-landslide-progressives-split.

39. Edward Fieldhouse et al., *Electoral Shocks: The Volatile Voter in a Turbulent World* (New York: Oxford University Press, 2019), 173.

40. 'Len McCluskey: The Free Movement of Labour Is a Class Question', Institute of Employee Rights, 8 November 2016, ier.org.uk.

41. This was the position associated with organisations such as Another Europe is Possible (anothereurope.org) and DIEM-25 (diem25.org).

42. John Curtice, 'Breaking the Conservative-Labour Duopoly', *IPPR Progressive Review* 26, no. 2 (September 2019): 213–22.

43. Keir Milburn, *Generation Left* (London: Wiley, 2019).

44. Joe Chrisp and Nick Pearce, 'Grey Power: Towards a Political Economy of Older Voters in the UK', *Political Quarterly* 90, no. 4 (October 2019): 755.

45. Axel Honneth, *The Struggle for Recognition: The Moral Grammar of Social Conflicts*, Studies in Contemporary German Social Thought (Cambridge, MA: MIT Press, 1996), 164–5.

46. Nancy Fraser and Axel Honneth, *Redistribution or Recognition? A Political-Philosophical Exchange* (London: Verso, 2003).

47. Jospeter M. Mbuba, 'Attitudes Toward the Police: The Significance of Race and Other Factors among College Students', *Journal of Ethnicity in Criminal Justice* 8, no. 3 (26 August 2010): 201–15; Amie M. Schuck, Dennis P. Rosenbaum and Darnell F. Hawkins, 'The Influence of Race/Ethnicity, Social Class, and Neighborhood Context on Residents' Attitudes Toward the Police', *Police Quarterly* 11, no. 4 (December 2008): 496–519.

48. Darrell Hudson et al., 'Surviving the White Space: Perspectives on How Middle-Class Black Men Navigate Cultural Racism', *Ethnic and Racial Studies*, 12 November 2020, 1–19.

49. Anoop Nayak, 'Critical Whiteness Studies: Critical Whiteness Studies', *Sociology Compass* 1, no. 2 (November 2007): 737–55.

50. Kathy J. Ogren, *The Jazz Revolution: Twenties America and the Meaning of Jazz* (New York: Oxford University Press, 1992).

51. Kimberly Chabot Davis, *Beyond the White Negro: Empathy and Anti-Racist Reading* (Urbana: University of Illinois Press, 2014).

52. Frantz Fanon, *Black Skin, White Masks*, 2020; James Donald and Ali Rattansi, eds., *'Race', Culture, and Difference* (London: SAGE, 1992).

53. Paul Gilroy, *The Black Atlantic: Modernity and Double Consciousness* (London: Verso, 1993).

54. Frédéric Lordon and Gabriel Ash, *Willing Slaves of Capital: Spinoza and Marx on Desire* (London: Verso, 2014), 29.

55. Chris Crass, *Towards Collective Liberation: Anti-Racist Organizing, Feminist Praxis, and Movement Building Strategy* (Oakland, CA: PM Press, 2013); Jodi Dean, *Solidarity of Strangers: Feminism after Identity Politics* (Berkeley: University of California Press, 2018); Jonathan Matthew Smucker, *Hegemony How-to: A Roadmap for Radicals* (Oakland, CA: AK Press, 2017); Hicks, 'Cultural Marxism: Nonsynchrony and Feminist Practice'.

56. Lydia Sargent, ed., *Women and Revolution: A Discussion of the Unhappy Marriage of Marxism and Feminism* (Montréal: Black Rose Books, 1981).

57. Frédéric Lordon, *L'intérêt souverain* (Paris: La Découverte, 2011), 159–60; Lordon and Ash, *Willing Slaves of Capital*.

58. Lordon and Ash, *Willing Slaves of Capital*, 32–9.

59. Bruce J. Schulman and Julian E. Zelizer, eds., *Rightward Bound: Making America Conservative in the 1970s* (Cambridge, MA: Harvard University Press, 2008). Of particular relevance are the chapters by Matthew D. Lassiter and Marjorie J. Spruill.

60. Beatrix Campbell, *The Iron Ladies: Why Do Women Vote Tory?* (London: Virago, 1987).

61. Manuel Castells, *The Power of Identity*, Information Age 2 (Malden, MA: Blackwell, 1997), 134–242.

62. George Lakoff and Mark Johnson, *Metaphors We Live By* (Chicago: University of Chicago Press, 2003).

5 Platform Power

1. In this Gramsci is distinguishable from his most notable successors, Ernesto Laclau and Chantal Mouffe, whose conception of hegemonic struggle as discursively articulated equivalence formation tends to see all influence of infrastructure merely as economism to be warded off. In particular, we note that the layout and functionality of platforms do not tend to follow the language-like mechanics of Laclau and Mouffe's political ontology. See Alex Williams, *Political Hegemony and Social Complexity: Mechanisms of Power after Gramsci* (Basingstoke: Palgrave Macmillan, 2019); Ernesto Laclau, *New Reflections on the Revolution of Our Time* (London: Verso, 1990); Ernesto Laclau and Chantal Mouffe, *Hegemony and Socialist Strategy* (London: Verso, 1985); and Ernesto Laclau and Chantal Mouffe, 'Post-Marxism without Apologies', in *New Reflections on the Revolution of Our Times* (London: Verso, 1990), 97–132.

2. Antonio Gramsci, *Selections from the Prison Notebooks*, trans. Quintin Hoare and Geoffrey Nowell Smith (London: Lawrence & Wishart, 1971), 350.

3. Kalwant Bhopal and Farzana Shain, eds., *Neoliberalism and Education: Rearticulating Social Justice and Inclusion* (London: Routledge, 2016), routledge.com; Stephen J. Ball, 'Performativity, Commodification and Commitment: An I-Spy Guide to the Neoliberal University', *British Journal of Educational Studies* 60, no. 1 (1 March 2012): 17–28.

4. Matthew Watson, 'Michael Gove's War on Professional Historical Expertise: Conservative Curriculum Reform, Extreme Whig History and the Place of Imperial Heroes in Modern Multicultural Britain', *British Politics* 15, no. 3 (1 September 2020): 271–90.

5. James Trafford, *The Empire at Home: Internal Colonies and the End of Britain* (London: Pluto Press, 2020); John Elledge, 'The

History of the British Empire Is Not Being Taught', *New States-man*, 12 June 2020, newstatesman.com.

6. Paul Gilroy, *Postcolonial Melancholia* (New York: Columbia University Press, 2004).

7. Didier Fassin, 'Are "Woke" Academics a Threat to the French Republic? Ask Macron's Ministers', *Guardian*, 12 March 2021, theguardian.com.

8. Ross Clark, 'Minorities of Woke Students Now Govern Our Universities', *Telegraph*, 9 June 2021, telegraph.co.uk.

9. Christy Kulz, *Factories for Learning: Making Race, Class and Inequality in the Neoliberal Academy* (Manchester: Manchester University Press, 2017).

10. For an early take on the idea, see Gregory Bateson, *Steps to an Ecology of Mind* (London: Jason Aronson, 1973), and for a thorough summary, see Dietram Scheufele, 'Framing as a Theory of Media Effects', *Journal of Communication* 49 (March 1, 1999): 103–22.

11. Nathan J. Russell, 'An Introduction to the Overton Window of Political Possibilities', 4 January 2006, Mackinac Center for Public Policy, http://www.mackinac.org/7504.

12. Sebastián Valenzuela and Maxwell McCombs, 'The Agenda-Setting Role of the News Media', in *An Integrated Approach to Communication Theory and Research*, ed. Don W. Stacks, Michael B. Salwen and Kristen C. Eichhorn, 3rd ed. (London: Routledge, 2019).

13. Annabelle Gawer, 'Platform Dynamics and Strategies: From Products to Services', in *Platforms, Markets and Innovation*, ed. Annabelle Gawer (Cheltenham: Edward Elgar Publishing, 2009), 45–76; Nick Srnicek, *Platform Capitalism* (Chichester, UK: John Wiley & Sons, 2016); Carliss Baldwin and Jason Woodard, 'The Architecture of Platforms: A Unified View', in *Platforms, Markets and Innovation*, ed. Annabelle Gawer (Cheltenham: Edward Elgar Publishing, 2009), 19–44.

14. David Beer, *The Data Gaze: Capitalism, Power and Perception* (Los Angeles: SAGE, 2019).

15. William C. Wimsatt, *Re-engineering Philosophy for Limited Beings: Piecewise Approximations to Reality* (Cambridge, MA: Harvard University Press, 2007), 133–4.

16. Gawer, 'Platform Dynamics and Strategies'.

17. Karl Kautsky, *Das Erfurter Programm* (Stuttgart: Verlag von J. H. W. Diek, 1892).

18. Laclau and Mouffe, *Hegemony and Socialist Strategy*, 76.

19. Gramsci, *Prison Notebooks*, 137, 366.

20. Jonathan Joseph, *Hegemony: A Realist Analysis* (New York: Routledge, 2002), 120.

21. Gramsci, *Prison Notebooks*, 366.

22. Keller Easterling, *Extrastatecraft: The Power of Infrastructure Space* (London: Verso, 2014), 2.

23. James Gibson, 'The Theory of Affordances', in *Perceiving, Acting, and Knowing: Toward an Ecological Psychology*, ed. Robert Shaw and John Bransford (Hillsdale, NJ: Lawrence Erlbaum Associates, 1977), 62–82.

24. For an example of this kind of thinking from a typically conventional political science academic, see Steven Fielding, 'How Starmer Can Beat Boris?', *Spectator*, 11 June 2021, spectator. co.uk. For a discussion of this phenomenon, see Jonathan Dean, 'On Corbyn, Book-Eating and the Future of UK Political Science', Political Studies Association, 13 June 2017, psa. ac.uk.

25. Erik J. Engstrom, *Partisan Gerrymandering and the Construction of American Democracy* (Ann Arbor, MI: University of Michigan Press, 2013), 191–206.

26. Ivan D. Margary, *Roman Roads in Britain* (London: John Baker, 1973).

27. Philip Mirowski and Dieter Plehwe, *The Road from Mont Pèlerin: The Making of the Neoliberal Thought Collective* (Cambridge, MA: Harvard University Press, 2009); Damien Cahill, *The End of Laissez-Faire? On the Durability of Embedded Neoliberalism* (Cheltenham: Edward Elgar, 2014); Williams, *Political Hegemony and Social Complexity*, chap. 10.

28. Tim Wu, *The Attention Merchants: The Epic Scramble to Get Inside Our Heads* (New York: Knopf, 2016).

29. John T. Cacioppo, James H. Fowler and Nicholas A. Christakis, 'Alone in the Crowd: The Structure and Spread of Loneliness in a Large Social Network', *Journal of Personality and Social Psychology* 97, no. 6 (December 2009): 977–91.

30. Nick Davies, Graham Atkins and Sukhvinder Sodhi, 'Using Targets to Improve Public Services', Institute for Government, 16 June 2021, instituteforgovernment.org.uk.

31. Will Davies, 'How "Competitiveness" Became One of the Great Unquestioned Virtues of Contemporary Culture', *British Politics and Policy at LSE* (blog), 19 May 2014, blogs.lse.ac.uk/politicsandpolicy.

32. Mario Tronti, *Workers and Capital*, trans. David Broder (London: Verso, 2019).

33. Thomas Perroud, 'Privately Owned Public Spaces: A Comparative Study of the Legal Responses to Their Development and a Proposal for Reform', *Oxford Law Faculty* (blog), 22 March 2020, law.ox.ac.uk/research-and-subject-groups/property-law/blog/.

34. Shagun Jhaver, Christian Boylston and Amy Bruckman, 'Evaluating the Effectiveness of Deplatforming as a Moderation Strategy on Twitter', *Proceedings of the ACM on Human-Computer Interaction* 5, no. 381 (2021).

35. Safiya Umoja Noble, *Algorithms of Oppression: How Search Engines Reinforce Racism* (New York: New York University Press, 2018).

36. Sarah O'Connor, 'The Gig Economy Is a Symptom of Bigger Problems', *Financial Times*, 9 November 2020, ft.com.

37. Kiran Stacey, 'Washington vs Big Tech: Lina Khan's Battle to Transform US Antitrust', *Financial Times*, 10 August 2021, ft.com.

38. Costas Lapavitsas, *Profiting without Producing: How Finance Exploits Us All* (London: Verso, 2013).

39. Richard Dienst, *The Bonds of Debt* (London: Verso, 2011).

40. Geoffrey E. Schneider, 'An Institutionalist Assessment of Structural Adjustment Programs in Africa', *Journal of Economic Issues* 33, no. 2 (1 June 1999): 325–34.

41. Gerald F. Davis and Suntae Kim, 'Financialization of the Economy', *Annual Review of Sociology* 41, no. 1 (2015): 203–21.

42. Stephen E. G. Lea, 'Debt and Overindebtedness: Psychological Evidence and Its Policy Implications', *Social Issues and Policy Review* 15, no. 1 (2021): 146–79.

43. Miguel Coelho, Sebastian Dellepiane-Avellaneda and Vigyan Ratnoo, 'The Political Economy of Housing in England', *New Political Economy* 22, no. 1 (2 January 2017): 31–60.

44. Keir Milburn, *Generation Left* (Cambridge, UK: Polity, 2019).

45. Nicholas Shaxson, *Treasure Islands: Tax Havens and the Men Who Stole the World* (London: Vintage, 2012).

46. Davis and Kim, 'Financialization of the Economy'.

47. We can distinguish the elites of the tech and finance worlds in terms of their relationship to the counterculture of the 1960s and '70s: tech elites were shaped in a period where the influence of post-hippie counterculture was omnipresent. Conversely, elite finance workers tend to be less reconstructed capitalists. Both are largely neoliberals, but one set via the *Whole Earth Catalog*, the other via Thatcher-Reagan and organic Hayekianism.

48. For an example of the kind of dispute that leads to substantial fines see, 'WTO Dispute Settlement – DS593', World Trade Organization, 12 November 2020, WTO.org.

49. Quinn Slobodian, *Globalists: The End of Empire and the Birth of Neoliberalism* (Cambridge, MA: Harvard University Press, 2018).

50. Ibid., 13.

51. Robin Murray, 'Fordism and Post-Fordism', in *New Times: The Changing Face of Politics in the 1990s*, ed. Stuart Hall and Martin Jacques (London: Lawrence & Wishart, 1989), 38–53.

52. Daniel Yergin, *The Prize: The Epic Quest for Oil, Money, and Power* (New York: Simon & Schuster, 1991).

53. Matthew Lawrence, *Future Proof: Britain in the 2020s*, Institute for Public Policy Research, 2016, ippr.org.

54. Shoshana Zuboff, *The Age of Surveillance Capitalism: The Fight for a Human Future at the New Frontier of Power* (London: Profile Books, 2019); Shoshana Zuboff, ' "The Goal Is to Automate Us": Welcome to the Age of Surveillance Capitalism', *Observer*, 20 January 2019, theguardian.com.

55. Zuboff, *Surveillance Capitalism*, 15.

56. See Jamie Bartlett, *The People vs Tech: How the Internet Is Killing Democracy* (London: Ebury Press, 2018); Yael Eisenstat, 'Perspective: I Worked on Political Ads at Facebook. They Profit by Manipulating Us.' *Washington Post*, 4 November 2019, washingtonpost.com; and Julia Carrie Wong, 'Revealed: The Facebook Loophole That Lets World Leaders Deceive and Harass Their Citizens', *Guardian*, 12 April 2021, theguardian.com.

57. Zuboff, 'The Goal Is to Automate Us.'

58. Zuboff, *Surveillance Capitalism*, 484.

59. Siva Vaidhyanathan, *Antisocial Media: How Facebook Disconnects Us and Undermines Democracy.* (Oxford: Oxford University Press, 2019).

60. McKenzie Wark, *Capital Is Dead: Is This Something Worse?* (London: Verso, 2021).

61. Joshua A. T. Fairfield, *Owned: Property, Privacy, and the New Digital Serfdom* (Cambridge, UK: Cambridge University Press, 2017).

62. Indeed, shortly before his death, political economist Robin Murray argued that tech platforms demonstrate an emergence of a post-post-Fordism. See Robin Murray, Jeremy Gilbert and Andrew Goffey, 'Post-Post-Fordism in the Era of Platforms', *New Formations* 84, no. 84 (20 October 2015): 184–208.

63. Ian Kershaw, *The 'Hitler Myth': Image and Reality in the Third Reich*, repr. (Oxford: Oxford University Press, 2001).

64. As Dimitar Gueorguiev has put it, Xi practices an 'inclusive authoritarianism' that requires some degree of voluntary participation by the Chinese citizenry, which we would characterise as almost classically hegemonic in nature. See Dimitar Gueorguiev, *Retrofitting Leninism: Participation without Democracy in China* (Oxford: Oxford University Press, 2021).

65. Richard Seymour, *The Twittering Machine* (London: Verso, 2020).

66. Leslie Berlin, *Troublemakers: Silicon Valley's Coming of Age*, repr. (New York: Simon & Schuster, 2018).

67. John Markoff, *What the Dormouse Said: How the Sixties Counterculture Shaped the Personal Computer Industry* (New York: Penguin, 2006).

68. Farhad Manjoo, 'Silicon Valley's Politics: Liberal, with One Big Exception', *New York Times*, 6 September 2017, nytimes.com.

69. Steven Levy, *Hackers: Heroes of the Computer Revolution* (Newton, MA: O'Reilly Media, 2010).

70. Jennifer Burns, 'Godless Capitalism: Ayn Rand and the Conservative Movement', *Modern Intellectual History* 1, no. 3 (November 2004): 359–85; Anne C. Heller, *Ayn Rand and the World She Made* (New York: Knopf Doubleday Publishing Group, 2009).

71. Paulina Borsook, *Cyberselfish: A Critical Romp through the Terribly Libertarian Culture of High Tech* (New York: PublicAffairs, 2001).

72. Luc Boltanski and Eve Chiapello, *The New Spirit of Capitalism*, trans. Gregory Elliot, rev. ed. (London: Verso, 2018).

73. Ibid., 356–58.

74. Eden Medina, *Cybernetic Revolutionaries Technology and Politics in Allende's Chile* (Cambridge, MA: MIT Press, 2011).

75. *British Social Attitudes Survey, 1995: Version 2*, Interuniversity Consortium for Political and Social Research, 2001.

76. Peter Blackburn, 'Outsourced and Undermined: The COVID-19 Windfall for Private Providers', British Medical Association, 8 September 2020, bma.org.uk.

77. Reijer Hendrikse, 'Neoliberalism Is Over – Welcome to the Era of Neo-Illiberalism', *openDemocracy*, 7 May 2020, opendemocracy.net.

6 Strange Times

1. Couze Venn, *After Capital* (London: SAGE, 2018).
2. Richard G. Wilkinson and Kate Pickett, *The Spirit Level: Why Greater Equality Makes Societies Stronger* (New York: Bloomsbury, 2010); Olivia Sagan and Eric D. Miller, eds., *Narratives of Loneliness: Multidisciplinary Perspectives from the 21st Century* (London: Routledge, 2018); Mark Fisher, *Capitalist Realism: Is There No Alternative?* (Winchester, UK: Zero Books, 2010).
3. 'Amazon Hopes Pandemic Habits Stick after Profits Triple', *BBC News*, 29 April 2021, bbc.com.
4. Meagan Day and Micah Uetricht, *Bigger than Bernie: How We Go from the Sanders Campaign to Democratic Socialism* (London: Verso, 2020).
5. Karen Weise and Michael Corkery, 'Amazon Workers Vote Down Union Drive at Alabama Warehouse', *New York Times*, 9 April 2021, nytimes.com.
6. Joe Tenebruso, 'If You Bought $10,000 of Zoom Stock at the Beginning of 2020, Here's How Much You'd Have Today', Nasdaq, 27 December 2020, nasdaq.com.
7. 'Protecting the Right to Organize Act', *Wikipedia*, wikipedia.org.
8. 'Fifth of UK Covid Contracts "Raised Red Flags for Possible Corruption," ' *Guardian*, 22 April 2021, theguardian.com.
9. Darren Dodd, 'Macron: Time to Think the Unthinkable', *Financial Times*, 17 April 2020, ft.com.
10. 'What Is the UK Government's Levelling Up Fund?', *Independent*, 24 August 2021, independent.co.uk.
11. 'The Left Has Slightly Loosened the Cold Grip of Austerity under President Biden', *Jacobin*, 16 February 2021, jacobinmag.com.
12. Paul Ian Campbell, 'Taking the Knee in Football: Why This Act of Protest Has Always Been Political', *The Conversation*, 16 June 2021, theconversation.com.

13. Lester K. Spence, *Stare in the Darkness: The Limits of Hip-Hop and Black Politics* (Minneapolis: University of Minnesota Press, 2011).

14. Keeanga-Yamahtta Taylor, *From #BlackLivesMatter to Black Liberation* (Chicago: Haymarket Books, 2016).

15. Martin Jacques, 'There Should Be an International Investigation into Why the West Failed so Disastrously', *Global Times*, 28 June 2021, globaltimes.cn.

16. Zhiqun Zhu, 'Interpreting China's "Wolf Warrior" Diplomacy', *Pacific Forum* 26 (2020): 2.

17. For a book-length analysis of the UK experience with some comparative reference to the American, see Jeremey Gilbert, '2020 Analysis', *jeremygilbertwriting* (blog), 4 June 2021, jeremygilbertwriting.wordpress.com.

18. Jeremy Gilbert, 'It Was the Centrist Dads Who Lost It', *openDemocracy*, 13 January 2020, opendemocracy.net.

19. Kara Voght, 'Bernie Sanders Lost the Black Vote. That's Probably a Problem Going Forward.' *Mother Jones*, 1 March 2020, motherjones.com.

20. Jeremy Gilbert, 'History Is Clear: Labour Must Lead an Alliance for Democratic Reform', *openDemocracy*, 18 January 2020, opendemocracy.net.

21. Jeremy Gilbert, 'We Lost Because We Weren't Big Enough', *openDemocracy*, 9 September 2020, opendemocracy.net.

22. Micah Uetricht, *Strike for America: Chicago Teachers against Austerity*, Jacobin Series (London: Verso, 2014); Jane McAlevey, *A Collective Bargain: Unions, Organizing, and the Fight for Democracy*, (New York: Ecco, 2020).

23. We must also note that in other places, particularly Europe, there are some signs of a reversal of fortunes for more traditional social democratic parties, often in alliance with green parties.

24. Adolph Reed, 'The Post-1965 Trajectory of Race, Class, and Urban Politics in the United States Reconsidered', *Labor Studies Journal* 41, no. 3 (September 2016): 260–91.

25. James Meadway, 'Neoliberalism Is Dying – Now We Must Replace It', *openDemocracy*, 3 September 2021, opendemocracy.net.

26. Olivier Henri Bonnerot, 'In Memoriam: Romain Rolland, Un Compagnon de Route de Roger Drouin', *Cahiers de Brèves*, no. 40 (January 2018): 2; Antonio Gramsci, *Letters from Prison* (New York: Harper & Row, 1975), 159–60.

7 Strategies for Future Wars

1. Chantal Mouffe, *For a Left Populism* (London: Verso, 2019).

2. Kate Aronoff et al., *A Planet to Win: Why We Need a Green New Deal* (London: Verso, 2019).

3. Mike Makin-Waite, *On Burnley Road: Class, Race and Politics in a Northern English Town* (London: Lawrence & Wishart, 2021), Didier Eribon and Michael Lucey, *Returning to Reims* (London: Penguin, 2019).

4. Adam Harris, 'America Is Divided by Education', *Atlantic*, 7 November 2018, theatlantic.com; 'How Britain Voted in the 2019 General Election', *YouGov*, 17 December 2019, yougov.co.uk.

5. Brian Manning, *The English People and the English Revolution*, 2nd ed. (London: Bookmarks, 1991).

6. Uetricht, *Strike for America*.

7. Jeremy Gilbert, *Twenty-First Century Socialism* (Cambridge, UK: Polity Press, 2020), 59–64.

8. Maurrizio Lazzarato and Robert Hurley, *Capital Hates Everyone: Fascism or Revolution*, Semiotext(e) Intervention Series 29 (South Pasadena, CA: Semiotext(e), 2021).

9. Rodrigo Guimaraes Nunes, *Neither Vertical nor Horizontal: A Theory of Organization* (London: Verso, 2021), 51–80.

10. Ibid., 97–111.

11. See Nick Srnicek and Alex Williams, *Inventing the Future: Postcapitalism and a World without Work* (London: Verso, 2015), chap. 8.

12. Mikhail Aleksandrovich Bakunin and Sam Dolgoff, *Bakunin on Anarchy: Selected Works by the Activist-Founder of World Anarchism* (New York: Vintage, 1972); Robert Michels, *Political Parties: A Sociological Study of the Oligarchical Tendencies of Modern Democracy*, repr. (New York: Free Press, 1968).

13. Georg Lukács, *Lenin: A Study in the Unity of His Thought* (London: Verso, 2009), 24–37; Antonio Gramsci, *Selections from the Prison Notebooks*, trans. Quintin Hoare and Geoffrey Nowell Smith (London: Lawrence & Wishart, 1971); Jodi Dean, *Crowds and Party* (London: Verso, 2016).

14. Gramsci, *Prison Notebooks*, 123–205.

15. Jeremy Gilbert, 'Labour Should Have Argued against the Last 40 Years, Not Just the Last Ten', *openDemocracy*, 15 January 2020, opendemocracy.net.

16. Perry Anderson, *English Questions* (London: Verso, 1992). We acknowledge the fierce debate between Anderson and his collaborator Tom Nairn on the one hand, and their great interlocutor E.P. Thompson, on the other, partly on this question of how far such anti-intellectualism really is endemic to the 'English' 'left'. Our own observations and experience as well as our own theoretical perspective lead us to conclude that both parties to this debate offered significant insights, which could all be accommodated by the observation that English *elite* culture has been, historically, unusually anti-intellectual and anti-theoretical in character, and that this tendency has been reproduced within middle-class and working-class culture and institutions *except* in those instances wherein deference to that elite culture has been weakest and/or most self-consciously resisted.

17. Jeremy Gilbert, 'The Joy of Co-production', *IPPR Progressive Review* 26, no. 2 (12 August 2019): 161–72; Jeremy Gilbert, 'Platforms and Potency: Democracy and Collective Agency in the Age of Social Media', *Open Cultural Studies* 4, no. 1 (31 December 2020): 154–68.

18. Jeremy Gilbert, *Anticapitalism and Culture: Radical Theory and*

Popular Politics (Oxford: Berg, 2008), 223–35; Gilbert, *Twenty-First Century Socialism*.

19. Srnicek and Williams, *Inventing the Future*; Gilbert, 'Platforms and Potency'.

20. Nick Couldry and Ulises Ali Mejias, *The Costs of Connection: How Data Is Colonizing Human Life and Appropriating It for Capitalism*, Culture and Economic Life (Stanford, CA: Stanford University Press, 2019); Richard Seymour, *The Twittering Machine* (London: Verso, 2020); Shoshana Zuboff, *The Age of Surveillance Capitalism: The Fight for a Human Future at the New Frontier of Power* (London: Profile Books, 2019).

21. Srnicek, *Platform Capitalism*, 2017.

22. Gramsci, *Prison Notebooks*, 279–87.

23. See Zuboff, *Surveillance Capitalism*; Couldry and Mejias, *Costs of Connection*; and Srnicek, *Platform Capitalism*.

24. Ann Pettifor, *The Production of Money: How to Break the Power of Bankers* (London: Verso, 2018).

25. Amartya Sen, *Commodities and Capabilities* (New Delhi: Oxford University Press, 2008); Martha C. Nussbaum, *Creating Capabilities: The Human Development Approach* (Cambridge, MA: Belknap Press of Harvard University Press, 2011).

26. Asad Haider, *Mistaken Identity: Race and Class in the Age of Trump* (London: Verso, 2018).

27. See Keeanga-Yamahtta Taylor, ed., *How We Get Free: Black Feminism and the Combahee River Collective* (Chicago: Haymarket Books, 2017).

28. Judith Butler, 'We Need to Rethink the Category of Woman', *Guardian*, 7 September 2021, theguardian.com.

29. Barbara Epstein 'What Happened to the Women's Movement?', *Monthly Review*, 1 May 2001, monthlyreview.org.

30. 'Notes Towards a Theory of Solidarity', *jeremygilbertwriting* (blog), 1 May 2018, jeremygilbertwriting.wordpress.com.

31. Prerna Singh, *How Solidarity Works for Welfare: Subnationalism and Social Development in India*, Cambridge Studies in Comparative Politics (New York: Cambridge University Press, 2015);

David Featherstone, *Solidarity: Hidden Histories and Geographies of Internationalism* (London: Zed Books, 2012).

32. Gramsci, *Prison Notebooks*, 350.

8 The Promise of Neosocialism

1. Ben Little and Alison Winch, *The New Patriarchs of Digital Capitalism: Celebrity Tech Founders and Networks of Power* (Abingdon, UK: Routledge, 2021).

2. Jeremy Gilbert, 'Labour Should Have Argued against the Last 40 Years, Not Just the Last Ten', *openDemocracy*, 15 January 2020, opendemocracy.net; Maria Sobolewska and Robert Anthony Ford, *Brexitland: Identity, Diversity and the Reshaping of British Politics* (Cambridge, UK: Cambridge University Press, 2020).

INDEX